INSPIRING LITERACY

INSPIRING LITERACY

Literature for Children and Young Adults

Edited by
Sam Sebesta and Ken Donelson

Transaction Publishers
New Brunswick (U.S.A.) and London (U.K.)

Library of Congress Catalog Number: 92-42713
ISBN: 1-56000-668-4
Printed in the United States of America

Library of Congress Cataloging-in-Publication Data

Inspiring literacy : literature for children and young adults / edited by Sam Sebesta and Ken Donelson.

  p. cm.

 ISBN: 1-56000-668-4

  1. Reading—United States—Language experience approach. 2. Children—United States—Books and reading. 3. Literature—Study and teaching United States. I. Sebesta, Sam Leaton. II. Donelson, Kenneth L.

LB1050.35.I57 1993

372.64'044—dc20

                       92-42713
                         CIP

To the memory of
JOHN DONOVAN

Contents

Children's Books: The State of the Art

Young Adult Literature

I
Children's Books: The State of the Art

1

A Renewed View of Children's Literature

Sam Sebesta

Many colleges of education offer a course on materials designed specifically to teach reading. To some people, the existence of such a course is evidence of error. They say that we should not need materials designed to teach reading. We should use real things—the current term is *authentic text*. We should dispense with graded word lists, readability, prepared passages loaded with a designated comprehension factor, and other things that have been done to reading materials to soften or shape them to teach children how to read.

You may shake your head yes, no, or in a quandary over the above paragraph, depending on your experience, training, or disposition. Some believe that special materials are necessary. To dismiss them is to relinquish what we need for good instruction. Others argue for literature-based programs, where whole books (trade books, not textbooks) predominate. Some urge a complete integrated literature-based curriculum, *sans* textbooks.

This chapter and most of the other chapters in this book are really not about that issue. The issue needs to be acknowledged, for it is pertinent, and then set aside, for it will not be resolved. What does need attention here is the importance of children's literature in all classrooms and, we hope, in all children's lives.

Why Children's Literature?

Reading experts come close to agreeing that the more actual reading children do, the better they will do it. Allington (1977) found this to be true in the classroom, and Fielding et al. confirmed it (1984) in the wider context of independent reading. In one study (Anderson et al., 1987) "interestingness" accounted for thirty times more variance in comprehension scores than did readability. These seem to be powerful arguments for turning to the source, children's literature, as the content of what children read and the means of accessing interest.

Beyond utilitarian reasons, what are the intrinsic ones? You, no doubt, can think of many. Lukens (1990) and others list some of them: enjoyment, self-understanding, world knowledge, empathy, multicultural awareness, language growth, problem solving, cognitive structure. Beyond such lists, a comprehensive theory of literary experience needs attention, for it may help bring cohesion when we present literature to children.

One prominent theory derives from Louise Rosenblatt (1983). Reading literature is a "performing art," not necessarily in the sense of oral interpretation or staged drama but in the sense that readers of any age must bring it to life. It is called a *transaction* theory: readers transact with literature on the page to construct meaning and feeling. Ushered by text (which in children's literature includes visual art), readers reconstruct imagery, re-create characters, and relate their own experience to what the literature "says" to them. Nor is this transaction confined to narrative fiction or *belles-lettres*. It applies, perhaps equally, to expository nonfiction. It might even apply to a recipe for lasagna.

Rosenblatt defines stages in transaction. The first is *evocation*, requisite to any further authentic transaction. It is the stage of "living through" the reading experience. You see it in children when they stop milling around and devote rapt attention to what is being read to them or what they are reading themselves. You discover it in yourself when a part of you forgets where you are and what page you are on as you surrender to the substance and spirit of what you read.

Evocation cannot last forever. You enter a second stage when you put the book aside or go back and scrutinize some passage, or when you think about it as you wash dishes or go out to the playground or talk with your friends about it. If evocation is strong, you may try to recapture it. This is what Hickman (1979) found when she sat in literature-rich classrooms, where children would search for ten minutes to find a book they had enjoyed in order to bring it to her and tell her about it. But, eventually, evocation gives way to more considered consciousness. We begin to look more closely. For example, we examine a story from a different point of view of a character or of other readers. We are in a stage of considering *alternatives*.

Consider an easy example: that third little pig was smart. The first time we heard, saw, or read the story, we reveled in his triumph over the bad wolf. Come to think of it, though, he's a tricky little beast. Reminds me of a neighbor we had—I wouldn't wan *him* for a neighbor! Or, if you prefer an extreme alternative, turn to *The True Story of the Three Little Pigs* purportedly by A. Wolf (Scieszka, 1989).

Consider a hard example: Cynthia Rylant's *Missing May* (1992). Three very different people undertake an epic journey to find a spiritualist to contact a loved one who is dead. Only one of the travelers really believes that this will happen. Why, then, the journey? When it is over, who had benefited from it? Only as we consider alternatives can we arrive at an interpretation—not necessarily the author's but our own.

We generalize; we relate our thinking about alternatives to our lives and the rest of the world. Thus we have reached a stage of *reflective thinking*. It is a thematic level, where literature significantly touches life. It is a realm that the ancients knew, perhaps better than we do. They took their story-tellers and sages more seriously. How clever shall we be next time the wolf or some other threat comes to our door or playground? What do we know now about the possible rewards of what appears to be a fruitless endeavor?

These three levels represent the major part of Rosenblatt's transaction theory. (1) Evocation, the reader's absorption or surrender to the work, merges into (2) an alternative stage in which the reader interprets the work from many perspectives, arriving at (3) a reflective thinking level, where generalization, or theme, derived from the transaction relates to the reader's life or the world in general. In part, the theory is a reaction against text-bound theories in which the reader is perceived as passive. A question such as "What is the author's theme?" becomes, in the Rosenblatt model, something like this: "What theme do *you* get from your reading of *Missing May*?" In part, the theory attempts not to *prescribe* but to *describe* what happens when readers transact with literature. It attempts to look long and deep at the "why" of literary experience.

How to Present Children's Literature

Literary experience begins with evocation. It follows that teacher's first task is to stimulate evocation. How? To begin with, some literature requires little stimulation. It seems instantly to engage attention, stir the emotions, and connects to the reader's vivid experience.

If you visit different classrooms in different regions, you discover a great range in literature that evokes interest. Here you find series books, pop-ups, and cartoons. There you find elaborate picture books, chapter books with sustained suggestions of theme, and books of information. You may try to account for the difference by citing vocabulary and comprehension levels. Something else, though, seems to be operating.

Sometimes teachers help evocation without seeming to realize that they are doing so. Their enthusiasm shows, and it is genuine. They approach a book as an invitation to engage interest. They model reading with a spirit of inquiry. One teacher worried aloud about what happened to a horse named Penny, who in colonial times escaped from a cruel owner and ran off into the woods. The book, *Meet Felicity* (Tripp, 1991), didn't say. Another teacher tried to figure out how, in *The Wright Brothers: How They Invented the Airplane* (Freedman, 1991), Orville moved his hips and shoulders to steer the aircraft.

These are small but specific invitations to evocation. They may be more effective than direct instruction. Sometimes, indeed, we have set purposes for reading, our own or the textbook's, without engaging the reader's own sense of inquiry. Sometimes, too, we structure too tightly. You do not need a whole "schema" lesson on sheepherding in order to begin *Babe the Gallant Pig* (King-Smith, 1983).

Many children today read in order to share (Hickman, 1979). Sharing is part of evocation. Yet there are classrooms in which sustained silence reading stops there—with silence. And there are well-intentioned classrooms where the only discourse about literature is the teacher-pupil conference. Something more is needed: interaction.

One way to stimulate interaction is by literature circles, a "new" strategy that harks back to a family seated around the kitchen table trying to outguess the author of an eight-part serial in *The Saturday Evening Post*. Several readers (not more than seven) get together daily to share their thoughts about their reading, thus increasing the chances for evocation. They have a chairperson, and they can be coached initially by the teacher, who steers them toward "grand conversations" rather than interrogation (Eeds and Wells, 1989). When all members of the literature circle have read the same selection, their talk more easily shifts from evocation to alternatives such as these:

(1) Each person takes the point of view a character, posing as that character as the action unfolds. What are the different views of what is happening? Try this POV (point of view) technique, for instance, with the characters in a Newbery Medal book such as *Shiloh* (Naylor, 1991).

(2) Let the group decide ahead of time on a Big Question and come prepared to discuss it, packing their discussion kits or journals with evidence from first-hand experience and other reading. Sometimes the Big Question is weighty and very relevant. Students reading Paula Fox's *Monkey Island* (1991) ask: "What should a homeless kid do?"

Whether or not you choose to try literature circles, some provision for interaction is needed. It takes a dynamic leader to involve a whole class in literary discussion, but some teachers prove that it can be done. Paired reading, where two well-matched students read a selection and transact with it together, is another choice.

Response is learned; it "matures within a social context" (Probst, 1991, 660). But conversations about literature may lose the name of action and become stock response. We say a book is exciting, its characters true to life, such and such a scene terribly sad, the outcome thrilling. How do you rechannel such stock response? How do you keep alive the evocation, alternatives, and reflective thinking of literary transaction?

Children may not be very good at talk isolated from action. They are doers: activity as a mode of response is their thing. Thus, primary-age children can sit and talk about the strange and beautiful illustrations the Dillons have made for *Northern Lullaby* (Carlstrom, 1992), or they can get up and *be* the Moon, Star, Mountain, River, Moose, Hare, and all the rest personified by human figures in an Alaskan setting. Put music behind their mime (Brahms? Mahler?) and you have dance response while the text is read aloud. Return to the illustrations. Now they mean something more to the children, who have portrayed them.

In the past, activities have sometimes been selected randomly from a list. But if they are to be authentic extensions of response, they must be true to the literature. Clay figures may make memorable the positioning of *The Bremen Town Musicians* (Wilhelm, 1992) when they scare off robbers. The intricate action in *Mattimeo* (Jacques, 1990) can be better connected if the frontispiece map is enlarged on an overhead, sketched large, and routed like a military campaign to see how the hero followed Slagar the fox. Drama must also be authentic. Dialogue showing character contrast central to plot, such as conversations written by Jerry Spinelli or Betsy Byars, becomes readers' theater. Crucial scenes briefly told, especially those in distanced genres such as historical fiction and biography, are promising material for creative dramatics. Story theater, a recent technique, enlivens folklore: children mime the action as someone reads or tells the tale. These and other varieties of drama are within reach. You'll find them explained in Nellie McCaslin's *Creative Drama in the Classroom* (1990). teaching ideas applying specific extensions to current literature are featured widely in *Invitation to Reading*, edited by Cullinan (1992).

Over the past ten years, evidence from research and experience has grown: it shows that children's response to literature need nurture, using techniques such as those suggested above. Without that initial stage—evocation—little else will happen; hence the need to engage interest and encourage its expression. Some early observers thought that young children might not be capable of higher response levels, such as reflective or thematic thinking. Studies by Lehr (1988) and Louis (1991) show otherwise. It now appears that young children can respond to literature on many levels, including abstract ones, *if* the mode of response is appropriate (Don't ask them to write a paper discussing theme!) and if they are well guided. It is also a matter of finding literature that fits.

What Literature?

One reason for the rise in interest in children's literature is its increased availability. There are more books at all levels (4,500 new titles each year, 73,000 different titles in print), including a widening range in genres and multicultural representation. Another reason is that teachers, librarians, and other adults are themselves responding. From Maple Valley (Washington) to Shasta (California) to Midland (Texas) to Duluth (Minnesota)—all over the country you will find groups of adults who read so widely and enthusiastically in children's literature that they take your breath away.

A good program in children's literature begins with genre representation. Consider *realism*, a cluster of genres that attempts to transact with readers about *what is*. That cluster includes modern realistic fiction and historical fiction, informational nonfiction and biography. Consider the *fanciful*, a cluster that urges us to consider *what if*. Here you find the many varieties of folklore (myth, legend, fable, folktale), and modern fantasy and its technological off-shoot science fiction. Poetry—personal, narrative, lyric—has a place of its own. And picture books you will find to encompass all genres, from biography to folktale, and perhaps to be considered a visual literacy genre all their own. You can spend a day sorting a stock of books into genres. It isn't an idle endeavor if, as you sort, you consider the unique invitation of each to reader response.

Beware. All books are not of equal quality. Beware, too, of books recommended only by adults. Few adults include series books on their recommended lists, but children nearly always do. Pop-ups, pull-tabs, and "gross" cartooned books and outrageous sitcoms get passed around whether adults like them or not. They are often a first invitation to evocation. Remember them, and include some of them on your own reading list. The sign of progress is not when children stop reading books that adult critics don't mention or approve. The sign of progress is when they begin to select more widely and carefully, responding to all genres.

Genre variety. Current and class. The "good" and the popular. Books for easy evocation and books that lead firmly to reflective thinking. How do you find them? Here are some useful guides:

1. If you can find *Publishers Weekly*, browse through recent issues. They buzz with plans of publishers. Once a month they chart bestsellers in children's books in several categories. Note especially the series paperbacks that children buy.

2. *The Horn Book Magazine*, available in many libraries, is considered an authority on the best. Its board of reviewers writes a "Booklist" of best choices, appearing in each of the six issues per year. "The Hunt Breakfast" column lists current award winners.

3. Each year since 1974, *The Reading Teacher* (elementary-level journal of the International Reading Association) publishes an annotated list of "Children's Choices." These are more than a hundred books per year selected by children as current favorites. Look in October issues.

4. *Subject Guide to Children's Books in Print*, published by R.R. Bowker, lists all titles, assembled under 6,000 categories. If you want books about elephants or dinosaurs or about a specific period in U.S. history or Chinese folklore, here is your most extensive source. A more selective source, arranged by subject and with summaries, is *The Elementary School Library Collection* (see its "Selection Policies" at the front of the guide). Both of these guides are revised annually.

5. Several textbooks on children's literature contain chapters devoted to criteria and examples of each genre. At this writing, the most recent is *Through the Eyes of a Child*, by Donna E. Norton (3d edition, Merrill, 1991). Most influential and longest-running is *Children and Books*, now by Zena Sutherland and May Hill Arbuthnot, in its eighth edition (HarperCollins, 1991). See also *Literature and the Child* by Bernice E. Cullinan (2nd edition, Harcourt Brace Jovanovich, 1989).

Conclusion

Suppose that the next time you come out of a movie, someone hands you a workbook or journal that tells you to write a summary of the plot, a brief character sketch of the three main players, at least two facts about the author, and definitions of several vocabulary words unfamiliar to you. How will this assignment affect your future moviegoing? You may curtail your movie attendance.

In like manner, children who are asked to turn their literary experience to such ends may lose interest. Still, we want them to grow in their reading ability and understanding; we want to instruct them. Several ways out of the dilemma have been suggested. Rosenblatt (1991) urges for a 50-50 balance between an *aesthetic stance*, which refers to the "living through" transaction described in this chapter, and an *efferent stance*, which asks the reader to "carry away" information to be used for some purpose after the reading act. Norton (1992) and others would insert efferent "mini-lessons" into the transaction framework, so that readers will see the pertinence of comprehension strategies, schema, and vocabulary to their literary experience. Zarrillo (1991) tackled the problem head-on. He attempted aesthetic stance teaching in a fourth grade, recorded his sessions, established an "aesthetic teaching" hierarchy, and sorted out the results. His conclusion: "I am *not* arguing that aesthetic teaching constitutes a complete reading program. I would argue that there is a place aesthetic teaching in every classroom" (p. 230).

This new view has implications for assessment, as most reading researchers agree. It's high time to rethink assessment anyway. How much reading are children doing voluntarily? What is the range of genres and taste in their choices? If we examine their responses according to what we now know about transaction, what is the coverage and quality? Portfolios (Valencia, 1990), videos, interviews, and other means of assessment seem to be forthcoming. A renewed view of literature will include them and welcome them.

Atop my VCR is a lump of plastic shaped into a man painted silver. It is the Tin Woodman. His creator, L. Frank Baum, was a showman who didn't aspire to make a classic. Yet here he stands, almost a century later.

He tilts a little, a man of action uncertain where to go. How far does he see, I wonder, across my living room?

He is vulnerable but brave, and I think he is filled with good intentions. We know him because he reminds us of ourselves. Like ourselves, he searches for a heart. Like ourselves, he is mostly the product of the literary imagination.

References

Allington, R.L. 1977. "If They Don't Read Much How They Ever Gonna Get Good?" *Journal of Reading* 21: 57–61.

Anderson, R.C., L.L. Shirey, P.T. Wilson, and L.G. Fielding. 1987. "Interestingness of Children's Reading Materials." In R.E. Snow and M.J. Farr, eds., *Aptitude, Learning, and Instruction*, 3, Cognitive and Affective Process Analysis, 287–299.

Cullinan, B.E. ed., 1992. *Invitation to Read: More Children's Literature in the Reading Program*. Newark, Del.: International Reading Association.

Eeds, M., and D. Wells. 1989. "Grand Conversations: An Exploration of Meaning Construction in Literature Study Groups." *Research in the Teaching of English* 23: 4–29.

Fielding, L.H., P.T. Wilson, and R.C. Anderson. 1984. "A New Focus on Free Reading: Role of Trade Books in Reading Instruction." In T.E. Raphael and R.E. Reynolds, eds., *The Contexts of School-based Literacy*. New York: Random House.

Hickman, J. 1979. "Response to Literature in a School Environment, Grades K–5." Doctoral dissertation: The Ohio State University.

Lehr, S. 1988. "The Child's Developing Sense of Theme as a Response to Literature." *Reading Research Quarterly* 23: 337–357.

Louie, B.Y. 1991. "Enhancing Children's Concept of Theme with Metacognitive Instruction." Doctoral dissertation: University of Washington.

Lukens, R.J. 1990. *A Critical Handbook of Children's Literature*. 4th ed. Glenview, Ill.: Scott, Foresman/Little, Brown.

McCaslin, N. 1990. *Creative Drama in the Classroom*. 5th ed. New York: Longman.

Norton, D.E. 1992. *The Impact of Literature-Based Reading*. New York: Merrill.

Probst, R.E. 1991. "Response to Literature." In J. Flood, J.M. Jensen, D. Lapp, and J.R. Squire, eds., *Handbook of Research on Teaching the English Language Arts*. New York: Macmillan.

Rosenblatt, L.M. 1983. *Literature as Exploration*. 4th ed. New York: The Modern Language Association of America.

————1991. "Literature—S.O.S.!" *Language Arts* 68: 444–448.

Valencia, S.V. 1990. "A Portfolio Approach to Classroom Reading Assessment: The Whys, Whats, and Hows." *The Reading Teacher* 43: 338–340.

Zarrillo, J. 1991. "Theory Becomes Practice: Aesthetic Teaching with Literature." *The New Advocate* 4: 221–234.

Children's Books

Carlstrom, Nancy W. 1992 *Northern Lullaby*. Illustrated by Leo and Dianne Dillon. New York: Philomel.

Fox, Paula, 1991. *Monkey Island*. New York: Orchard.

Freedman, Russell. 1991. *The Wright Brothers: How They Invented the Airplane*. New York: Holiday House.

Jacques, Brian. 1990. *Mattimeo*. New York: Philomel.

King-Smith, Dick 1983. *Babe the Gallant Pig*. Illustrated by Mary Rayner. New York: Crown.

Naylor, Phyllis Reynolds. 1991. *Shiloh*. New York: Atheneum.

Rylant, Cynthia. 1992. *Missing May*. New York: Orchard.

Scieszka, Jon. 1989. *The True Story of the Three Little Pigs*. Illustrated by Lane Smith. New York: Viking Penguin.

Tripp, Valeria. 1991. *Meet Felicity, an American Girl*. Middleton, Wis.: Pleasant Company.

Wilhelm, Hans (reteller). 1992. *The Bremen Town Musicians*. New York: Scholastic.

2

Children's Book Publishing on the Ascent

John Donovan

The past decade has witnessed dramatic growth in children's book publishing. A decade ago 2,623 children's book titles were published according to R. R. Bowker's *Weekly Record;* five years later the total was 2,566; in 1990 the figure was 4,711. Book sales have also grown. According to Cahners Research, in 1980 combined hardcover and paperback sales for children's books amounted to slightly over $210 million; in 1985 sales were more than $336 million; in 1990, according to preliminary figures issued by the Industry Statistics Report of the Association of American Publishers, sales were well over $1 billion. Heady times for publishers. And a good time for those of us associated with publishing to take stock of the field.

Traditional Children's Book Publishers

A traditional publisher—and most well-known publishers are in this category—still relies heavily on the institutional market for the bulk of its sales, which are to libraries and schools. One way to ensure strong institutional sales is to have excellent reviews in a small number of publications that are read closely by potential children's book purchasers. Children's book publishers who are candid about this fact say that *School Library Journal* is the single most important reviewing publication to them. They also value highly reviews in the *Booklist* of the American Library Association, *The Horn Book Magazine,* and the *Bulletin* of the Center for Children's Books at the University of Chicago. This same list of publications would have been cited in respect to traceable sales of children's and young adult books ten or twenty years ago. About a dozen other regular reviewing sources together also appear to have an impact on sales figures, in particular the *Voice of Youth Advocates,* or VOYA, for young adult books, especially if reviews are favorable. Titles that are "starred," or emphasized in some other way, in these publications also appear to enjoy increased sales.

It is no news that when a book is honored with the Newbery or Caldecott Medal, its sales are substantial and it will probably remain in print indefinitely, and that the Honor Books for both of those awards programs also sell extraordinarily well. Publishers say that the other awards programs with substantial impact on sales are the various statewide, child-selected awards, but only in states that have organized these programs effectively. Having the winning title is not so important to publishers: the important thing is to have a title on the award reading list, usually fifteen or twenty titles that are read during the school year throughout the state. Other factors weigh heavily toward increasing institutional sales, including an author's "track record": few libraries or schools would *not* purchase new books by Paula Fox, Betsy Byars, Virginia Hamilton, Lloyd Alexander, Natalie Babbitt, Katherine Paterson, Mildred Taylor, or Jean Fritz, to cite easy examples.

Mass-Market Publishers

The more profitable market for children's books is in so-called mass markets. Until recently, Western Publishing, including Golden Books, and also Random House and Grosset & Dunlap, had a near-monopoly on mass-market children's book publishing. Currently, some firms with strong institutional lists have also entered mass-market publishing. When Putnam acquired Grosset & Dunlap, it was able to extend the Putnam publishing program into channels that Grosset opened to it. In mass-market children's book publishing, reviews and the other signs that institutional markets value highly are meaningless. Books tend to be sold not as titles, but as part of a line.

It is a mistake to conclude that if a book is part of a mass-market publishing program, it is not a very good book. Those who have studied the history of American children's book publishing know that some of the best titles in our literature have come from lists such as Golden Books, and that some of our foremost talents, such as the Provensens, have published comfortably for both traditional and mass-market houses. To oversimplify, a mass-market book can be found almost anywhere, while one has to look very hard to find the kind of book published in the more traditional way. The print run for a mass-market title is likely to be 75,000–100,000, while it is more likely to be 7,500–15,000 for a traditional title. The question that customarily follows is, Why don't publishers print larger numbers of so-called quality books, so they can be enjoyed by more children at cheaper prices? Alas, the customary and perfectly valid answer is that such books just do not seem to sell in mass-market outlets. When a traditional publisher does have a huge run for a new book, for a Chris Van Allsburg title, say, that book does not sell in mass-market outlets—which can be supermarkets, mall bookstores, drugstores, etc.—but sells in greater quantities in traditional outlets, namely to schools and libraries, and of course through bookstores.

Retail Markets

This brings me to the retail market for children's books. This is not a "new" market by any means, but it has become an important one for most children's book publishers only since the 1980s. It was always important for mass-market houses and it is still possible to visit some bookstores around the country and find only mass-market or series titles. Price is a big factor in such outlets. There have always been magic figures beyond which a title could not be sold; it was once 75¢, but of course it went up. Mass-market outlets today are uncomfortable with any children's title that has a price over $4.95, except for a will-be-in-the-family-forever title (poetry anthology) or you're-a-bad-parent-if-you-don't-buy-it title (Bible stories), which can tolerate prices of $9.95 or even $12.50.

I note that the retail market is not a new one, as the legendary children's book editor Louise Seaman—the first American exclusively children's books editor, at Macmillan, whose department she began in 1919—once assured me. In addition to generating a list of books for Macmillan, Louise Seaman had to pack up her new books twice a year and visit retail book outlets in major cities by train, to sell those titles to book buyers in department stores especially, but also in other important bookstores in Cleveland, Washington, D.C., Chicago, Boston, San Francisco, Los Angeles, etc. This was part of her job, and no second thought about it. It does not surprise that upon becoming Louise Seaman Bechtel within a decade, this estimable woman gave up children's book publishing, electing to spend a long career writing about others' books for the old *New York Herald Tribune*. The trail that Mrs. Bechtel blazed by railroad, was not, I think, hiked by the generations of legends who followed her as children's book editors, even though that function was later taken on by house staff whose principal function was to travel, though seldom to visit bookstores; *their* work involved libraries and school systems.

At the Children's Book Council (CBC) in the late 1960s, my colleagues and I found it interesting that so few good bookstores had a vigorous interest in selling children's books. It seemed odd in a great country like this one, with relatively successful bookstores, that children's books were such unimportant components of the stock offered for sale. After all, wasn't it obvious that there was a market for the books, that instead of waiting for patrons to reach fifteen before they shopped in the bookstore, they could and should begin to come at five, and even younger? Well, yes. And dozens of stores, maybe even hundreds, around the country, existed to prove the point. After a few years of wonderment on our part at CBC, it became clear that the one thing common to all the stores that sold children's books successfully was some-one—the owner, the owner's wife, a knowledgeable salesperson—who not only knew children's books (past and present) but loved them, and had the personality or ability to share that love and knowledge with customers. We set out to identify these people in 1971 and began to arrange for them to meet during the annual conventions of the American Booksellers Association. Our main purpose in arranging these meetings was to bring *them* together, so they could share their experiences and expertise with one another. After several years these people began their own association—the Association of Booksellers for Children, ABC—which now has about 450 bookstore members, an executive director, a newsletter, various national committees, and all the paraphernalia (baggage, some would say) of association life, and engages in many interesting cooperative activities.

This interest on CBC's part came at a time when many children's book publishers were retrenching from a boom in children's book sales that had accompanied post-Sputnik U.S. government largess to schools and libraries, which had been able to expand book collections, especially in the sciences. Children's book publishers benefited handsomely from these government programs for several years, and as they got phased out, or were diminished substantially, publishers had either to retrench or find new markets. For many houses—most, really—the retail trade was a new market. Although there may have been a dozen people around who knew of Louise Seaman's trips in the 1920s for Macmillan, nobody would follow that route more than fifty years later. Publishers did put together CBC's work with an emerging children's bookseller community, and their own needs for new markets, and within a couple of years, most publishers got the idea that they had found a "new" market.

It has been interesting to observe the growth of children's books-only bookstores in recent years. They have cropped up in most parts of the country, and more are opened (and, alas, closed) each year. The important characteristics of these stores—in contrast to, say, the many excellent general stores with strong holdings of children's books—is that they carry books in great breadth, from books for babies to (some, anyway) young adult fiction, though this second kind of book tends not to sell—certainly in hardcover— in such stores. Almost all of these stores have excellent selections of non-fiction titles, as is appropriate for a time when nonfiction is perceived to be "hot," anyway. While some remember that *The Horn Book Magazine* began its long life as the newsletter of the Bookshop for Boys and Girls, on Boylston Street in Boston, and there were other exclusively children's bookstores from the 1920s onward, there were not very many. By 1967, as far as we could determine at CBC, there was only one, The Magic Fishbone, in Carmel, California. This was a lovely little store in a posh town, where people had a lot of expendable income, there were a lot of tourists, and the U.S. Army had its Language School. A perfect place—economically—for a special-in-terest store. The Magic Fishbone was run by an imaginative former school-teacher who had customers and a mailing list that reached into all states of the union and several foreign countries within a few years of its opening. It was unique, for its day, and engaged in book fairs and autographing parties, published a newsletter, and advertised books in the local newspaper—all the things that most such bookstores do today. It was so successful that the owner was constantly sought out by others from around the country who wanted to open similar stores in their communities. The advice-giving got so time-consuming that the owner was forced, finally, to charge a substantial fee for a consultation—they continued unabated—and also started giving a course on children's bookstore operations.

Buying Children's Books in Bookstores

One interesting by-product of the reemergence of interest in retail sales of children's books—and not just in children's books-only stores, but in general stores and even in the chains—has been that there is now a more organized attempt to understand *who* is purchasing children's books. I shall allude to interesting experiences on the part of two individual publishers that spent time and money in attempting to understand their potential markets, but let me first mention a September 1990 survey by Cahners Research, as reported in the November 30, 1990 issue of *Publishers Weekly*. Cahners sent a questionnaire to 1,100 bookstores—general, including college; chain; and children's-only—and got a response from 30 percent, a high response rate in marketing. The information in the response was reported separately for the three types of stores—general, chain, and children's-only—and is telling, especially as it may help the stores (and also publishers supporting these stores with cooperative advertising) to focus their own marketing efforts toward people most likely to respond to them. Maybe it is no surprise that the single most active purchasers of children's books in all three types of stores are mothers, who are 38.9 percent of the customers in general stores and 44.7 percent in chain stores. Teachers make up 24.7 percent of the customers in children's-only stores, and I have the strong suspicion that many teachers spend their own money in such stores, as they comprise only about 10 percent of the customers for children's books in the other two types of stores. It is a big disappointment that fathers are not frequent purchasers of children's books in any of the three types of stores. And it is interesting that children themselves hardly darken the doorways of children's-only stores, at least as purchasers: they spend their own money in general bookstores and the chains. It is a big surprise that grandparents are infrequent purchasers. When I entered the children's book field, many stores around the country were known as grandparent stores: they stocked classics heavily, lots of books that Granny read as a child or read to her own children; these stores also customarily had a lot of prize-winning books. Booksellers often said, "Put a bright shiny sticker on the cover, any sticker will do, it makes customers think they are buying a book that someone—anyone—has honored, so it must be good." That sounds cynical, and it is, except it reveals, I think, how at loose ends most people feel when they buy books for children. If the salesperson is not familiar with children's books, the customer needs the assurance that she is not buying trash, or, if it's trash, at least it's trash that children really like.

A second survey by Cahners Research revealed which children's books— by type—people buy in bookstores. Although these survey results were published more than two years ago, and I think would be slightly different today (with more books being purchased for older children), they are interesting as the most current information we have. The most-purchased books are picture books (27%); books for younger readers amount to 20 percent of the purchases; middle readers, 19 percent; and books for babies and toddlers and for young adults each account for 17 percent of sales. Those who follow the monthly children's bestseller lists in *Publishers Weekly* will understand, from this survey, why that magazine lists ten titles for picture books in its reports; currently its four other categories, each of which includes five titles only, are "younger readers," "middle readers," "young adults," and "non-fiction."

Two Publishers Enter (and Leave) Children's Book Publishing

I noted that I would describe market research activities of two individual publishers. I feel at liberty to do this as in both instances what happened is now a part of children's book publishing history, albeit largely unreported. The first such activity was in the early 1980s, when the Hanes Hosiery people—manufacturers of the successful L'eggs product—considered becoming involved with children's books. After years of heavy market research, the Hanes people actually offered nearly two hundred children's books from most publishers' backlists in four markets: Rochester, N.Y., Kansas City, Mo., Milwaukee, and Salt Lake City. These were excellent titles, published as paperback "Starbooks," and retailing for from 69¢ to $1.69. People who purchased "Starbooks" also received a free copy of a book titled *Children's Reading Begins at Home: How Parents Can Help Their Young Children*, by Nancy Larrick. The cornerstone of the Hanes project was its distribution network: L'eggs were available in about 80,000 stores nationwide. Supermarkets and other outlets for L'eggs valued that product highly because it did not take up much room and offered a large 27 percent profit to vendors, whose profits on food, for example, are only about 2 percent. Hanes introduced "Starbooks" into its four test markets, with a TV and print advertising blitz, as a result of which the product was well received.

There were rumblings from retailers at the time: how could a regular bookstore sell a popular book at full price when it was available at the supermarket—albeit in a paperback edition with a special "Starbook" spine (but the same cover design)—for only a quarter of the price? Had the activity gone national, there would certainly have been court actions under the Sherman Antitrust Act, but it never did go national, not because it would not have been successful (it most surely would have), but because Hanes was testing a cosmetics line at the same time it was testing the children's book line, and saw that purchasers would be far more enthusiastic about makeup than about children's literature. So "Starbooks" was abandoned. A few months later, the man in charge of "Starbooks" called me to inquire whether CBC would be interested in purchasing the Hanes market research to share with our members. "How much?" I asked. "We'll let you have it for $13 million," was the answer.

The second market research activity, which actually ended up as a children's book publishing program, was a mid-1980s undertaking by Parker

Brothers, the game people. Within two years of introducing its first list, Parker Brothers became the third-highest-grossing children's book publisher for that year, after Western Publishing and Random House. Yet Parker concluded that, even with its enormous (by "our" standards) financial success, the money it realized seemed like petty cash; children's books pale next to the toy and game industries when it comes to making money, and so Parker immediately withdrew from publishing.

I think a lot of people in children's book publishing are in the field for a lot of wrong reasons. Their purpose is to make money, which makes no sense at all. If a company wants only to make money, why not go where the real money is? Parker Brothers tells us that this makes sense, and I admire it for recognizing in very short order that "real" money is not to be found in children's books, and for withdrawing from the field gracefully, even though it was clear that in our little world the company could have become a major publisher if it had chosen to stay.

Children's book publishers have adopted some of the unattractive business practices of our colleagues in publishing for adults. The worst practice is to fail to keep books in print. There are a lot of valid economic reasons for this. Not least among them is that warehousing older books is a huge expense, and one that often cannot be justified if a title sits unsold for two, three, or more years. But now that children's book publishers have accepted that they will declare some—most of their list, in many instances—titles out-of-print (O/P) within a year or so if the book has not sold well immediately, this has become the standard way to do business, not the exceptional one. There have always been publishers of ephemeral children's books that were not designed to last beyond a season or two—books about a popular athlete, books about computers, etc.—but the worrisome thing these days is that some publishers now factor in the O/P possibility right from the beginning, so there will always be room (and money) left for more and more new books, themselves destined for the O/P graveyard, nine titles out of ten. This approach was unthinkable in children's books previously, when most worthwhile houses thought they were publishing a title, if not for the ages, at least for the decade.

I am fortunate in my job in being able to see almost all new children's books published every year, and as a result I do not subscribe to the generally accepted perception that American children's book publishers aggressively do *not* seek out and publish books about diverse cultures in this country. I have to observe, however, that the "treasures" are few and far between; but I would say this about *all* children's books each year. This is not to say that individual writers and illustrators have not, themselves, made outstanding contributions to our literature, but to observe that the African American, Spanish-speaking, Native American, Asian American, handicapped, economically deprived, gay, or any other minority child has not exactly been on the front burner of most children's book publishers' publishing programs. I used to wonder about this quite a bit, but it no longer puzzles me so much, and for once the explanation is not rooted in economics. Publishers are basically reactive. They tend to evaluate what is in front of them; with the exception of overtly commercial projects, most good publishers do not construct ideas for authors and illustrators, though some often suggest possibilities to people already on their lists. In most publishing houses, there's hardly anyone who is in a position to seek out minority literature regularly and naturally. People used to wonder why so many books for boys and girls were set in boarding schools. It's simple: most of the old-time editors went to boarding schools. That isn't the case any more, but we do not yet have many people with decision-making editorial jobs who really know or are a part of a minority culture. Children's book publishers have a genuine personnel problem. A first step toward solving it would be to own up to it.

What is the near-term outlook for children's book publishing? Some factors are deeply satisfying to publishers as they think of their children's book plans for the next decade. According to the Book Industry Study Group, by 1994 children's book sales should amount to about $1.5 billion. The U.S. Department of Education projects that elementary school enrollments will not level off until the middle of this decade, while high school enrollments will certainly increase into the next century. As children's book publishers also publish young adult books, the prospects are encouraging, especially as parents in the United States—at least those who can spend money—are more than ever before committed to being certain that *their* children grow up as readers. Coincidentally, public and private institutions throughout the country appear to have a real interest in early reading programs for children whose parents cannot afford to purchase books for a home library. At the same time, budget cuts in public institutions nationwide are threats to these estimable programs.

Even so, while there is clear evidence that publishers' trade sales are increasing—though libraries and schools continue to receive the brunt of publishers' marketing efforts—aspects of this new situation surprise both the retailer and the publisher. For example, even though (according to the NPD Group report "What's Hot, What's Not") in the last quarter of 1990, U.S. independent bookstores (stores not affiliated with a chain store) sold five times as many children's hardcovers and paperbacks as they sold books in any other nine categories, publishers experienced an unsatisfying and unprofitable 24.8 percent children's hardcover books returns rate (from all sources) in the first quarter of 1991, according to the Statistics Program of the Association of American Publishers. While signs point to rosy expectations, only a reckless publisher would be complacent.

3

These Turbulent Times

Bernice E. Cullinan

NEWS ITEM: Children's Books Are Hot. The auction for rights to *Polar Bear, Polar Bear, What Do You Hear?* written by Bill Martin Jr. and illustrated by Eric Carle (Holt, 1991) closed at $400,000, giving Scholastic the right to publish a hardcover edition for the children's book club market. (*New York Times*, April 3, 1991 p. C-17)

NEWS ITEM: President George Bush announces a new education initiative, a plan giving the federal government major responsibility for improving the quality of secondary and elementary schools. The proposal calls for a national system of examinations, getting businesses involved in schools, and giving parents a choice about which school their children attend. (*New York Times*, April 21, 1991, sec. 4, p. 7)

NEWS ITEM: Reading Initiatives Take Hold. Literature-based, whole-language programs are spreading across the nation, changing the face of library programs and reading instruction in school curricula. (*School Library Journal*), April 1989, pp. 27–31)

Dramatic changes are occurring in the educational world, in book publishing, in government's role in education, and in school curricula. The changes are revolutionary. As one observer comments, we can't hope for a renaissance without a revolution. A renaissance in education, particularly in the attention to reading, writing, listening, and speaking, is possible. This review is limited to the revolutionary changes in methods and materials used to teach reading.

Review of the Literature

Trade books are used for instructional purposes more widely than ever before; textbooks are largely anthologies of good literature. Research that supports the changes toward literature-based programs comes from four areas: the effect of reading on writing, schema theory and narrative as a primary act of mind, research on writing, and studies of how children spend their time.

The Effect of Reading on Writing

Diane DeFord (1981) examined the kind of writing children do in first-grade classrooms in relation to the kind of reading program they have. She found that children taught in strong synthetic phonics programs write only the sounds of language they are taught to read. An example of writing from these classrooms: "I had a Dad. I had a gag." Children taught to read linguistically consistent word patterns write using only the patterns they know, for example: "I am Jill. I am Bill. Jill. Bill." In whole-language, or literature-rich, classrooms, where teachers surround children with books, newspapers, and magazines and encourage children to use invented spelling, they draw upon a richer fund of language. An example from these classrooms: "Iran is fighting U.S. 19 bombers down. 14 fighters. We olny have 3 bombers down. 6 fighters. We have droped 9 bombs over Iran. The hostges have been there long now. We head twards them. It's like a game of checers. We have destroyed Iran. Singing out. Jason." DeFord shows us that children draw upon the language used around them as they learn to write. If they read the interesting language of expository and narrative literature, that is what they will use in their writing. If they read stilted primerese language, that is what they will use in their own writing. DeFord's study was the first of many to show us that children write the kind of language they read.

Schema Theory and Narrative as a Primary Act of Mind

A group of theorists in England—Barbara Hardy (1978), James Britton (1970), and Harold Rosen (1973), among others—focus on the power of narrative and our hunger for story. Hardy reminds us that we remember the past in narrative, plan the future in narrative, and dream in narrative. In fact, narrative is the way we organize our minds. We live our lives as a story in which we are the central character. Another group of cognitive psychologists shows us that we remember new information better when we have a schema or a framework for remembering it. Anderson (1985) and other researchers at the Center for the Study of Reading gave subjects a list of thirty items to be picked up at the grocery store and a few minutes to study the list. Subjects remembered six to eight items. When researchers gave experimental groups the same list of thirty items but told them they were going to have a dinner party with an appetizer course, salad course, entrée, dessert, and coffee, subjects remembered twenty-six to twenty-eight items. When we have a schema for what we are learning, we remember much more. Story, or narrative structure, provides a schema or a framework for remembering.

Research On Writing

Leading writing researchers such as Don Graves (1983, 1991), Lucy Calkins (1990), Jane Hansen (1987), Nancie Atwell (1987), Jerome Harste (1988), and others found that teachers who provide models of good writing show children what real writers can do. They turn to children's literature for the good examples. In writing workshops, teachers read aloud and children read alone, from a variety of trade books, examples of high-quality writing. Children borrow from the models and use them to shape their own stories and expository pieces of writing. They learn that good writing has a structure by seeing the structures in their books; they adopt the patterns for their own writing. Children's literature is a vital part of writing workshops.

Studies of How Children Spend Their Time

The fourth research area to support an increase in the use of trade books in classrooms is the study of the amount of time students spend actually reading. For example, Richard Allington (1980, 1983) sat in classrooms with a stopwatch to measure the time spent in reading groups. He found that instructional periods for poor readers were much shorter than those for good readers. Teachers just could not tolerate the slow, laborious reading of poor readers and, therefore, cut the reading periods short. Thus students who need the most practice get the least.

We learned from Allington that remedial readers do not get as much practice reading as good readers, but what about all children in regular classrooms? Anderson (1985) reports a study by Dishaw (1977), who found that the amount of time most children spend reading in the average classroom is small. An estimate of silent reading time in the typical primary school class is seven to eight minutes a day. By the middle grades, silent reading time may average ten to fifteen minutes a day. Children spend most of their reading time at school filling in blanks or matching words and pictures.

Children do not spend much time reading at school, but what about outside school? Fielding, Wilson, and Anderson (1986) had children record their activities outside school in daily log books. For the majority of children, reading from books occupied 1 percent of their free time, or less. It is clear that children cannot develop fluency in reading unless they practice reading a lot. Reading seven to fifteen minutes a day at school and less than 1 percent of the time outside school does not provide adequate practice.

Teachers using whole-language and literature-based programs try to counter these statistics by giving children appealing books that they choose to read on their own. They also provide time to read in school. Attempts to increase the amount of reading children do include sustained silent reading, self-selected reading from trade books, and literature-based reading programs.

Survey of Statewide Reading Initiatives

In 1986, California State Superintendent of Schools Bill Honig stated, "A love of reading and books is one of the most important gifts we can give our young people. I want to encourage students to read and I want them to enjoy reading." With Honig's statement as the watchword, the State Department of Education launched the California Reading Initiative directed at teaching children to read well and to love doing it. Other states watched what was happening in California; some began their own reading and language arts initiatives.

Corollary to the spread of statewide initiatives, the whole-language movement, which includes the heavy use of literature in reading programs, was gaining momentum. The whole-language movement is a grassroots effort led by teachers and librarians who observe children learning to love to read through literature. The movement is grounded in three basic beliefs: children learn to read by actually reading, reading is part of language learning, and learning in any one area of language helps learning in other areas. Teachers and librarians who adhere to this philosophy provide unlimited opportunities for children to read suitable materials that support their desire to read.

In 1989, I conducted a survey of the state departments of education to see what was happening in literature-based programs. I received responses from all fifty states, most from state directors of reading and language arts but in a few cases from state presidents of the International Reading Association. The results, shown in Figure 1, indicate that nine states have statewide literacy-literature initiatives, seventeen have statewide integrated language arts initiatives with a literature strand, twenty-one have no statewide initiative but have many local districts using literature-based programs, and only three states report continuing their basic skills program.

Arizona, illustrative of the states with a statewide initiative, has three major components: Literacy Forum, Literacy Sites, and Bookstarts. The Literacy Forum, composed of university professors, district superintendents, curriculum coordinators, principals, librarians, teachers, consultants, and Department of Education specialists, serves as a guiding force to identify issues to be addressed and to propose possible solutions. The members of the Literacy Forum develop position papers, conduct research, and inform others about new approaches to literacy development.

A Literacy Site is a place where children learn to love to read and learn to do it well. The site may be an entire school, a library media center, or a classroom. The Arizona State Department of Education sends guidelines to every school in the state for the identification and establishment of Literacy Sites. One requirement for Literacy Sites is that they invite observers to their schools to see how they function.

Bookstarts is an ongoing series of annotated lists of book titles appropriate for children ages five to twelve. Each month, the Arizona State Department of Education publishes individual bookmarks to add to a packet featuring

FIGURE 1
LITERATURE AND LITERACY INITIATIVES

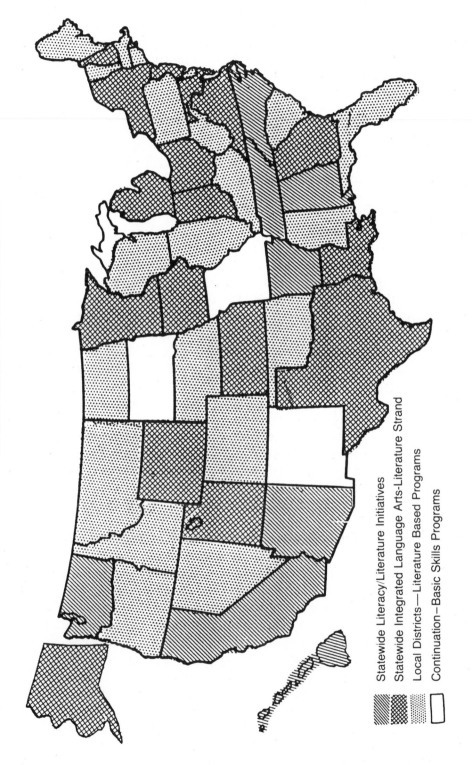

Statewide Literacy/Literature Initiatives

Statewide Integrated Language Arts-Literature Strand

Local Districts—Literature Based Programs

Continuation—Basic Skills Programs

different types of books. Teachers and librarians recommend for the lists titles of books that work well for them. Librarians, an integral part of the Arizona initiative, are involved in the development, implementation, and evaluation of the program.

Michigan, Minnesota, and New York illustrate the statewide integrated language arts initiatives. These states focus more broadly on an integrated curriculum in which literature is used widely. Leaders in these states suggest illustrative titles but are not ready to recommend a list of specific books. In Minnesota, for example, teachers use literature as a model for writing, as a way to understand cultural legends, and as the basis for listening, reading, writing, and speaking activities. Literature is a visible strand in all integrated language arts initiatives.

The twenty-one states with no statewide initiative but with many local districts using literature and whole-language programs are ones with strong local control of curriculum. Local districts reserve the right to select programs and materials. One state director of reading and language arts stated, "Our people would think we were part of a communist plot if we tried to tell them which books to read." Individual districts in each state have adopted whole-language and literature-based programs.

Three state directors of reading and language arts reported a continuation of the competency-based skills programs. Despite the state departments' official position, individual teachers in each state are using literature-based whole-language programs.

In summary, literature-based programs are spreading like wildfire across the country—not only through state departments of education but in individual teachers' classrooms. The grassroots movement in which teachers and librarians gain power to make curriculum decisions is growing. More trade books are used in instruction and for independent reading than ever before.

Sources of Influence on the Use of Trade Books

During the last decade a number of groups evolved to help teachers and librarians implement whole-language and literature-based programs. Some are totally new organizations created to support staff development, such as the Whole Language Umbrella group, the National Reading Initiative, and the American Association of Publishers Reading Initiative. Some are established professional organizations that expanded programmatic offerings, such as the International Reading Association, the National Council of Teachers of English, and the American Library Association. This review focuses on one organization, the International Reading Association, and its broadened offerings through publications, conference programs, and membership services.

In 1974, in cooperation with the Children's Book Council, the International Reading Association established Children's Choices, a national field test of newly published books that children like. Five regional teams of teachers and librarians try out hundreds of new books with children in classrooms and libraries. Children vote on their favorites. The top one hundred or so books selected by all of the regions are annotated; the final list appears in the October issue of *The Reading Teacher*.

The International Reading Association supports two other book selection projects: Teachers' Choices and Young Adult Choices. Both national field tests are patterned after the Children's Choices project. Teachers' Choices is a list of approximately thirty books that teachers find to be outstanding for curriculum use; they are books that students might not find on their own or without a knowledgeable guide. Young Adult Choices is a list of books that students in grades 7 through 12 like. Both Teachers' Choices and Young Adult Choices are annotated and appear in the November issue of *The Reading Teacher*.

The International Reading Association has a long and prestigious history of staff development through its publications and conference programs. One book, *Children's Literature in the Reading Program* (1987), contains chapters by seventeen leading children's literature specialists featuring ways to incorporate literature into reading programs. This book sold more than 100,000 copies. *Emerging Literacy* (1989) focuses on how children learn skills related to language and literacy. Experts in children's literacy development share ideas to be used with children ages two through eight years. Other publications directed to the use of literature in literacy programs include *Comics to Classics: A Parent's Guide to Books for Teens and Preteens*; *Young Children and Picture Books: Literature from Infancy to Six*; *How Children Construct Literacy: Piagetian Perspectives*; and *Our Daughter Learns to Read and Write: A Case Study from Birth to Three*.

IRA conference programs at local, state, regional, national, and international levels feature authors, children's literature specialists, and teachers using literature-based programs in their classrooms. In addition, IRA sponsors staff development courses and seminars through offerings developed by association members. Many of the seminars and courses focus on using literature in the classroom.

These recent developments signify a revolution in education that can lead to a renaissance. Children's books are produced in greater numbers and attract higher prices in rights-bidding auctions. George Bush claims to be the education president and makes proposals that will profoundly affect schools in the United States. Teachers and librarians clamor to use new trade books in classrooms and libraries. State departments of education spread literature-based programs in literacy, literature and integrated language arts initiatives throughout many states. Professional organizations continue to promote new ideas in teaching with literature. Whether or not we achieve the renaissance remains to be seen.

References

Allington, R. L. 1980. "Teacher Interruption Behaviors during Primary Grade Oral Reading." *Journal of Educational Psychology* 72:371–372.

————. 1983. "The Reading Instruction Provided Readers of Differing Ability." *Elementary School Journal* 83:255–265.

Anderson, Richard, et al. 1985. *Becoming a Nation of Readers: The Report of the Commission on Reading*. Washington, D.C.: National Institute of Education, U.S. Department of Education.

Atwell, Nancie. 1987. *In the Middle: Writing, Reading, and Learning with Adolescents*. Portsmouth, N.H.: Heinemann.

Baghban, Marcia. 1983. *Our Daughter Learns to Read and Write: A Case Study from Birth to Three*. Newark, Del.: International Reading Association.

Britton, James. 1970. *Language and Learning*. New York: Penguin Books.

Calkins, Lucy McCormick, with Shelley Harwayne. 1990. *Living Between the Lines*. Portsmouth, N.H.: Heinemann.

Cullinan, Bernice E., Ed. 1987. *Children's Literature in the Reading Program*. Newark, Del.: International Reading Association.

————. 1989. "Latching on to Literature: Reading Initiatives Take Hold." *School Library Journal* (April), 35, 8:27–31.

DeFord, Diane. 1981. "Literacy: Reading, Writing and Other Essentials." *Language Arts* (September), 58, 6:652–658.

Dishaw, M. 1977. "Descriptions of Allocated Time to Content Areas for the A-B Period." *Beginning Teacher Evaluation Study*. Technical Note IV-11a. San Francisco: Far West Regional Laboratory for Educational Research and Development.

Fielding, Linda G., Paul T. Wilson, and Richard C. Anderson. 1986. "A New Focus on Free Reading: The Role of Trade Books in Reading Instruction." In *The Contexts of School-Based Literacy*, ed. Taffy E. Raphael. New York: Random House, 149–160.

Goodman, Yetta M., Ed. 1990. *How Children Construct Literacy: Piagetian Perspectives*. Newark, Del.: International Reading Association.

Graves, Donald H. 1983. *Writing: Teachers and Children at Work*. Portsmouth, N.H.: Heinemann.

————. 1991. *Build a Literate Classroom*. Portsmouth, N.H.: Heinemann.

Hansen, Jane. 1987. *When Writers Read*. Portsmouth, N.H.: Heinemann.

Hansen, Jane, Thomas Newkirk, and Donald Graves, Eds. 1985. *Breaking Ground: Teachers Relate Reading and Writing in the Elementary School*. Portsmouth, N.H.: Heinemann.

Hardy, Barbara. 1978. "Narrative as a Primary Act of Mind." In *The Cool Web: The Pattern of Children's Reading*, ed. Margaret Meek, Aidan Warlow, and Griselda Barton. New York: Atheneum, 12–23.

Harste, Jerome C., Kathy Short, and Carolyn Burke. 1988. *Creating Classrooms for Authors: The Reading-Writing Connection*. Portsmouth, N.H.: Heinemann.

Jalongo, Mary Renck. 1988. *Young Children and Picture Books: Literature from Infancy to Six*. Newark, Del.: International Reading Association.

Reed, Arthea (Charlie). 1988. *Comics to Classics: A Parent's Guide to Books for Teens and Preteens*. Newark, Del.: International Reading Association.

Rosen, Harold, and Connie Rosen. 1973. *The Language of Primary School Children*. London: Penguin, Education for the Schools Council.

Strickland, Dorothy S., and Lesley Mandel Morrow, Eds. 1989. *Emerging Literacy: Young Children Learn to Read and Write*. Newark, Del.: International Reading Association.

4

"Have You Heard About an African Cinderella Story?": The Hunt for Multiethnic Literature

Violet J. Harris

I received a telephone call from a school librarian who wanted to ascertain whether an African variant of Cinderella had been published recently:

Dorothy: Have you heard a rumor that an African version of Cinderella has been published?

Violet: It's not a rumor. I have a copy of the book and the illustrations are extraordinary. Believe it or not, there is a fairy tale in which the prince is literally tall, dark, and handsome.

Dorothy: Well, I have to get a copy.

The fairy tale in question was *Mufaro's Beautiful Daughters* (Steptoe, 1987), a Zimbabwean variant of Cinderella. The book received numerous accolades, including designation as a Caldecott Honor Book and the *Boston Globe-Horn Book* award for illustration. The tale is even more important because it was John Steptoe's last book, the culmination of a brilliant career. Most people who see the book have an immediate response: they ooh and ahh. The illustrations are simply stunning. After that come expressions of astonishment: the listener or reader did not know that a range of Cinderella variants exists. Then people marvel at the nontraditional portrayal of an African country.

Steptoe commented upon this ground-breaking tale and spoke about the cultural influences, many negative and others positive, that led to his adaptation and illustration of the tale. He spoke of the need to create the tale in response to feelings of worthlessness because of the racial climate in the United States (Natov and De Luca, 1987, 122–129). Further, he stated, "I wanted to create a book that included some of the things that were left out of my own education about people who were my ancestors" (Steptoe, 1988, pp. 25–28). Steptoe recognized that the traits extolled in Cinderella—dignity, grace, strong sense of tradition, industriousness, kindness, and consideration—were apparent in the Zimbabwean variant and in his own family. Yet, the images of himself and his culture that he received through print and electronic media were decidedly negative (Steptoe, 1988):

> You know, being a child of the fifties, I was told in white magazines that Africans said "ooga booga": they didn't come from a complex society. So I wanted to find out about African culture. And my research took me to southeast Africa where there was trade with China as far back as 500 B.C. The story I found was a fairy tale recorded by a missionary. It was originally called "The Story of Five Heads." It took me about a year to research the story and about another year and a half to write and illustrate it. (Natov and De Luca, 1986, 128–129)

Steptoe's philosophical, historical, and psychological journeys enabled him to create a legacy in children's literature. Other books, such as *Aida* (Price, 1990), *The House on Mango Street* (Cisneros, 1989), and *Tales from Gold Mountain* (Yee, 1990), are capable of generating similar responses.

A market exists for these and other "multiethnic" books, though the market remains mainly unserved. In this article, I will examine some of the reasons why multiculturalism has reemerged as an influential philosophy in education, how this reemergence affects children's literature, the current boom in children's literature, the marginalized status of multiethnic children's literature vis-à-vis this boom, and some suggestions for publishers.

Reemergence of Multiculturalism in Education

Some educators have long noted a need for education that apprises students of this nation's cultural diversity. They have viewed these efforts as resulting in the development of tolerance and expanded knowledge about the history and contributions of various ethnic, racial, and linguistic "minorities" (Banks, 1990; Gay, 1988). A number of labels identify this rejuvenated movement, including cultural diversity, multiculturalism, pluralism, and cultural pluralism. Several groups of individuals are lumped under these various labels. Among them are ethnic and racial "minorities," women and girls, poor and working-class individuals, individuals with a range of proficiency in English, the elderly, religious minorities, lesbians and gays, and the disabled (Banks, 1990; Gay, 1988; Gollnick and Chin, 1986). However, not everyone agrees that each of these groups experiences similar treatment or suffers the same degree of racism, prejudice, or bigotry.

Various factors have acted as catalysts for the renewed emphasis on multiculturalism in schooling. First is the impact of the movements for equality, exemplified by the civil rights and women's rights struggles. Some of the individuals associated with these movements targeted educational institutions as significant in maintaining inequality and potentially powerful in eliminating inequality. Anderson (1988) documented why these conclusions were reasonable based on his analysis of the systematic limitations placed on African American education until the 1960s:

> From the end of Reconstruction until the late 1960s, black southerners existed in a social system that virtually denied them citizenship, the right to vote, and the voluntary control of their labor power. They remained an oppressed people. Black education developed within this context of political and economic oppression. Hence, although black southerners were formally free during the time when American popular education was transformed into a highly formal and critical social institution, their schooling took a different path. (p. 2)

Women and other ethnic and racial groups were denied equal educational access in a similar manner.

Second, changing demographics suggest the need for multicultural education. U.S. Census Bureau data suggest that approximately 55 percent of the U.S. population will be African, Asian, and Latino American by the year 2100 (Barbuto, 1991). Some shifts in power will occur as these groups acquire economic and political parity. Certainly, some will focus their attention on schools and the type of curricula offered. Some evidence of shifting political power can be seen in attempts to change "Eurocentric" curricula and in lawsuits filed in some states to equalize school funding. Further, because many schools, especially those in urban areas, are populated wholly by students of color, educators argue that teachers will have to possess some understanding of the students' cultures, histories, experiences, educational goals, and learning/communication styles (Banks, 1990; Gray, 1988).

A third catalyst for multicultural education results from increased incidents of "ethnoviolence" (violence precipitated because of a person's ethnicity or race), gay bashing, and abuse of the elderly and women (*Newsweek*, December 24, 1990). Once again, individuals place the burden of ameliorating or eradicating these conditions on schools. Schooling can help promote tolerance and reduce bigotry and prejudice, but other cultural institutions such as churches, the electronic media, the courts, and businesses will have to assume greater responsibility as well. For instance, the overwhelming majority of portrayals of African Americans in the news media are as entertainers, athletes, criminals, and individuals mired in abject poverty. These are realities, but they are not the only portrayals of African Americans possible.

Few, for example, know of the achievements of Dr. Raymond Massey, the current director of the National Science Foundation, or Dr. Mae Jemison, the first African American female astronaut-designee. The achievements of these and other individuals were profiled extensively in the African American press but not in the "mainstream" press.

A fourth catalyst that will affect literary curricula and publishing most is the effort to expand literary canons to include exemplars that depict multi-cultural experiences. Canons emerge as a result of several cultural, artistic, literary, and political processes. For instance, specific works appear on recommended reading lists; critics and scholars refer to these works continuously and compare new works to them; colleges and universities offer courses and seminars about the works; students in college preparatory classes read them, presumably, to help gain entrance into college; and "guardians of tradition" help perpetuate the notion that these works represent the best in Western literary traditions. Somehow, many of those engaged in the debates forget that many of the works enshrined in current canons are by authors who engendered new literary trends that were criticized at their inception.

The debates about expanding literary canons generated several terms that suggest opposition to or support for diversity. For instance, the phrase *race, class, and gender* elicits dichotomous responses. Some view it as an indication of the "new McCarthyism" or intolerance on the left (D'Souza, 1991; Ravitch, 1990); others perceive it as an end to ideological hegemony (Taxel, 1991). Moreover, some critics of analyses based on race, class, and gender abhor what they term the "politicization" of literature. Joel Taxel, editor of the *New Advocate*, penned an essay entitled "On the Politics of Children's Literature" (1991, pp. vii–xii). He argued that one cannot divorce evaluation of children's literature from the sociopolitical contexts that shaped that literature:

> The dominant approach to the study of children's literature *has been* to divorce the discussion of literature from issues of politics. During the 60s and 70s, for example, when the civil rights and women's movements were gathering national and international attention there were many within children's literature circles who steadfastly insisted that issues of race and gender bias had little to do with the evaluation and selection of books for young people. (p. vii)

He continued by asserting that discussions about literature have always been depoliticized, allowing for exclusion of the political: "the very claim of such a separation itself *must* be seen as profoundly political because it effectively masks and thereby removes from the realm of possible discussion that which is denied but, if we are honest, must be finally acknowledged" (p. x). Taxel contends that children need books that "address social issues of our day" and that "we must insist that important issues and themes be presented in ways that make their development inseparable from that of plot, story, and character" (p. xi). For Taxel, the works of Mildred Taylor, Vera Williams,

Lloyd Alexander, and others combine literary excellence with political and social consciousness.

Canon wars will continue even after multiculturalism becomes an integral tenet of literary curricula or the movement loses some of its prominence in schooling. Nevertheless, the resurgence of the movement affects children's literature and has brought about the demand, again, for multicultural and multiethnic literature.

Demands for Multiethnic Literature

Requests and demands for multiethnic literature are not of recent origin. Abolitionist literature in the 1800s forged a path for modern-day multiethnic literature. For example, a children's journal, *The Slave's Friend* (1836–1838), published poetry, stories, and essays that were pleas for the emancipation and equitable treatment of freed persons. The early 1900s saw a continuation of this trend for equality in literature. For instance, W. E. B. DuBois, the editor of the *Crisis Magazine*, the official publication of the National Association for the Advancement of Colored People, published several statements that decried the depiction of African Americans in school texts, literature, and the periodical press. His remedy for children was the creation of a periodical that he named *The Brownies' Book* (1920–1921) and a publishing company that published a collective biography for children as alternatives to the mainstream press (Harris, 1990). Carter G. Woodson, like DuBois, protested the depiction of African Americans. He, too, published journals, *The Negro History Bulletin*, for example, which devoted several pages to materials for children. He established a publishing company, The Associated Publishers, which is the oldest publishing company established by African Americans still in existence. The Associated Publishers had one of the most varied backlists, in terms of genre and number of books, of any African American publishing company until the 1960s (Harris, 1991).

Asian Americans, Latinos, and Native Americans have comparable literary and publishing heritages. Palomino (1988), for example, analyzed the portrayal of Japanese Americans and found that their portraits in children's literature were limited. Most books portrayed quaint customs or model Japanese Americans. Alternatives depicting Japanese Americans as multifaceted individuals existed, albeit outside mainstream publishing. Palomino labeled many of the works of authors such as Toshio Mori, Momoko Iko, and Milton Murayama as working-class novels, plays, and poems. Native Americans also have small presses that provide a forum for voices excluded from mainstream presses. One press, The Greenfield Review Press, publishes literature that reflects authentic cultural traditions of a variety of nations. Many Latino authors rely on Arte Publico for publication (Barbuto, 1991).

Authors, intellectuals, parents, children, and activists continually requested multiethnic literature. The role of librarians cannot be underestimated. Librarians such as Augusta Baker, Charlemae Rollins, and Doris Seale published articles, reviews, and recommended reading lists that contained books apprising children of the achievements and literature of people of color.

Occasionally clichés such as "out of the mouths of babes" capture a significant truth. This happened in 1965, when Nancy Larrick visited a preschool in New York City. A five-year-old African American girl asked her why the children in books were always white. Larrick did not have the answer, but she conducted a survey of children's publishers to determine why. Larrick (1965) queried publishers about the books published that contained illustrations of Negroes or had plots which featured Negroes. Of the 5,206 books published between 1962 and 1964, 349 or 6.7 percent included one or more Negroes. The four publishers with the largest lists, Franklin Watts, Macmillan, Doubleday, and Harper & Row, published a total of 866 books with 4.2 percent featuring Negroes; eight publishers produced only "all-white" books (p. 64).

The Children's Interracial Book Council grew, in part, out of Larrick's article and responses to it. Elinor Sinnette, commenting upon the CIBC, stated: "It is no accident that Negro history and Negro identification have been forgotten. Our society has contrived to make the American Negro a rootless person. The Council for Interracial Books for Children has been formed to relieve this situation" (Larrick, 1965, p. 85).

A transformation occurred in publishing. Publishers heeded the requests of parents, teachers, children, librarians, and other interested adults. The number of books about African Americans increased dramatically in the 1970s. Chall et al. (1979) reported that the numbers had increased to 14.4 percent for African Americans. The number of books about Asian, Latino, and Native Americans increased, but not so dramatically (Nieto, 1982; Asian American Book Project, 1981; Stensland, 1979).

Sims (1983) reexamined the "all-White world" of children's books to determine whether progress has been maintained and assessed the status of African Americans specifically. She argued that a literary census could not gauge fundamental changes in content. Sims found that three issues were still apparent: (1) the relationship between choice of primary audience and presentation of character and events; (2) the author's interpretation of the term *Afro-American experience*; and (3) the author's perspective as an insider or outsider in relation to the cultural group portrayed. Further, she found that three categories of books emerged. The first was social conscience books, apparently designed to create a social conscience among white children. Melting-pot books, the second category, presented a homogeneous portrait of America with no racial conflicts; these were primarily picture books. The last category, culturally conscious books, were portrayals told from the point of view of African American characters; these books were set in African American families or communities. Sims considered these books as literature written for African American children.

Sims Bishop (1990) reported that a "total of nineteen books about Hispanics, fifteen nonfiction and four books of folk stories and legends" were published in the previous publishing cycle. Far fewer books about Asian and Native Americans were published during the same cycle. Indeed, publishing seems to have reverted to the world that Larrick critiqued in 1965.

Finally, Mildred Taylor (1990), author of *Roll of Thunder, Hear My Cry*, a Newbery Medal winner and one of the few books about people of color to sell more than 100,000 copies in 1990, discussed the reasons why she writes books that reflect African American experiences. She wrote about the pain and embarrassment she felt when her class discussed "the Negro":

> Though I was a good student, there were times when I did not want to go to school, and at no time was that greater than when we studied the Civil War, because it meant that we would also be studying the Negro. And there was never any pride in that for me, not the way the Negro was depicted. Too often the history books we read in class, and the educational movies we saw, portrayed blacks as docile, subservient, almost moronic people, contented and happy with slavery. They taught of a people happy and contented with their way of life still, a people with no past except slavery and not much future. I remember there was no pride in that history; no pride like that I felt when I heard the stories told by my father and other members of my family. (p. 740)

The need to see oneself positively, truthfully, and heroically prompted Taylor to write her seven historical novels. These same needs prompt Asian, Latino, and Native American authors as well and keep parents searching for literature that does not cause their children pain or embarrassment.

The literature that Taylor and others write is often difficult to find. The literature, to use a popular term, is marginalized. Author John Wideman (1990) provided a perceptive explanation of marginalization:

> Since we're seen as marginal politically, economically, and culturally, African-American writers have a special, vexing stake in reforming, revitalizing, the American imagination. . . . As has always been the case, in order to break into print we must be prepared to deal with the extra-literary voices that have conspired to keep us silent, or our stories, novels, and poems will continue to be treated as marginally as our lives, unhinged, unattached to the everyday reality of "mainstream," majority readers. Magazine editors know that their jobs depend upon purveying images the public recognizes and approves, so they seldom include our fictions, and almost never choose those which transcend stereotypes and threaten to expose the fantasies of superiority, the bedrock lies and brute force that sustain the majority's power over the other. Framed in foreign, inimical contexts, minority stories appear at best as exotic slices of life and local color, at worst as ghettoized irrelevancies. (pp. v-vi)

The authors address a number of themes reflective of current trends, the art in many of the picture books wins critical awards occasionally, and some of the authors experiment with form. Yet many of the authors cannot transcend the marginalized status they inherit, and many of their books are unavailable in spite of the boom in children's literature. What are the critical aspects of that boom, and why is multiethnic children's literature not a part?

Current Status of Children's Literature: Publishers' Best Dream

Many articles detailing the boom in children's literature were published during the first years of the decade (Roback, 1990b; 1990c; 1990d; 1991). Book sales doubled between 1980 and 1985 and were expected to double again by the end of 1990. Industry analysts expected sales of children's books to exceed 1 billion in 1991 and increase to 1.5 billion by 1994. Vast changes in children's book publishing occurred between 1970 and 1987 (McDowell, 1988). Multinational corporations purchased smaller concerns. For example, Harper & Row was acquired by Rupert Murdoch's publishing empire. Other acquisitions included Robert Maxwell's purchase of Macmillan and Matsushita Electric Industrial Company's purchase of G. P. Putnam's Sons (Elie, 1991). Children's book publishing became a key component of publishing companies' profits. These acquisitions will reshape the relationships that existed in publishing. It is quite possible that the "genteel" enterprise of children's book publishing will have to accommodate greater adherence to marketing strategies and bottom lines.

Additional evidence of significant changes in children's book publishing is found in the growth of bookstores specializing in children's literature (Roback, 1990c; McDowell, 1988). In the early 1980s, fewer than 350 bookstores specializing in children's literature existed in the United States. By the end of 1990, the number had increased significantly. Further, children's independent, chain, and specialty bookstores indicated that the amount of space devoted to children's books would increase during 1991 (Roback, 1990c). Most of these stores planned to expand their stock and increase the amount of space devoted to ancillary materials such as audiotapes.

Several trends in book sales were evident in 1990. The vast majority of titles sold in bookstores were selections from publishers' backlists, numbering half to two-thirds of sales (Roback, 1990c). Most of the backlists consisted of titles written by authors such as Judy Blume, Chris Van Allsburg, Dr. Seuss, and Beverly Cleary, books written by celebrities, books with a Christmas or winter theme, books with gimmicks, books with crossover appeal, and books with Sesame Street characters (Roback, 1991). Several Newbery Medal winners were among bestselling backlist titles, such as *Dear Mr. Henshaw* (Cleary, 1983), *Sarah, Plain and Tall* (MacLachlan, 1985), *Hatchet* (Paulsen, 1987), and *Bridge to Terebithia* (Paterson, 1977). After remaining on the *New York Times* bestseller lists for seemingly endless weeks, the Waldo books represented the tops in hardback sales in children's books. These books accounted for

20 percent of all hardback books sold (Roback, 1991). Paperback bestsellers were the Berenstain Bears series, books by Mercer Mayer, and the Babysitters Club series (Roback, 1991).

Many of these books were purchased by adults and children who did not seek the advice of librarians or teachers. Book buyers no longer require the assistance of children's book specialists. The proliferation of children's bookstores and the selling of children's books in every conceivable venue shifted the balance of critical and advisory power (Reid and Reuter, 1990). Publishers would have to adopt different strategies for marketing books to libraries, classroom teachers, bookstores, and parents. Mothers purchased most of the children's books in general, independent, specialty, chain, and children's bookstores (Roback, 1990c). The number of fathers purchasing children's books in all categories was "quite small" (Roback, 1990c). Surprisingly, children were the second largest group of purchasers in general bookstores, and grandparents were number two in chain bookstores (Roback, 1990c). The most effective methods for promoting books in children's bookstores were author signings and readings, and storytelling. In other types of bookstores, in-store displays and newsletters proved beneficial, too (Roback, 1990c).

Other factors fueling the surge in children's book sales were the renewed emphasis on literacy, especially emergent literacy and the influence of the whole-language movement (Ohanian, 1991). However, shrinking textbook budgets and state regulations made switching to literature-based instruction difficult. Further, the influence of baby boomers cannot be underestimated. Many possessed the discretionary income that enabled them to purchase extensive libraries for their children, as evidenced by the set of children's classics offered by F. A. O. Schwartz in 1990.

A number of other trends were evident (Reid and Reuter, 1990; Roback, 1990a, 1990d). These included more efficient distribution systems, increased specialization, the rise of the mega-selling hardback, tie-ins with other entertainment forms, book club wars, greater demand for picture books, application of FTC antitrust laws, and the invasion of the market by adult and celebrity authors. One minor trend was the recognition of the need for multiethnic and multicultural literature: "Changing social realities and concerns are being mirrored in children's books—most notably in books reflecting multicultural experiences, and in titles on the importance of protecting the environment and endangered species " (Roback, 1990a, p. 117). However, an analysis of one survey noted that only 4.5 percent of respondents (booksellers and subscribers to *Publishers Weekly*) reported a strong demand for multicultural titles (Roback, 1990c).

Herein lies the paradox. Many educators cite a need for multicultural/multiethnic literature (Sims Bishop, 1990), yet few booksellers note a concurrent increase in demand for the books. Independent publishers delineated a number of factors that limited their efforts to provide books to readers (Igus, 1990). Frequently cited barriers were the reluctance of major chain bookstores to handle the works of smaller publishers; the reluctance of distributors to stock books; a perception among many that a limited market exists for the books; and the lack of capital to promote books in a manner comparable to that employed by major publishers.

One major factor contributing to the marginalization of multiethnic literature in general and African American literature in particular is the belief that the books lack universal themes or character types or that the books appeal only to members of the group portrayed (Sims Bishop, 1990; Spears-Bunton, 1990). Consequently, many well-written and wonderful books go unread. This is not to suggest that these books will appeal to every child, but rather to acknowledge the fact that most children do not have the opportunity to read the literature at all. Some evidence supporting this contention is found in the annual review of bestsellers appearing in *Publishers Weekly*.

For the calendar year 1990, only eleven books featuring people of color were either paperback or hardback bestsellers (Roback, 1991). These included *Roll of Thunder, Hear My Cry* (M. Taylor, 1976), *Sounder* (Armstrong, 1972), *The Cay* (T. Taylor, 1979), *Lon Po Po* (Young, 1989), *The Indian in the Cupboard* (Banks, 1982), *The Return of the Indian* (Banks, 1987), *Sadako and the Paper Cranes* (Coerr, 1979), *The Secret of the Indian* (Banks, 1989), and two Babysitters Club books—*Jessi and the Superbrat* (Martin, 1989) and *Jessi's Babysitter* (Martin, 1990). Only *Roll of Thunder, Hear My Cry* and *Lon Po Po* can be labeled "culturally conscious." That is, they reflect the perspectives, traditions and culture of the portrayed group in an authentic manner. The Babysitters Club books, *Jessi and the Superbrat* (Martin, 1989) and *Jessi's Babysitter* (Martin, 1990), and *Sadako and the Paper Cranes* (Coerr, 1979) respectively, present credible African-American and Asian heroines whose experiences are realistic. If books were purchased on the basis of quality alone, then 1990 tradebooks such as *Cousins* (Hamilton), *Baseball in April and Other Stories* (Soto), and *Aida* (Price) would be runaway bestsellers.

Despite these barriers, some cause for optimism exists. The next section examines challenges to the marginalized status of multiethnic literature, using African American children's literature as the touchstone.

Breaking the Barriers

A number of individuals concerned with their inability to purchase books about African Americans opened publishing companies and bookstores, and created book clubs. For instance, Wade and Cheryl Hudson (1991) founded Just Us Books after having difficulty locating positive images in literature for their child. The Hudsons described the factors that precipitated their involvement in publishing. Wade Hudson referred to the negative effects of growing up in a segregated community and seeing no reflections of himself in electronic or print media. The need to read something about himself also prompted the creation of the publishing company. Cheryl Wade, too, encountered few images of herself or for her child and decided to assume the responsibility of providing children with literature that embodied specific features: value-centered, actual/factual, culturally authentic, positive, encompassing a range of perspectives, self-affirming, possessed of strong, three-dimensional characters, well-written, attractive, and affordable. She believes that publishers can and should foster this kind of literature. Moreover, she contends that the resulting literature need not be propaganda or pabulum.

Just Us Books attempts to improve the status of literature written by African Americans through the publication of *Harambee*, a newspaper for young readers, coloring/activity books, concept books, picture books, and information books. Thus far, in three years, they have sold over 350,000 copies of books with titles such as *Afro-Bets ABC Book*, *Afro-Bets Book of Black Heroes*, and *Bright Eyes, Brown Skin*. In addition, they have entered into special agreements with distributors and wholesalers such as Red Sea Press and Book Source as well as with individuals who assume responsibility for sales in a particular geographic location.

A new generation of bookstores emerged as well. These new bookstores, for instance HueMan in Denver and The Shrine of the Black Madonna in Atlanta and Detroit, devote considerable shelf space to children's literature. Several offer mail order services. Many are beginning to sponsor author readings, which are not numerous in African American communities. Other African American organizations generate publicity and support for these ventures. For example, *Essence* magazine, the major periodical marketed to African American women, featured a profile of Clara Villarosa, the owner of HueMan bookstore. In addition, the magazine highlights children's books in its book review column and the section of the magazine devoted to parenting. These booksellers and others like them are crucial to the marketing of multiethnic literature. A few are located in integrated communities, but many serve African American communities. Relatively few major chain bookstores are located in African American communities or they provide limited selections of multiethnic literature. Therefore, the role of these independents becomes even more essential.

Book clubs offer individuals the opportunity to purchase books in specific categories, and shop-at-home convenience. School book clubs such as Lucky, SeeSaw, Trumpet, and Tab offer extensive selections and reduced prices that appeal to parents and children. Janus Adams attempted to provide the same services for individuals who wanted to purchase literature featuring African Americans by founding the Harambee Book Club in 1989. Response was immediate and overwhelming; the book club has been featured in newspapers such as the New York Times.

Publishers can help sustain these positive efforts if they implement what Cheryl Hudson of Just Us Books characterized as an "aggressive and fair policy which involves the recruiting, training, and retaining of people of color" (1991). Publishers can initiate a number of actions that may ameliorate the marginal status of multiethnic literature.

Suggestions for Publishers

First, publishers should heed the exhortation of Cheryl Hudson: they should recruit, train, and retain people of color. Elie (1991) assessed the status of African Americans in publishing. He found that a few highly qualified individuals such as Adrienne Ingram, editor and vice-president of G. P. Putnam's Sons, and Carol Hall, executive editor of Simon and Schuster, acquired key positions in the top echelon of publishing. According to Elie, their progress is exceptional. African Americans comprise 4.0 percent of publishing officials and managers, 6.1 percent of professional and technical staff, and 4.5 percent of sales workers (p. 104). One could assume that comparable figures exist for Asian, Latino, and Native Americans. The argument is not that percentages employed should equal percentages in the national population, but rather that a more diverse workforce might yield greater diversity in types of books published.

Second, publishers should reinstitute the writer's contests of the late sixties and seventies. Past contests resulted in the discovery of writers such as Walter Dean Myers and Virginia Driving Hawk Sneve. However, in order to attract potential authors, publishers should place advertisements in literary magazines as well as in periodicals directed to a particular group such as *Ebony* and the *Bilingual Review*. This action has the potential to generate significant numbers of manuscripts. *Ebony*, for example, sponsors a short-story contest each year. The contest yields hundreds of submissions culminating in judgment by a panel of nationally known authors and public figures, a monetary prize, and publication of the winner's story. A similar contest for children's stories should generate comparable responses.

Third, publishers should consider entering into joint ventures with small, independent publishers such as Arte Publico, the Children's Press, or the Greenfield Review Press. These joint ventures could provide smaller presses with larger advertising budgets, the benefit of experience, and increased access to major chain bookstores, distributors, and wholesalers. The smaller presses, in turn, could provide larger publishing houses with access to the specialized markets they serve. In addition, school book clubs could provide the offerings of small presses.

Fourth, author visits to schools motivate students to read and write. Publishers might consider sponsoring writer- and illustrator-in-residence programs. However, school districts selected should be those least likely to have literature-based literacy programs, whole-language programs, or the discretionary income to fund authors' and illustrators' visits to urban and rural school systems. Author Walter D. Myers (1991) spoke about the writing program he conducts with "inner-city" adolescents and the ways in which they shaped the content of his novels. He found that their lives were absent from literature, and he desired to validate their perspectives, dreams, and pain. Certainly, these adolescents benefit from the guidance in writing they receive from Myers.

Fifth, a number of "minority" publications reach markets that mainstream publishers cannot. The phenomenal success of Johnson Publications with its *Jet, Ebony,* and *Ebony Man* publications and radio and television stations demonstrate the potential for reaching this largely untapped market. Mainstream publishers should consider advertising in these media.

Sixth, publishers should consider establishing marketing agreements with fraternal, social, and religious organizations. Again, Johnson Publications provides a model. The company encourages various institutions to sell subscriptions to its magazines. In return, the organizations receive a generous profit from the publisher. Such joint ventures offer numerous benefits for all.

Finally, publishers might consider lowering the prices of books sold to financially strapped districts. Granted publishing is a for-profit endeavor, but a dire need exists for some philanthropic actions. Consumers can assist by writing government representatives to encourage tax incentives.

These recommended actions, if implemented, can help provide a foundation for ensuring that children's literature depicts and celebrates the country's diversity. Then, perhaps, ten- to fifteen-year reviews of the "all-white world" of children's books will no longer remain a publishing staple.

References

Anderson, J. 1988. *The Education of Blacks in the South, 1865–1930.* Chapel Hill: University of North Carolina Press.

Asian American Book Project. 1981. "How Children's Books Distort the Asian American Image." *Interracial Books for Children Bulletin* 7, 2 & 3:3–33.

Banks, J. 1991. *Teaching Strategies for Ethnic Studies.* 5th ed. Boston: Allyn and Bacon.

Barbuto, J. 1991. "Latino Writers in the American Market." *Publishers Weekly* 238 (February 1):18–21.

Chall, J., E. Rashburn, V. French, and C. Hall. 1979. "Blacks in the World of Children's Books." *The Reading Teacher* 32:527–533.

D'Souza, D. 1991. "Illiberal Education." *The Atlantic* 267 (March):51–58, 62–65, 67, 70–74, 76–79.

Elie, L. 1991. "A Career You Can Book On." *Black Enterprise* 21 (February):102–106, 108.

Gay, G. 1988. "Designing Relevant Curricula for Diverse Learners." *Education and Urban Society* 20:327–340.

Gollnick, D., and P. Chin. 1986. *Multicultural Education in a Pluralistic Society.* 2d ed. Columbus: Merrill.

Harris, V. 1990. "African-American Children's Literature: The First One Hundred Years." *Journal of Negro Education* 59:540–555.

———. 1991. "Helen Whiting and the Education of Colored Children, 1930–1960: Emancipatory Pedagogy in Action." Paper presented at the annual meeting of the American Educational Research Association, Chicago, April.

Hudson, C., and W. Hudson. 1991. "Dialogue: The Publisher's Perspective." Paper presented at the Multicolored Mirror: Cultural Substance in Literature for Children and Young Adults Conference at the annual meeting of the Cooperative Children's Book Center, Madison, April 5–6.

Igus, T. 1990. "Publishing Books for Black Kids." *ABBWA Journal* 4:13–18.

Larrick, N. 1965. "The All-White World of Children's Books." *The Saturday Review* 48:63–65, 84–85.

McDowell, T. 1988. "Profitable Renaissance for Children's Books." *The New York Times,* April 18, pp. 63–65, 84–85.

Myers, W. 1991. Speech presented at the annual children's literature conference at Ohio State University, Columbus, January 24–26.

Natov, R, and G. De Luca. 1986. "An Interview with John Steptoe." *The Lion and the Unicorn* 6:122–127.

———. 1987. "An Interview with John Steptoe." *The Lion and the Unicorn* 7, 1:122–129.

Nieto, S. 1982. "Children's Literature on Puerto Rican Themes -Part I: The Messages of Fiction." *Interracial Books for Children Bulletin* 8, 1 & 2:6–9.

Ohanian, S. 1991. "Learning Whole Language." *Publishers Weekly* 238 (February 1):123–125.

Palomino, H. 1988. "Japanese Americans in Books or in Reality? Three Writers for Young Adults Who

Tell a Different Story." In B. Bacon, ed., *How Much Truth Do We Tell the Children?: The Politics of Children's Literature*, pp. 125–134. Minneapolis: MEP Publications.

Ravitch, D. 1990. "Diversity and Democracy." *American Educator* 14:16–20.

Reid, C., and M. Reuter. 1990. "Confounding Doomsayers, Industry Figures See Rosy Present and Future." *Publishers Weekly* 237:13–15.

Roback, D. 1990a. "Fall 1990 Children's Books." *Publishers Weekly* 237 (July 27):117.

———. 1990b. "Children's Booksales: Past and Future." *Publishers Weekly* 237 (August 31):30–34.

———. 1990c. "Bookstore Survey: Zeroing in." *Publishers Weekly* 237 (November 30):36–38, 42–44.

———. 1990d. "The Names in Games." *Publishers Weekly* 237 (October 26):34–37.

———. 1991. "Commercial Books Scored Big With Kids." *Publishers Weekly*. 238 (March 8):30–35.

Sims, R. 1982. *Shadow and Substance*. Urbana, Ill.: National Council of Teachers of English.

———. 1983. "What Has Happened to the "All-White" World of Children's Books?" *Phi Delta Kappan* 65:650–653.

———. 1985. "Children's Books About Blacks: A Mid-Eighties Status Report." *Children's Literature Review* 8:9–13.

Sims Bishop, R. 1990. "Windows, Mirrors, and Sliding Glass Doors." *Perspectives* 6:ix–xi.

Spears-Bunton, L. 1990. "Welcome to My House: African American and European American Students' Responses to Virginia Hamilton's *House of Dies Drear*." *Journal of Negro Education* 59:566–576.

Stensland, A. 1979. *Literature by and about the American Indian*. Urbana, Ill.: National Council of Teachers of English.

Steptoe, J. 1988. Acceptance speech for the 1987 *Boston Globe–Horn Book* Award for illustration. *The Horn Book Magazine* 64:25–28.

Taxel, J. 1991. "On the Politics of Children's Literature." *The New Advocate* 4:vii–xii.

Taylor, M. 1990. "Growing Up with Stories." *Booklist* 87 (December 1):740–741.

Wideman, J. 1990. Preface. In T. McMillan, ed. *Breaking Ice*. New York: Penguin Books.

Literature Cited

Armstrong, W. 1972. *Sounder*. New York: Harper & Row.

Banks, L. 1982. *The Indian in the Cupboard*. New York: Avon.

———. 1987. *The Return of the Indian*. New York: Avon.

Banks, J. 1989. *The Secret of the Indian*. New York: Avon.

Cisneros, N. 1984; 1989. *House on Mango Street*. New York: Vintage Books.

Cleary, B. 1983. *Dear Mr. Henshaw*. New York: Morrow.

Coerr, E. 1979. *Sadako and the Thousand Paper Cranes*. New York: Dell.

Gardiner, J. 1983. *Stone Fox*. New York: Harper & Row.

Hamilton, 1990. *Cousins*. New York: Harcourt Brace Jovanovich.

MacLachlan, P. 1985. *Sarah, Plain and Tall*. New York: Harper & Row.

Martin, A. 1989. *Jessi and the Superbrat*. New York: Scholastic.

———. 1990. *Jessi's Babysitter*. New York: Scholastic.

Paterson, K. 1977. *Bridge to Terebithia*. New York: Crowell.

Paulsen, G. 1987. *Hatchet*. New York: Bradbury.

Price, L. 1990. *Aida*. New York: Harcourt Brace and Jovanovich.

Soto, G. 1990. *Baseball in April and Other Stories*. New York: Harcourt Brace and Jovanovich.

Steptoe, J. 1987. *Mufaro's Beautiful Daughters*. New York: Lothrop, Lee & Shephard.

Taylor, M. 1976. *Roll of Thunder, Hear My Cry*. New York: Dial.

———. 1990. *Road to Memphis*. New York: Dial.

Taylor, T. 1979. *The Cay*. New York: Avon.

Yee, P. 1990. *Tales from Gold Mountain*. New York: Macmillan.

Young, E. 1989. *Lon Po Po*. New York: Philomel.

5

Trade Books and the Social Studies Curriculum

Dianne L. Monson and Kathleen Howe

One seeks to equip the child with deeper, more gripping, and subtler ways of knowing the world and himself.
—Jerome Bruner

Social studies in the elementary grades is the study of people and their interactions with one another. A primary concern of social studies education is to teach young learners the skills and knowledge necessary to become responsible and informed citizens. A second major concern is to help students begin to perceive themselves as part of a larger human community within the context of time and space. To accomplish this, it is important that children begin to understand other peoples and cultures and to consider similarities and differences in contrast to their own lives. History, government, and geography are the traditional major topics of study in the elementary grades. Opportunity to experience life in other times and places through the eyes of the people involved should be a major focus of social studies instruction, but too often this opportunity is not provided. Children's books can offer that very important dimension.

Although the content and skills of social studies are particularly suited for helping children understand more about themselves and their role in the larger human community, social studies as an elementary subject has been rated by upper elementary students as one of the least liked subjects taught in school (Goodlad, 1984). Status studies comparing student attitudes toward different subject areas in the elementary and secondary grades have consistently found that social studies was rated poorly when compared to other curricular subjects. As early as 1949, Jersild reported that social studies was the least liked subject in school. More recently, social studies was named as the most favorite subject by only 3 percent of nine-year-old students surveyed, while 48 percent chose mathematics and 24 percent chose language arts as the favorite subject (*Science Education Databook*, 1980). Although topics from the social studies curriculum were often highly rated, interest in social studies as a school subject was consistently rated low in comparison with other subjects. "The topics of study become removed from their intrinsically human character, reduced to the dates and places readers will recall memorizing for tests" (Goodlad, 1984, p. 212). Children's literature can play a role in changing that situation.

The Research Base for Social Studies and Literature

What do children want to know about other places? Student interests should certainly guide development of the social studies curriculum and the choice of reading materials to support the curriculum, yet there is little evidence that children are often consulted about such matters. In order to find out about student interests, we questioned more than two hundred U.S. children, ages nine to eleven. We asked what they would like to learn about a child from another country, in this case Australia. We invited them to raise questions they would ask an Australian child who visited their school. The results were interesting, though perhaps not surprising. When the responses were clustered into broad categories, these nine questions emerged:

1. What kinds of foods do you eat?

2. What kinds of clothes do you wear?

3. What are your houses like?

4. What kinds of pets or animals do you have?

5. What are your schools like?

6. What is your weather like?

7. Do you have any brothers or sisters?

8. Do you have many friends?

9. Do you ever get lonesome?

This set of questions was derived from the actual, more specific questions such as: Do you have pizzas? Do you eat kangaroos? Do you have kangaroos for pets? How big is your house? What is it made of? What are your schools like? Are your teachers nice? What do you learn in science? (Monson, Howe, and Greenlee, 1989).

The need to know is one of the developmental needs identified by Abraham Maslow. And that need to know is often associated with the kind of curiosity that engages children in reading so that they want to gain as much as possible from a book, regardless of whether it is fiction or nonfiction. Therefore, having identified some questions of interest to children, we examined units on Australia in eight social studies texts commonly used in the elementary school. We also read fifteen works of fiction for children, all of them with Australian settings. The authors of fiction included Robin Klein, Ruth Park, Joan Phipson, Ivan Southall, Colin Thiele, Elizabeth Wilton, and Patricia Wrightson. Our purpose was to determine whether children might find answers to their questions through the textbooks and through fiction.

When we consulted our notes from all sources, it was clear that both textbooks and novels provided information about the country. However, the novels answered many more of the children's questions and gave far richer descriptions of the details of daily life and the emotions of children living in Australia. The social studies texts gave facts about the country; the novels brought out implications of those facts for children's lives. From social studies books, children learned about the country; the novels provided the experience of living in the country, as shown through actions, thoughts, and conversations of story characters.

A recent study conducted by Howe (1990) focused on the use of children's literature in elementary social studies to supplement and enrich textbook lessons. This school-based study involved 168 fifth-grade students from a relatively large, middle-class, racially homogeneous suburban school district. Teachers of the treatment group read aloud two selections of historical fiction that related directly to the periods of American history studied in that school district's curriculum. While the students studied the westward movement, the teachers read aloud *Prairie Songs* by Pam Conrad (1985) to help them gain a more empathic understanding of the people who were part of that period in U.S. history. Based on historical documents and oral histories, this is the story of a young girl and her family living on the Nebraska prairie during the early nineteenth century.

While the students studied the American Civil War period, the teachers read aloud *Charley Skedaddle* by Patricia Beatty (1987), the story of a twelve-year-old Bowery boy from New York City who runs off to join the Union Army. Charley wants to avenge his older brother's death at Gettysburg but learns the horrors of war firsthand as he sees his best friend killed on the battlefield.

Students in the control group also heard stories read aloud, but their teachers chose two humorous selections of realistic fiction that did not relate to the topics studied in American history. Throughout the study, students in both the treatment and control groups had ready access to reading centers in their classrooms. These centers contained a variety of genres of children's books written at a wide range of reading levels. All of the books dealt with the westward movement or the Civil War.

Results indicated that the books of historical fiction that teachers read aloud to students in the treatment group directly affected the book choices those students made from reading centers for their independent reading. Two books were chosen most often as free reading choices by these fifth graders. *The Golly Sisters Go West* by Betsy Byars (1985) and illustrated by Sue Truesdell was most often chosen by students in the treatment group to read while they were studying the westward movement in social studies. This "I Can Read" picture book is full of fun and humor. The story tells of the slapstick adventures of two sisters, May-May and Rose Golly, a singing and dancing team, as they travel west in a covered wagon and entertain the people they meet along the way.

Nettie's Trip South by Ann Turner (1987) and illustrated by Ronald Himler was most often chosen by the fifth-grade students for their free reading while they were studying the American Civil War. Based on the real diary entries of the author's great-grandmother, this picture book is the powerful and deeply moving story of Nettie, a young girl from Albany, New York, who travels to visit Richmond, Virginia, just before the Civil War. The book offers an emotionally descriptive account of Nettie's reaction to slavery in the South and especially of her experience at a slave auction where a woman is sold "like a sack of flour."

Both selections were historical fiction picture books and both were of high literary and artistic merit, yet they were quite different in major themes and writing styles. Surprisingly, the fifth-grade students in the study chose these books most often to read on their own even though both books were written at about the second- or third-grade reading level. Although most of the fifth-grade students in the study read at or above grade level, they chose books written at a much easier level for their free reading choices.

Results of the study demonstrated that when teachers read aloud selections of historical fiction to supplement and enrich social studies textbook lessons, students showed considerable gains in achievement. These findings indicate that historical fiction can play an important role in social studies learning and provides a welcome change from the use of the textbook as the sole resource for teaching social studies.

Rationale for Including Children's Literature in Social Studies

Both children's literature and social studies have people as their common focus. Fiction written for children tells the stories of human activities and intentions, and often includes the institutions, traditions, and values that give structure to people's lives.

Because of this common human focus, children's books are a valuable source for enriching the social studies curriculum. The range of children's books published today reflects an awareness of children's diversity in interests and background. The content of both social studies and children's literature can be effectively integrated in the elementary classroom to help children learn more about themselves and others in their world.

Our purpose is not to argue for discontinuing the use of social studies textbooks. Well-written social studies textbooks are useful as references and provide a needed framework of organization for the curriculum. However, even at an early age, children should have access to a variety of sources of reading material to gain an understanding of the different structures and functions of language, and more specifically, printed text (Durkin, 1966; Cullinan and Carmichael, 1977; Strickland and Morrow, 1989).

Children's literature and all of its genres (folk tales, tall tales, myths and legends, fantasy, poetry, realistic and historical fiction, as well as biography and informational books) can provide this variety in written structure. Odland argues that all genres of children's literature are appropriate for teaching social studies content, especially American history. She asserts that "a strong case can be demonstrated for the *interrelated* nature of the study of literature and the people whose joys and dilemmas are reflected in that literature" (Odland, 1980, p. 474).

Responding to History through Fiction

The Howe study gives evidence that children's literature can contribute to learning about several periods of U.S. history. Consider the possibilities literature offers for other areas of the social studies curriculum.

The Revolutionary War is just a milestone in history for many young people. It happened a long time ago and, if any of their ancestors were involved, students in the 1990s are unlikely to know that. The event becomes simply an historical episode unless students can experience it through the eyes of someone living at the time. *My Brother Sam Is Dead* by James Lincoln Collier and Christopher Collier (1974) offers that opportunity, for we come to know a very real conflict among family members, a conflict that results from political disagreements. As Tim Meeker tells his story, we learn just how torn he is between loyalty for the Tory parents he respects and support for his brother, Sam, who has run away to fight on the side of the Patriots. This human perspective on the conflicts and death that resulted from the war can have more influence on readers than a host of facts about the dates and places of battles and the names of heroes. Perhaps the most compelling aspect of *My Brother Sam Is Dead* is the representation of both sides in this war, as told by members of the Meeker family.

The opportunity to experience history from more than one point of view is present as well in *The Sign of the Beaver* by Elizabeth George Speare (1983). Here the historical setting is earlier, Maine in the mid-1700s. The conflict is, in large part, man against nature as the son of a westward-bound family is left to look after newly claimed land while his father returns home to bring back his mother and their newborn baby. Matt, who is thirteen, survives despite theft by a dishonest itinerant and hardships imposed by lack of food. He survives because an Indian boy, Attean, and his grandfather, Saknis, of the nearby Beaver Clan, teach him the tools of wilderness survival. Influences of the westward movement are clear. The good fortune of settlers seeking land to claim is surely a misfortune for the Indians who have lived on that land for generations. The good and bad experiences of settlers are shown clearly through Matt's feelings. The unfortunate outcomes for the Indians are expressed through the voices of Attean and Saknis. A young person who reads this book can respond to the expressed feelings of the characters and come to respect the many examples of courage shown by Indians and settlers alike.

Not far from Maine and a century later, Katherine Paterson's *Lyddie* (1991) describes the poverty that sent many young women from farms to the factories of Massachusetts. In this case, Lyddie Worthen is left with only her younger brother, Charlie, to tend the family farm in Vermont. We move, with Lyddie, through the events that lead to her mother's decision to lend out the farm in order to pay debts and to send the two children into service. Lyddie's work at the local inn comes to a halt when she is dismissed. But, at the same time, her encounter with an escaped slave arouses her sympathy for his desire to be free. It also encourages her to seek her freedom as an independent wage earner, a factory girl. Lyddie's goal is to repay the farm debt and reclaim the land. She does not succeed, but she does learn to read and sets herself another goal, to attend Oberlin College in Ohio, where women as well as men are welcome as students. Paterson's finely crafted story shows the struggle for independence as Lyddie deals with the kinds of difficulties many had to contend with during that period in history.

On another frontier in the same century, Patricia MacLachlan's *Sarah, Plain and Tall* (1985) provides a look at the lives of homesteaders on the midwestern prairie. Through the eyes of Anna Witting, and Sarah Wheaton, the mail-order bride who came to live with Anna, her father, and her younger brother Caleb, we come to know the loneliness of prairie life. We also experience the beauty of the prairie seasons and the contrasting beauty of coastal Maine. The period of westward movement has been described vividly in other books, to be sure, but this story underscores the courage needed to leave home and family for a totally different life in the West.

Dakota Dugout by Ann Turner (1985), illustrated by Ronald Himler, offers another glimpse of pioneer life. Through beautifully sensitive pencil drawings and image-filled, economical text, a woman tells her granddaughter what it was like to move to the Dakota prairie as a young bride and live in a sod house with her new husband, Matt. The loneliness and hardship of the first year are overcome, and the young couple finally get the crops to grow and are able to make a happy life for themselves on the prairie. As the woman talks, she reflects that "sometimes the things we start with are the best."

Details and the drama of pioneer life are eloquently told through the words of Brett Harvey and the pencil drawings of Deborah Kogan Ray in *My Prairie*

Year (1986). In 1889, the author's grandmother Elenore Plaisted, then nine years old, moved west with her family from Maine to become homesteaders on the Dakota prairie. There are vivid descriptions of commonplace things like "sweet-smelling sheets and clothes flapping in the sun" and of the sudden, raging prairie fire that threatens the pioneer family's barns and home. Such images make life on the Dakota plains come alive in the eyes of the reader.

Alice Fleming's *The King of Prussia and a Peanut Butter Sandwich* (1988), illustrated by Ronald Himler, illuminates a little-known aspect of American history in the late 1800s. This book of nonfiction tells the story of the peace-loving Mennonites and their journey to a new land, which began in warlike Prussia and ended on the Great Plains of Kansas. It is the story of how these hard-working farmers fled from their homeland to the steppes of Russia. There they developed Turkey Red winter wheat, and the young children helped their parents to hand-pick only the healthiest seeds from the harvest to bring to America and grow on the American prairie.

A Caldecott Honor Book, *When I Was Young in the Mountains* by Cynthia Rylant (1982), illustrated by Diane Goode, tells the warm story of a very special childhood growing up in the Appalachian Mountains at the turn of the century. The author's family memories offer a description of a past way of life in American history that was both peaceful and loving.

Set in the twentieth century, *Number the Stars* by Lois Lowry (1989) provides a close-up of what it was like to be Jewish during the German occupation of Denmark in World War II. It also shows the courage of Danes who risked their lives so that some of their Jewish neighbors could escape to neutral Sweden. Along with Ellen Rosen and Annemarie Johansen, readers experience the terror of Nazi soldiers searching the house for the Rosen family. In that one brief scene and throughout the book, the horror of war is dramatically shown from a child's perspective.

Sadako and the Thousand Paper Cranes by Eleanor Coerr (1977) is the moving story of a young Japanese girl living in Hiroshima after World War II. She was only two years old when the atom bomb was dropped on her city. Now, ten years later, she is dying from leukemia caused by fallout from the bomb. Based on the actual events in the life of Sadako Sasaki, this is the story of hope and a plea for peace. Each year on August 6, Peace Day, paper cranes made by children from around the world are placed at the foot of Sadako's statue in Hiroshima Peace Park. Engraved on the base of the statue are the words: "This is our cry, this is our prayer; peace in the world."

Social studies includes contemporary lives and cultures as well as historical periods. Today, as never before, it is crucial for young people to understand the problems faced by people of races and cultures different from their own. Those important understandings must be nourished through interaction with the lives of people who represent diverse groups within the United States and, indeed, throughout the world. In order for children to gain a sense of the diversity within our society, they need books like Laurence Yep's *Child of the Owl* (1977). In *Child of the Owl*, Casey must struggle with the dilemma of trying to maintain and respect the traditional Chinese culture of her grandmother, Paw-Paw, and at the same time fit into the cultural ways of her non-Chinese classmates. Fortunately, Paw-Paw's stories provide the bridge for this blending of cultural values and allow Casey to feel secure in the old values while moving into a different cultural milieu. The dignified treatment of traditional cultural values is an important aspect of this fine book, along with the interpretation of those values through the eyes and voice of Paw-Paw. Such point-of-view experiences are important for young readers.

In much the same way, Katherine Paterson's *Park's Quest* (1988) provides a contemporary view of the prejudice shown toward children born of Vietnamese mothers and fathers who were U.S. military personnel stationed in Vietnam. Here, the situation is seen from the perspective of a boy whose father was killed in the Vietnam conflict and who is seeking to know more about his paternal family. He discovers his half-sister who has come from Vietnam to live with their grandfather. Park's dislike for the girl and his prejudice toward her is clear, but so is her view of the way Park and other people in the United States have treated her. Readers who enter into a transaction with this story become engaged with the plight of Park's half-sister as well as with Park's own feelings about his father. The ill will between the two young people is a very real consequence of war and immigration and the multicultural diversity of our country. Yet it is an example of the kinds of problems that are seldom, if ever, dealt with in social studies texts.

Three books published in 1990 offer young readers insight into the lives of people from different cultures around the world. *The Kapok Tree: A Tale of the Amazon Rain Forest*, written and illustrated by Lynn Cherry (1990), is a thought-provoking modern folk tale of a young woodsman who enters the Brazilian rain forest to chop down a giant kapok tree. He becomes weary and lies down to take a nap. As he sleeps, creatures from the rain forest come to beg him not to chop down their home. Finally, a child from the Yanomamo tribe pleads, "When you awake, please look upon us all with new eyes, Senhor." This book speaks to both children and adults as it makes an unsentimentalized plea to save the animals and the plants of this delicate, endangered tropical environment.

The gentle tale *My Grandpa and the Sea*, by Katherine Orr (1990), gives a view of life on the island of St. Lucia in the Caribbean. Lila's grandfather works as a fisherman, but when large commercial fishing boats begin to overfish the sea, her grandfather must find another way to make a living. Grandpa believes that "if we give back something for everything we take, we will always meet with abundance." This philosophy and his respect for the sea help him to become a farmer of sorts, growing seamoss on large floating rafts in the ocean. The text and colorful illustrations depict the beauty of this island setting.

Loving by Ann Morris, with photographs by Ken Heyman (1990), is a photographic study of love and how people around the world express this emotion in the same ways: by holding, caring, feeding, teaching, and sharing. This nonfiction book is a fine resource to use in the elementary classroom for teaching about cultural diversity in the world. While showing that there are differences among people, it illustrates how we are all really alike.

The problems grappled with by people in the stories summarized here can scarcely be described outside the context of the kinds of social interactions that are best portrayed through literature. Similarly, children can best experience life in other countries through books of fiction authentically set in those countries and accurately reflecting their cultural values.

We have discussed a small number of books that interpret for contemporary U.S. children the lives of children in other times and places. Increasingly, such books are becoming available, but there is still a need to provide new books written at a wide range of reading levels for all elementary school grades and to provide books dealing with more of the topics, issues, and concepts that are included in elementary social studies programs. There is a particular dearth of books for younger readers, books that will allow children as young as seven or eight to experience the lives of their peers in a variety of U.S. cultural backgrounds as well as peers in other countries. Certainly there are some books that offer such experiences, books by Eloise Greenfield, Mildred Pitts Walter, Angela Johnson, Patricia McKissick, Yoshiko Uchida, Sharon Bell Mathis, Bette Bao Lord, and others. But the challenge remains to provide more literature, for all ages and reading levels, that will add the crucial human dimension to learning about others which is a major concern of social studies programs.

This is not to ask for fiction that is written to instruct, for that is not the role of literature. The request is for books that will encourage children to gain a sense of respect for all people. It has been said that literature offers the opportunity to live many lives within our single lifetime. Children must have access to that opportunity if their world is to be a better place to live.

References

Cullinan, B. E., and C. W. Carmichael. 1977. *Literature and Young Children*. Urbana, Ill.: National Council of Teachers of English.

Durkin, D. 1966. *Children Who Learn to Read Early: Two Longitudinal Studies*. New York: Teachers College Press.

Goodlad, J. I. 1984. *A Place Called School*. New York: McGraw-Hill.

Howe, K. 1990. "Children's Literature and Its Effects on Cognitive and Noncognitive Behaviors in Elementary Social Studies." Doctoral dissertation, University of Minnesota.

Jersild, A. I. 1949. *Children's Interests and What They Suggest for Education*. New York: Bureau of Publications, Teachers College, Columbia University.

Monson, D. L., K. Howe, and A. Greenlee. 1989. "Helping Children Develop Cross-Cultural Understanding with Children's Books." *Early Child Development and Care* 48: 3–8.

Odland, N. 1980. "American History in Fact and Fiction: Literature for Young Readers." *Social Education* 44: 474–481.

Science Education Databook. 1980. Washington, D.C.: National Science Foundation.

Strickland, D. S., and L. M. Morrow. 1989. "Environments Rich in Print Promote Literacy Behavior During Play." *The Reading Teacher* 43: 178–179.

Children's Books

Beatty, Patricia. 1987. *Charley Skedaddle*. New York: William Morrow and Company.

Byars, Betsy. 1985. *The Golly Sisters Go West*. Illustrated by Sue Truesdell. New York: Harper and Row.

Cherry, Lynn. 1990. *The Kapok Tree: A Tale of the Amazon Rain Forest*. New York: Harcourt Brace Jovanovich.

Coerr, Lynn. 1977. *Sadako and the Thousand Paper Cranes*. New York: Dell Publishing Co.

Collier, James Lincoln, and Christopher Collier. 1974. *My Brother Sam Is Dead*. New York: Four Winds Press.

Conrad, Pam. 1985. *Prairie Songs*. New York: Harper & Row.

Fleming, Alice. 1988. *The King of Prussia and a Peanut Butter Sandwich*. Illustrated by Ronald Himler. New York: Charles Scribner's Sons.

Harvey, Brett. 1986. *My Prairie Year: Based on the Diary of Elenore Plaisted*. Illustrated By Deborah Kogan Ray. New York: Holiday House.

Lowry, Lois. 1989. *Number the Stars*. Boston: Houghton, Mifflin.

MacLachlan, Patricia. 1985. *Sarah, Plain and Tall*. New York: Harper & Row.

Morris, Ann. 1990. *Loving*. New York: Lothrop, Lee & Shepard.

Orr, Katherine. 1990. *My Grandpa and the Sea*. Minneapolis: Carolrhoda Books.

Paterson, Katherine. 1991. *Lyddie*. New York: Lodestar/Dutton.

———. 1988. *Park's Quest*. New York: Lodestar/Dutton.

Rylant, Cynthia. 1982. *When I Was Young in the Mountains*. Illustrated by Diane Goode. New York: E. P. Dutton.

Speare, Elizabeth George. 1983. *The Sign of the Beaver*. Boston: Houghton, Mifflin.

Turner, Ann. 1985. *Dakota Dugout*. Illustrated by Ronald Himler. New York: Macmillan.

———. 1987. *Nettie's Trip South*. Illustrated by Ronald Himler. New York: Macmillan.

Yep, Laurence. 1977. *Child of the Owl*. New York: Harper & Row.

6

Exciting Nonfiction

James Cross Giblin

Children's and young adult nonfiction used to have a reputation for being dull and boring, and in the case of many books that reputation was justified. The writing in these books had about as much life as a routine encyclopedia entry. The research for science and history titles was frequently thin, and made-up dialogue lessened the credibility of many biographies.

Even when nonfiction authors had done a good job, their efforts did not necessarily result in an appealing and successful book. At some publishing houses, nonfiction books were treated like stepchildren. They appeared in small, cramped formats, and were illustrated with just a smattering of line drawings or a few grainy photographs.

The very word *nonfiction* came to have a negative connotation for many people. It seemed to imply that informational books were on a lower level than their fictional counterparts, and should not aspire to being treated as literature, let alone as works of art.

But all this changed ten or fifteen yeas ago. Imaginative children's authors and editors saw a fresh interest in nonfiction topics, fueled by informational television programs. The result was a new type of nonfiction book for young people.

What are the chief characteristics of these books? First, the writing is entertaining as well as informative, and employs humor and suspense to bring the material to life. Unlike many nonfiction books of the past, the treatment is closely focused rather than encyclopedic. For example, instead of attempting to cover six or eight famous volcanic eruptions in one slim volume, Patricia Lauber in her Newbery Honor-winning *Volcano* tells the story of just one eruption, that of Mt. St. Helens. She still conveys a great deal of information about volcanoes in general, but the tight focus enables her to do it in a more effective way.

Another characteristic of the new nonfiction is the inclusion of additional material at the back of the book. Even books for young children usually have a reading list or bibliography and an index. As an added bonus, many also contain supplementary information that youngsters or adults working with them can go on to read if they wish to. A good example of such information can be found in Betsy Maestro's picture book, *The Story of the Statue of Liberty*. Its backmatter features a table of dates connected with the statue, a list of people who helped with its construction, and notes on recent repairs to it. In my forthcoming picture book biography of George Washington, I use the backmatter to tell the real story of George and the cherry tree, to describe the building of the Washington Monument, and to take readers on a brief tour of Mount Vernon today.

The most visible difference between the new nonfiction and the old is a vastly greater emphasis on design and illustration. Nonfiction books for all age groups, from those aimed at preschoolers to titles directed toward young adults, are being given what one art director has called "the Tiffany treatment."

Visually striking titles abound at every age level. For the youngest, author-illustrator Gail Gibbons has created a long line of simple, colorful picture books about everything from clocks to sunken treasure. Aliki found ways to make history come alive for the picture book audience in such titles as *A Medieval Feast* and *The King's Day*. Moving up the age scale, Joanna Cole has discovered her own unique way to inform and amuse young readers in the "Magic Schoolbus" series, illustrated by Bruce Degen. Seymour Simon conveys the special features of the planets in the solar system through concise texts and vivid color photos. Russell Freedman used archival photographs to portray the humanity and pathos of our Civil War leader in *Lincoln: A Photobiography*.

But while the visual aspect of nonfiction has become increasingly important in recent years, the ultimate impact of any book depends on the depth and quality of the writing. *Lincoln* provides an excellent example of this. Although its design and illustrations certainly play an important part in drawing young people to the book, the way it is organized and written is what holds them once they begin to read. It is also what led to the book's being awarded the 1988 Newbery Medal as the year's "most distinguished contribution to American literature for children"—the first time, incidentally, that a nonfiction title had won the Newbery since 1956.

Different nonfiction authors use different methods in order to catch and hold the attention of their readers. Here I'd like to share some of those that I've employed in my own books. If they seem similar to the techniques used by novelists, that's deliberate. For I—along with many of my colleagues— believe that a nonfiction writer is also a storyteller. The only difference is that the stories we tell are true.

The first and foremost consideration is choosing a good subject for a book. It has to be one that arouses my curiosity deeply; otherwise, I'd find it hard to sustain interest during the two to four years it usually takes me to research and write a book. All of my books are histories of one sort or another, and I love doing the research for them. As I discover things I didn't know before, I feel as if I'm getting a marvelous crash course in the subject. I only hope the books have a similar effect on young readers.

Finding the right title for a book is another important consideration. I like a title that implies a question, such as *The Truth About Santa Claus* (What is the truth?) or *The Riddle of the Rosetta Stone* (Did anyone ever solve it?). If the question is intriguing enough, perhaps the young reader will be inspired to open the book and seek the answer.

When I outline a book I spend a lot of time deciding how to begin the first chapter, for I know the first few paragraphs may determine whether the reader will go any farther. Ideally, I try to start each book with a dramatic factual scene like the one that opens *The Riddle of the Rosetta Stone*:

> The place: The Egyptian Sculpture Galley of the British Museum in London. The time: Now.
>
> Near the entrance to the long, high-ceilinged room stand two mag-nificent granite statues of Pharaoh Amenophis III, who ruled Egypt about 1400 B.C. Farther on is a colossal head of Pharaoh Rameses II dating back to 1250 B.C. And beyond it, resting on a simple base, is a slab of black basalt, a volcanic rock.
>
> Next to the statues and the head, the slab seems unimpressive at first glance. It is roughly the size of a tabletop—three feet nine inches long, two feet four and a half inches wide, and eleven inches thick. But many experts would say that this rather small piece of rock was more valuable than any of the larger objects in the room. For it is the famed Rosetta Stone, which gave nineteenth-century scholars their first key to the secrets of ancient Egypt.

During the research for a book I'm always on the lookout for colorful and amusing anecdotes that will help to bring the topic to life. For example, when I was researching *Chimney Sweeps* I was pleased to find the following anecdote which explains why sweeps are associated with good luck:

> A person who meets a sweep and bows to him three times is supposed to have good luck. According to a story told in England, the first person who experienced this kind of "chimney sweeps' luck" was King George III, who ruled during the 1700s.
>
> One afternoon the King was out riding in a London park when a rabbit ran across the bridle path and frightened his horse. The terrified animal began to buck and rear while the King's companions watched in horror. A chimney sweep who was passing by dropped his brushes

and bag of soot when he saw what was happening. He hurried over, grabbed the reins of the King's horse, and managed to calm him down.

If the sweep hadn't come to his rescue, the King might have been thrown from the horse and trampled to death. In gratitude, the King removed his hat and bowed three times to the dirty sweep. All the King's companions did the same, and soon people everywhere began to link bowing to a sweep with good luck.

Note that I was careful to say this was a story told in England. Anecdotes should always be identified as such so that trusting readers won't confuse them with facts.

Where appropriate, I like to include material on the contributions of non-Western peoples since I feel it adds a multicultural dimension to a book. For example, *From Hand to Mouth*—which is an account of eating utensils and table manners in various eras and cultures—features a chapter on chopsticks and how to use them. *Let There Be Light: A Book About Windows* contains sections on the unusual ways people have found to bring light and air into their dwellings in Africa, the Middle East, and Asia, as well as in Europe and America.

And in *The Truth About Unicorns*, along with the traditional European unicorn, there is a description of the very different Chinese unicorn—the *ki-lin*. (Besides the multicultural aspect, this excerpt is also an example of how folklore can be used to add color to a nonfiction text.)

In Chinese tales, the *ki-lin* was described as being a solitary animal that lived in deep forests and high in the mountains. It never appeared to humans unless it came on a special mission. Whenever a ki-lin showed itself to an emperor, it was thought the ruler would enjoy a long and peaceful reign.

The Buddhist religion spread to China from India in the first century A.D., and after that stories about the ki-lin endowed the animal with many Buddhist virtues. Buddhists disapproved of the unnecessary taking of life. So it was said that the ki-lin refused to eat any living thing, animal or vegetable.

To preserve life, the Chinese unicorn would not step on an ant or even a blade of green grass. A soft, fleshy tip grew over the end of its horn so that the ki-lin could never use it to harm a living creature.

A Buddhist scholar writing in the second century A.D. summed up the virtues of the Chinese unicorn in these words: "The ki-lin often attains the age of a thousand years, and is the noblest form of animal creation, the emblem of perfect good."

Librarians and teachers today, unlike some in the past, are opposed to the use of invented scenes and dialogue in nonfiction, especially biographies. How can authors work within this limitation and still manage to breathe life into their subjects? By recounting the known facts in a vivid fashion and incorporating actual quotations into the text. Here's an example from *The Truth About Santa Claus*, which tells of the early life of St. Nicholas:

Little is known of Nicholas's life—so little, in fact, that in 1969 the Roman Catholic Church questioned whether he had ever really lived.

According to biographies of Nicholas, written long after his death, he was born in the village of Patara in Asia Minor about A.D. 280. His father and mother had been married for some years and had begun to fear they would never be blessed with a child. They were overjoyed with their first-born son and christened him Nicholas, which means "hero of the people" in Greek.

Although he was sometimes lonely, being an only child, Nicholas enjoyed school and went faithfully to religious services. His parents didn't spoil him. Instead they taught him to be modest and think of others before himself. As one biographer wrote, the family was "not so rich as to be boastful, but they had enough to support themselves and still give to the poor."

Then, when Nicholas was twelve or thirteen, his happy, carefree life was shattered. A plague hit Patara and both of his parents were infected. Within a week they died, leaving Nicholas an orphan.

Nicholas wasn't content to sit back and live on his inheritance, though. He gave much of the money to charity and devoted himself even more seriously to his religious studies. At the age of nineteen he was ordained a priest in the Christian church and made a pilgrimage to the holy city of Jerusalem. Soon after his return he was named Bishop of Myra, a city near Patara. Nicholas was still so young that people called him the "Boy Bishop."

Humor is as much of an asset in nonfiction as in any other kind of book, and often harder to find. So I was delighted when I came across the following precepts by Erasmus while I was researching *From Hand to Mouth*. They're from a guide to manners, "On Civility in Children," that the Dutch thinker wrote in 1530. This was before people in Europe started eating with forks. Here is some of the advice Erasmus gave his young readers, who included the crown prince of France:

"Take the first piece of meat or fish that you touch, and don't poke around in the pot for a bigger one."

"Don't pick your nose when eating and then reach for more food."

"Don't throw bones you have chewed back in the pot. Put them on the table or toss them on the floor."

Drama, like humor, is another desirable attribute of nonfiction. It can often be achieved through an accurate representation of actual historical events, with the emphasis placed on action. An example is this account of the infamous *Kristallnacht* from *Let There Be Light*:

The background to *Kristallnacht* was complicated. In the fall of 1938 Nazi Germany ordered all foreign-born Jews to leave the country, including the parents of seventeen-year-old Hershl Grynszpan, who was away at school in Paris. Although the Grynszpans were Polish citizens, they had lived in Germany since 1914, and Poland refused to allow them to reenter the country. Instead they and hundreds of other Poles who had been expelled were forced to stay in a detention camp on the Polish-German border.

When young Hershl heard what had happened to his parents, he lost control of himself. Taking a handgun, he went to the German embassy in Paris on November 7, 1938, and shot the first person he met, a minor official named Ernst von Rath. The Nazis played up the incident in the German press, calling it a typical example of Jewish treachery. And when von Rath died of his wounds two days later, it gave the Nazis an excuse to launch a huge new crackdown on the Jews in Germany.

On the night of November 10, with the encouragement of Adolf Hitler, Joseph Goebbels, and other German leaders, members of the Nazi party and the dreaded S.S. attacked Jewish synagogues and stores throughout Germany and Austria. The mobs smashed one store window after another and threw rocks through the priceless stained-glass windows in many of Germany's largest synagogues.

So much broken glass littered the streets that it gave the night the name by which it has been known ever since—*Kristallnacht*, Night of Broken Glass.

Over 700 Jewish stores were wrecked during *Kristallnacht*, 76 synagogues were destroyed, and 191 others were damaged. Nearly a hundred Jews were killed, and thousands of others were arrested when they tried to defend themselves and their businesses. But the Nazis made no apologies. Instead, when insurance payments were made to Jews, the Nazis arranged to confiscate the money. And the Jews were still made liable for repairing the damage—including all the cracked and broken windows.

The narrative techniques I've described so far—an effective beginning, lively anecdotes and multicultural material, a liberal use of actual quotations, and frequent injections of humor and of dramatic true-life episodes—all point toward the book's last chapter. In fiction, this chapter contains the climax of the story and the resolution of its major conflicts. So does the concluding chapter of a nonfiction book, but instead of tying up the plot it usually features a summary of the book's content and a final statement of its theme.

This statement can have a serious tone, like the final paragraphs of my book *Milk*:

> The fight for pure milk—like the fight for the purity and safety of other consumer items—is far from over. Pasteurization, as we have seen, is not always foolproof. . . . Extensive atomic testing may be resumed, or another nuclear accident like Chernobyl could pollute the atmosphere and threaten the milk supply.
>
> To guard against such things happening, people in the future will have to be as alert to possible dangers as were the concerned citizens of the past. Only then will the children of the next century be assured a safe, healthful supply of that essential food—milk.

Or the tone can be lighter, like the final sentences in *From Hand to Mouth*. (They follow a discussion of the fact that more and more Japanese today are using knives, forks, and spoons, while many Americans are trying to eat with chopsticks.)

> What's likely is that people in both East and West will continue to experiment with one another's table utensils. And who knows? Perhaps in time they will find a common solution to that age-old question: how to get food as swiftly, gracefully, and neatly as possible from hand to mouth.

It can even be lyrical, like the conclusion of *Let There Be Light*:

> The need for windows has survived wars, riots, and the collapse of great civilizations. It will no doubt continue to endure as long as people have eyes to see, hearts to feel, and a healthy curiosity about the world around them.

Whatever tone seems most appropriate, the ending should leave open—as these three do—the possibility of future changes and developments. For virtually every nonfiction topic, from science to history and even biography, is subject to new discoveries and interpretations. And the young readers of today's nonfiction books are likely to make many of these discoveries and write these interpretations. Why not help point the way for them?

The nonfiction author faces a challenge in trying to braid together all the diverse strands in a true story and bring it to a satisfying conclusion. But the rewards of success are great. Chances are young readers will abandon any preconceptions they may still have about nonfiction. Instead of thinking it is dull and boring, they will probably conclude that nonfiction books can be just as exciting as novels—maybe even more exciting.

7

Writing for Today's Child

Judy Delton

When I began writing in 1971, all my editors told me I was too prolific. They said slow down. Find a hobby. Go to Tupperware parties. Make Christmas tree ornaments out of egg cartons.

But I was driven, as all beginning writers are driven. It's fun to write when you don't know how. I was enamored of my own words, and I got up at six A.M. to set up my cardtable in the living room and commit every incident in my kids' lives to paper. Jamie asked me, "What color is rain?" and I wrote a book about it. Jina said, "The principal moved bathtubs into the library today to read in." I wrote about it. I wrote about being a selfish mother. I wrote about Jamie's first day of kindergarten. I wrote about garage sales and farm auctions and then I turned my mother into a duck and wrote *Two Good Friends*. When my husband lost his job (before it was popular to lose jobs) I wrote *My Daddy Lost His Job Today*. When it didn't sell, I changed the title to *My Mother Lost Her Job Today* and it did. This was 1971. Role reversal books like *William's Doll* were just coming into print.

Everything I saw or heard or smelled or touched was grist for my mill. I had four small children to support, and I was going to do it by becoming a famous author. I wasn't going to work in a bakery and I wasn't going back to teaching second grade. I was going to be a famous writer.

The lucky part of all this is that I was in a small Wisconsin town, isolated from other writers, and had no idea that I could not develop skills overnight. (It's a misconception lots of my students have today.) In those days children's books were written by a handful of familiar names like Wanda Gág and Ludwig Bemelmans and Beverly Cleary—people I wrote about on little index cards in college for Children's Lit. Writing and painting were done by artists, and everyone out of work did not write a book. It was a good time for writers because there was lots of money for libraries. And the slush pile was not ten feet deep.

The other lucky thing I did was to protect myself. I didn't read my manuscripts to my children or parents or husband or neighbors or the man on the street. I knew criticism would destroy me. I never let anyone see my things until they were published. Then I was safe. I had my three dollars for my poem or five hundred for a picture book and I was off and running and no one could stop me.

My only problem was (as I said when I began a page or so back) that editors said I wrote too much. They couldn't publish so many of my children's books every year. And they didn't like an author who "slept around" so to speak—publishing with lots of houses. One editor told me she had one author who "took ten years to write a picture book," implying that the longer a writer took to write, the better the quality.

I always worked fast. My daughter is an artist and does her assignments very quickly, too. We are a fast family. We feel that overwriting and over-drawing muddies up the product.

Some children's book editors told me they would publish two books a year, but no more. Well, I couldn't support my family of five with one thousand dollars a year, especially when I could produce many more books and loved to do it.

And this leads me to one of the few things about publishing trends that I know: I was twenty years too soon to be prolific. I published hardcover children's books for ten years and barely earned a living holding myself back to two a year.

After all those editors in the seventies told me to "slow down," the 1980s finally came, and with it the blessed word SERIES. I met George Nicholson of Dell at an International Reading Association convention, and he asked me to write ten books a year for him. My life has not been the same since. At last I could merge my productivity with the series market need, and find, as they say, my niche.

In the 1970s, most books were fancy hardcover full-color books for parents or librarians to read to children. There were a few series like Nancy Drew and Betsy Tacy, but these were hardcover and not mass market. By 1986, when I met George, the trend had begun of having books that children could choose themselves, afford to buy themselves, and could read themselves. My halcyon days were here at last. Since that meeting I have done twenty Pee Wee Scout Books with Dell, six Condo Kids books , many picture books, and I am working on six new space books for Dell Young Yearling. So that's what I know about trends. Series.

Another thing I know about trends is how important timing is. When I first wrote *Kitty in the Middle* and my other Kitty books for Houghton Mifflin in the late seventies, I wrote about growing up Catholic in the forties. *Roots* had just been published. Ethnic cultures were trendy. I thought, now is the time for me to write about my childhood and get away with it. If I'd waited till now, I'd be out of luck. The market is saturated with growing-up-Catholic books. Timing is important.

I also know that in the seventies writing about a grandparent dying was considered brave and new. Just the concept of death for children was risky. But it caught on, and there must be hundreds of books about dying grandparents now, as well as books about social problems like divorce, foster children, child molesting, rape, incest, murder, and other sundries. I personally don't like social issues disguised as children's books, but then I have always written to entertain, not to teach. Children learn when they read, but only by accident. First they have to pick up the book and like the content. It has to be something they have experienced in some way, not boring, move fast, have some humor, and *then* they learn from it.

Once my editor at Houghton asked me to take President Roosevelt out of my Kitty book. She said children would not know who he was. Of course they wouldn't! But they remember his name, when they read it. I know I learned all the facts I remember today from reading *fiction*, not history. My daughters always are quoting some fact they learned from *The Boxcar Children* or *Curious George*.

I never tried to write a "good book." The pressure would be too great. I have to give myself permission to write a bad book. Or I'd be scratching every word out, and throwing away all that paper you see people in movies doing when they write. I can't "try" to write a good book. I can't really try for anything. I do what I do and try to be honest.

Before I go into honesty, I want to say something about why writers write. I always am reading about authors who write to "hook" kids (which I think is deceitful). Or "turn them on." (Ditto). I find my motives infinitely more selfish. I find I write to entertain myself. I write because I like an audience. Because I can't talk all the time. Because it's easier than acting. Because I can't tap dance like Shirley Temple.

I write because editors tell me I make them laugh, they like what I write (if someone likes what you do, you try twice as hard). I write to support my house, I write because I'm not in therapy (and writing is cheaper than therapy), I write to discover my past, and I write because I'm too far into it to turn back. Twenty years is the longest I've stayed at any one thing. (I'd tried painting plates, playing guitar [the kids were really glad when that didn't work out], and raising tropical fish before this.)

I find this reversal of writing for myself instead of for kids serendipitous. Because only when I write for myself can I write for others. It's like making people happy. You can't go out and "make" people happy. You have to be happy yourself and then hope that it affects others.

Writing for oneself allows honesty, and honesty is what gives fiction depth and substance.

For years I went to visit schools (when I was writing two books a year instead of ten). And I used to ask the children the difference between fiction and nonfiction. All the hands would wave, and I'd call on someone, and without fail, he or she told me that nonfiction was TRUE and fiction was made up. I always shocked them by saying it is just the opposite of that. Nonfiction can be anything, but *fiction must be honest*. I can spot dishonest fiction across a crowded room. I recognize it right away because I start bristling around the edges.

There is a difference between honesty and truth. Everything you write in a children's fiction book doesn't have to be the truth, but it does have to be honest.

In one of my last Pee Wee Scout books, Molly wanted to earn a baby-tending badge, and she had no baby. In another book she had looked for a fire hazard; now she would look for a baby the same way. She'd look for an orphan, she'd steal a baby, she'd get one someplace. To be *truthful*, I never stole a baby. But in all *honesty*, I did have Molly's feeling of desperation. The compelling need to get something, to accomplish something, to not be the only one without a badge. And that feeling is what has to be real. It is that emotion that must be honest. Or else children's books aren't worth paper.

In my Kitty book I have a scene with giant paperdolls. Kitty and Margaret Mary cut them out of old boxes in Kitty's back yard. They were lifesize. They drew faces on them, and clothes and lockets and shoes. When they finished, Margaret Mary's was beautiful. She had blond curls and a blue hair ribbon and a gold locket and most important, her arms and legs were the right length. Her knees bent in the right place and her sweater looked soft and cuddly.

Kitty's doll had too long a neck and too short an arm and the knees bent almost at the hips. She wanted a doll just like Margaret Mary's. Kitty cried and begged and pleaded but Margaret Mary refused to make her an identical doll. Finally Margaret Mary said, "Oh, all right, you can have this one. I'll make myself another one. But I'm going to make mine better."

Kitty had her way now, but she was distressed. She wanted a doll better than Margaret Mary's. She didn't want her to make a prettier one for herself.

I am Kitty. It was not easy to admit to myself and the world that I was that selfish. I was selfish back before psychologists said it was OK to be selfish. So were other children. Children are not sweet, angelic creatures as people think. They are basically selfish, base, loving beings, and it is important to transmit how they really are, not how we want them to be. Margaret Mary wanted her doll to be best, and Kitty wanted hers to be best. That is a simple truth about children. If you lose touch with the real child in your own self, you can't write for children.

I often think it is necessary to be hypnotized to write good fiction. (Fiction for children is no different from fiction for adults.) Once you are inside a character you know, once you are under a spell in that other world, the truth flows. You are away from sentiment and falsity, deep deep down where real things are. You are on the inside writing out, not on the outside trying to write like a writer.

When I taught writing classes, most of the manuscripts I read lacked that honesty. The writers were not willing to take that risk. They were not willing to spill their guts all over the sidewalk. So they wrote about characters named Tiffany and Bruce and they were cardboard people doing cardboard things. One in every hundred manuscripts I read was honest and saleable.

Students would say, "I can't write about Aunt Martha till she dies; she might read it and be hurt." I told these students: (1) She probably won't read it. (It's amazing how few people read your books. One of my series alone has sold over three million copies and yet most of my friends and relatives have not read them.); (2) You can't be a nice person and still be an honest writer. You have to get the body on paper before it's cold. You have to have a notepad at the funeral. If you worry that the mourners will complain, writing isn't your field.

To me the sine qua non of good writing for children (and adults of course) is humor and pathos. When it is very honest it can be funny and sad at the same time. The lightest humor must have a sweet dark side. The happiest child has fears and forebodings—if you capture the real child. The kinds of things that last in literature, the classics, have this honesty. I'm not positive a writer can do this on purpose. I don't think you can start out to write series books that will sell in the millions by saying, "I will be funny and sad. My books will be funny but have a lot of depth." I think it is something you either have naturally or you develop. And honesty comes from taking risks. Giving yourself permission to write badly. Breaking through the façade to who you really are, to the real child inside, not just from memory but from gut feeling, without fear that someone will think you are mean or nasty or selfish.

I didn't know all this when I began writing. I didn't start out to be a writer. I worked at the telephone company, I was a dental assistant. (I hated this so much I broke my leg in five places to get away from it.) I didn't have any background in writing, no journalism courses in college, no creative writing classes, no A's on essays, no parents who were novelists, and I didn't write journals in a pile of red notebooks like my daughter does.

I did write good notes to the milkman and my children's teachers, and good letters to my friends. But real letter writing today is a lost art, and it never did pay well.

I had only one writing lesson in my life and that was from my dad when I was in fifth grade. He taught me more in a half-hour than I learned in a lifetime in school. My homework was to write an essay. I groused about it, and he said, "What did you do today?" I said nothing. He said, "What happened at school?" Nothing. Home? Nothing. In disgust, I said "I didn't have any lunch because I forgot my key."

He probed. He said I had an essay here. So I wrote, "I got home at noon and couldn't get in the house so I had no lunch because my mom wasn't home."

He showed me how to give it a beginning (I was hungry. I ran all the way home, thinking about what kind of sandwich my mom would have to eat. Olive and nut? Tuna fish?) A middle. (I got to the back door and my mom wasn't home. She was shopping downtown with Aunt Marge.) And an end. (I could see my lunch through the window but I couldn't eat it, because I'd forgotten my key.) It was a simple thing, but it was structure.

Save the surprise for the end. Set the background. The facts did not have to be all truthful, but the feelings were honest.

That was my background for writing series books. In 1971 I was thirty-nine-years-old and casting about for something to add meaning to my life and support my family and I wrote a poem and said, "This is wonderful, I will be a writer." No one said I couldn't, so I plunged ahead. In 1974 my first children's book was published, *Two Good Friends*. The scrupulous duck was my mother, and the messy bear was me. I wrote it like it was. (Except that my mother really wasn't a duck.) I had to take my shoes off when I came in the house, so did Duck. When the book was an ALA notable, I stuck my mother in more books, like *Penny Wise* (my mother was an ostrich who collected coupons), *Rabbit's New Rug* (my mother was a rabbit who had a lovely rug but wouldn't let anyone walk on it; Rabbit lost a lot of friends and so did my mother).

When I exhausted my mother I tried my dad and wrote *A Walk on a Snowy Night* (Harper), which was about all the walks my dad and I took on blizzardy nights while the people in the warm houses were listening to the war news on the radio.

Then I invaded the lives of my children. I told Jamie to go out and play one day when I was busy writing, and he said, "Boy, you're sure crabby in winter," and I immediately wrote, *My Mom Hates Me in January*. Spring becomes the resolution to that book.

I decided to try novels for children, and my first attempt was the Kitty series. Kitty was all me. Like Maud Hart Lovelace, I committed my childhood to paper, with a plan. The war bond drives, the Legion of Decency, the pagan babies, novenas, proms, best friends, and lots and lots of nuns. I didn't have to make it funny. If I just told it, it was funny from a child's view. The Catholic things didn't matter as long as the feelings were real and the kids could identify.

When I began the Angel series, I had only an image. It was of my third daughter, Jennifer, sitting on the back steps in our old house in Wisconsin, pouting. She didn't smile until she was five. When I related this at a lecture in Omaha, a concerned librarian asked, "What happened to Jennifer? Is she still troubled?" I replied that Jennifer is now twenty-four, living with her boyfriend, and smiling all the time (and I don't even want to *know* why). I based the whole series on that lonely character on those steps and found out why she didn't smile (she wanted a friend).

In *Only Jody* I was the eccentric mother who watered plants in her tap shoes. She appears again in Condo Kids were she owns her own faucet company and moves her kids to the suburbs just when they are settled in a city school.

Jennifer reappears in Pee Wee Scouts (*Spring Sprouts*) as Molly planting a garden to earn a badge. When Jennifer was eighteen (instead of six) she planted some radishes and a month later said, "Shouldn't I have some radishes on my plants by now?" The word "on" worried me. I told her to pull one up and see. She said, "PULL ONE UP?"

Jennifer graduated from the university with a 4.0 GPA, and yet at eighteen she did not know that radishes grew underground. (The American education system has a lot to answer for.)

It was too good a thing to waste, and it made a fine theme for Molly, who is the only one without a vegetable when the scouts are due to collect their badges. Even Sonny, my mama's boy, the only Pee Wee with training wheels on his bike at a bike race, knew radishes grew underground.

Another trend I might mention is that midlist authors get a few scatterings of fan mail a month, but when you take the plunge into series it comes by the barrel. Most of them are a class assignment and very similar, but every once in a while there is one that is so original and fresh and honest that I treasure it. A recent one said, "Dear Judy Delton, I love love love your books. You are my favorite author. Love, Robin. PS: I haven't read any of your books yet, but I am going to soon."

Another letter told me, "I can't go to sleep without reading one of your books."

But the one I'll always love the most is this hand-typed-by-the-child-herself one:

Dear Judy Delton,

Hi, how are you, I am fine. I am going to tell you a little story about the Condo Kids to you. My story will begin about if we get a good report card we get to go to the book store and spend five dollars. Well last time I went my brother and I both got good report cards. My brother got a couple of books that were not yours. I was looking to see if you wrote any more Pee Wee Scout books but there were no new ones. So I went to the other side and and I saw THE CONDO KIDS books, *AND I JUMPED FOR JOY!* I only had a little bit of money left and I wanted another thing *but I put the other thing back and bought your book.* I am going to read it when I finish another book called . . . ha ha ha. You will find out latter on in theis letter. By the way I got Condo Kids no. 1. As I was saying you will find out the other book latter on in theis letter [sic]. Right now I guess it is latter on [sic] so I will tell you now. It's an Angel book! It's called ANGEL IN CHARGE but I do not know what no. it is because it does not tell you. I love Angel and I love all your books so, so, so, so, so, so, so, much. I am your biggest fan. I have to go eat dinner now so bye.

Love, Erica.

And that's what being a series author is all about. It's the most any author could hope for. That a child will go to a book store with his report card money hot in his fist, *"put the other thing back,"* and choose mine. That's what happiness is.

8

Envisioning Experience: The Potential of Picture Books

Barbara Kiefer

"Read it again," is a refrain familiar to many parents and teachers who realize that picture books play a significant role in the lives of young children. Research shows, in fact, that children who are read to in the preschool and early grades gain significantly in language and literacy development over the years. Yet while focusing on the development of children's oral language and reading abilities in the context of picture storybook reading, many studies of children and picture books have neglected what may be the book's major attribute, the *visual* context it provides for literacy, and for literary and aesthetic understanding. Such studies have also neglected to consider the picture book as an *art object*, a combination of image and idea in a sequence of turning pages that can produce in the reader an effect greater than the sum of the parts (Marantz, 1977; Bader, 1976).

In studies of emergent reading, for example, much attention focuses on the verbal aspect of the storybook reading sessions. In many analyses, researchers devise complex categories for discourse that centers on the printed verbal text and limit comments about the illustrations to one or two categories (Harker, 1988; Yaden, Smolkin and Conlon, 1989). Even when illustrations were the focus of reading comprehension or word recognition studies, researchers often isolated words and pictures from the context of the whole book or story, destroying the aesthetic nature of the book. In one such study, for example, Samuels (1967) presented groups of kindergarteners with four words on index cards either with pictures or without. When the "no picture" group gave significantly more correct responses to the printed words than did the "words and pictures" group, Samuels concluded that pictures inter-fered with word learning and recommended that books for beginning readers contain no illustrations (1970). Fortunately, other researchers (Schallert, 1980; Levin, 1981) have since concluded that both listening and reading compre-hension are facilitated when illustrations overlap and extend the printed words in books, a characteristic inherent in the definition of the picture book as an art object.

Other studies whose object has been the artistic qualities of the picture book and whose results have been directed toward informing book publishers and purchasers have also neglected the unique aesthetic nature of the picture book. Often these studies were efforts to determine children's preferences for style, media, or content of illustrations, and researchers reduced their testing instruments to single pictures or slides that controlled for variables like color, pictorial content, or style and asked children to choose the picture that they liked best (Martin, 1931; Rudisill, 1952; Smerdon, 1976). Such studies found, for example, that children preferred color over black and white, re-alism over abstraction, and familiar content over the fantastic.

Moreover, in many of these studies children's reactions were observed only momentarily. For example, in Smerdon's (1976) study children were asked to look at pairs of slides flashed on a screen at five-second intervals and then directed to mark their preference for a picture on a checklist. In this fashion not only was the artistic object oversimplified but so also was the event of picture viewing. Like Smerdon, other researchers have not taken into account the complex nature of aesthetic response, the fact that it involves affective as well as cognitive understanding or that it might change over time (Rosenblatt, 1976; Purves and Beach, 1972). Nor have they considered the social and cultural nature of the reading that is part of children's experience with picture books (Hickman, 1981; Heath, 1983).

Furthermore, researchers may have neglected the power of picture books to evoke emotional response. For example, researchers working to under-stand how meaning is constructed linguistically in the context of picture book reading have certainly contributed much to our understanding of how pic-tures support or extend the meaning of the verbal text, but less about how books capture children's hearts as well as their minds. Yet the power of art to evoke emotions may be the picture book's most significant contribution to children's cognitive and aesthetic understanding. Langer (1953) has ar-gued, for instance, that artwork is an expression of the artist's idea, "i.e., something that takes shape as he articulates an envisagement of realities which discursive language cannot properly express. What he makes is pri-marily a symbol to capture and hold his own imagination of organized feeling, the rhythms of life, the forms of emotion" (p. 392). I believe it is this powerful quality of the visual art of the picture book that gives rise to the deepest responses on the part of children, what Rosenblatt has referred to as "the full lived—through fusion with the text" (1978, p. 47). Surely we must consider this aspect of the picture book as well as its power to instruct or inform, so that the question to ask is not How do picture books help children learn to read? or What kind of pictures do children like? but To what kind of picture books do children respond most deeply?

To answer this question and resolve previous difficulties concerning picture book research, I sought to use naturalistic research techniques, entering classrooms where I might find children regularly interacting with and responding to picture books in order to study and describe the dimensions of their responses. My initial research began in first/second-grade classrooms in alternative schools in a suburb of Columbus, Ohio. These classrooms were modeled on the British informal system, one that might currently be called "whole language." Children's literature and not textbooks formed the core of the curriculum, with learning activities organized around themes. There were between three hundred and five hundred picture books in the classroom libraries. The teachers read aloud to children and discussed books with them several times a day, and children had opportunities to read alone and with other children, to talk about books with each other, and to respond to books through art, writing, drama, and other avenues.

I entered the classrooms as a participant observer, first for ten weeks and, the following year, for twelve weeks. Initially my role was observational. I kept a field notebook, noting behaviors and comments during read-aloud sessions and during individual and group work times, and I recorded some sessions on audio tapes. During the second observation period, I also conducted and taped interviews with children both singly and in pairs. In one set of interviews I presented children with two recently published picture books that differed in style and content and asked them to show me how they liked to look at a new picture book and to talk about each book as they looked through it. In the second group of interviews, I read children a Grimm's fairy tale without showing them the pictures, asking them to try to imagine pictures in their heads. Later I showed pairs of children three versions of the tale illustrated in different styles and media and asked them to talk about their responses to the books.

During my early observations, as I reviewed field notes and tape transcripts, several general themes began to emerge concerning children's responses to picture books. These themes or domains involved the variations in children's responses, the changes in responses over time, and the stylistic and content differences among the picture books. Then, as I reviewed data gathered from further observations and interviews, I developed a descriptive framework for children's responses to picture books (Kiefer, 1982, 1986).

Although I did not quantify children's responses, the categories and subcategories that emerged were useful for observations conducted in other settings and with other populations in subsequent years. These further studies were conducted in a third/fourth-grade combination classroom in the same school I had initially visited in suburban Columbus; in a university preschool in Houston, Texas; in a second grade in an urban Houston school with a multicultural population; and in a below-grade-level multicultural fifth-grade classroom in a suburban Houston school. In all these settings, by using the ethnographic techniques discussed, I have been able to describe a variety of possible responses to picture books that reinforces the validity of the descriptive framework. In addition, by looking at children's responses at different ages I have also been able to note developmental differences in children's awareness of stylistic factors relating to the art in picture books. In this article, I will discuss the dimensions of response that I found among the children I observed and the types of aesthetic awareness that also may develop as children have time to respond to picture books as they mature developmentally.

A Descriptive Framework for Response to Picture Books

Unlike studies of children's preferences for illustrations which sought norms for particular styles, media, or content of books, my own observations have identified the wide *variation* in individual responses. Thus, the descriptive framework I developed for looking at children's responses includes the many behaviors that grew out of children's contact with picture books, how they chose picture books, how they looked at them, how they talked about them, and what they said they saw in the illustrations. Moreover, I believe that the classroom context—that is, the many picture books available, the actions of teachers and peers, and the changes over time in children's responses—was essential to the range and depth of responses that occurred. Often responses to books occurred during group read-aloud sessions or during the times teachers had set aside for children to read for pleasure either alone or with another student. When teachers gave children encouragement, opportunity, and time to respond to picture books beyond these types of sessions, children often chose a variety of ways to extend their initial reactions to books. Many chose some form of artistic response, either two-dimensional (paintings, collages, murals) or three-dimensional (dioramas, sculpture, displays). Children often chose to write in response to books in informal journals, in short personal pieces telling about their personal reaction, in poetry, or in more formal reports. Often these responses involved small groups of children who wanted to work together. Creative drama (puppet shows or plays) was one result of such group response.

Talking About Picture Books

Within all the different contexts in which I observed children responding to books, the category of response that accounted for the most data was children's verbal responses. As I observed children in all settings, I found an enthusiastic willingness to immerse themselves in the contents of their picture books, and language seemed to give them the tools for understanding this complex art object. In reviewing transcripts of read-aloud sessions and interviews, I noticed that children seemed to employ many different functions of language as they talked about books within the larger social context of each particular classroom. This brought to mind M. A. K. Halliday's (1975) work on language development titled *Learning How to Mean*. Because the children I observed seemed to be intent on making meaning regarding picture books, I developed a classificatory scheme for children's verbal responses to picture books based on four of Halliday's functions of language: informative, heuristic, imaginative, and personal. These categories are useful, I believe, for helping to understand how it is that children *learn how to mean* in the world of the picture book.

Informative Language

Many children used language to convey information about picture books, often pointing to the pictures as they spoke. For example, a first grader looking at Plume's version of *The Bremen Town Musicians* pointed to the picture and stated, "Here's the dog and here's the cat and here's the donkey." Other children seemed to use the picture to retell or reconstruct events in the story. A fifth grader looking at Galdone's version of *Hansel and Gretel* explained, "Here you see the witch looking right through the curtain. You don't even see the witch talking to them. You just see them sleeping there and the witch leaving and then you see her trying to get her [Gretel] to go in."

The informative function also helped children to compare the illustrations to the real world or to other books. Children of all ages made comments such as "this looks like wood" or "this reminds me of the other book." A second-grade child noticed the small game box under the tree on the title page of Van Allsburg's *Jumanji*. "That's like his other book," she told me, and indeed, the box, an inch across, did seem to have the topiary figures that decorated the cover of Van Allsburg's first book, *The Garden of Abdul Gasazi*.

Children also provided information about the process of illustration as well as the content of the pictures. They talked not only about the elements of art ("He used brown") but also about processes of composition. A fifth grader pointed out the white spaces on several of the pages in Zwerger's version of *Hansel and Gretel*:

Rhonda: The white kinda lets you just focus on the illustration, like it lets you see white and you look in the middle.

Interviewer: It draws your attention to the picture.

Rhonda: Yeah, cause you look at this [the center] and then you look at the corners too.

Heuristic Language

Many children wondered about the illustrations or made inferences and predictions about the contents, characters, or events in the illustrations. These remarks show children using the heuristic or problem-solving function of language. For example, two fifth-grade boys discussed the children's lack of shoes in Galdone's version of *Hansel and Gretel*:

Colby: I think they would have some kind of shoes for them because if they stepped on a twig they would have got real hurt.

Jay: Well they were poor so they may not have been able to afford shoes for them.

Colby: See they would have stepped on those pebbles and they'd be going down the path in real pain with those pebbles.

Another fifth grader made inferences about the stepmother in Browne's modern-day version of *Hansel and Gretel*:

In this story she's the one getting all the attention and the money spent on her. See the makeup on her face? See how she's dressed and she has makeup and her hair is done? Is that a cigarette? And she's wearing high heels out in the forest and the leopard coat. They [the family] may be running out of money because all the money they spent on her.

In addition to applying heuristic language to understand the story, children also seemed to be interested in understanding art techniques or the illustrator's intentions. A first grader speculated that Bloom had used paint in *We Be Warm Till Springtime Come* because she could "see the brush strokes coming down." Looking at Zwerger's *Hansel and Gretel* a fifth grader explained, "This looks like water color because how the bottom's real dark and it's, like, wet."

Imaginative Language

The imaginative function of language allowed children to participate in an imaginary world created by the author or artist or to create their own mental images. Some children assumed the roles of characters and created imaginary dialogue as they viewed the illustrations, while others discussed mental images evoked by the illustrations. Two fifth graders looked at an illustration in Zelinsky's version of *Hansel and Gretel* in which Hansel is dropping bread crumbs on the path:

Patrick: He's pausing and he's throwing them down and she's looking back telling him like, "Come on!" She's thinking, "Would you hurry up!"

Rhonda: And you can really think in your mind that can really happen.

The imaginative function also allowed children, particularly young children, to use verbal imagery in formulating unusual comparisons. A first grader, for example, looked at ripples behind a boat in Shulevitz's *Dawn*. "That's like whipped cream that men put on to shave," he explained. On other occasions first and second graders described Tomie de Paola's distinctive clouds as "pumpy" or "like mashed potatoes."

Personal Language

Children often related personally to books, either connecting the books to something in their own lives or discussing feelings or opinions about the books. A story event or illustration often triggered a personal connection that might seem to have little relation to the book itself. "We got a blanket colored like that," reported a first grader of a picture in Chaffin's *We Be Warm Till Springtime Come*. The dog character in Domanska's *The Bremen Town Musicians* reminded another first grader, "I love dogs. They're so cute. We were going to get one but my grandma had to come [live with us] because she kept messing up the [her] house." A fifth grader noticed the witch's red eyes in Zelinsky's *Hansel and Gretel*: "She can't see that good cause her eyes are real red. You can't see that good cause after you get out of the swimming pool—you can't see that good and your eyes are still red."

The pictures also evoked expressions of emotion. As they looked at a close-up of a dog's face filled with porcupine quills in Carrick's *Ben and the Porcupine*, first and second graders exclaimed, "Don't show that picture. It makes me so sad." Third, fourth, and fifth graders recognized the effects of color on their emotions, reporting that bright green made them feel happy or that browns and grays made them feel sad or scared.

At all grade levels I found children willing to express opinions about books and to evaluate their quality. As Applebee (1978) found in studying children's responses to stories, the younger children whom I observed evaluated books based on their own subjective responses rather than on some objective quality in the book itself. When asked to explain why she had stated that Domanska's *What Do You See?* was a good book, for example, a first grader replied, "Because I liked it." In observing third through fifth graders, however, I found children more apt to back up their subjective reactions to a book with objective criteria. Looking at the landscape paintings on the endpapers of Zelinsky's version of *Hansel and Gretel*, two fifth graders explained:

Rhonda: This looks like you're really standing outside and seeing birds and clouds.

Patrick: I think the illustrator did a good job because I like realistic illustrations.

Interviewer: And you don't think the other books were realistic, huh?

Rhonda: Not that much.

Interviewer: What is the difference?

Rhonda: The details and the colors.

Patrick: [turning the pages]: And they look really poor because look at his pants. They're all torn. . . . He used a lot of detail because the walls are cracked.

Rhonda: And look at their faces.

Such exchanges show how fluid and dynamic all these functions of language were, one function quickly giving rise to another, one child supporting or extending the understanding of another, all in the context of making meaning through picture books.

The Development of Aesthetic Awareness

As I examined these verbal responses to picture books in a variety of classroom contexts and began to articulate a theory of style in picture books (Kiefer 1982, 1988), I noted developmental differences in children's awareness of stylistic factors relating to the art in picture books. I noted first of all that children seem to see the small details that many illustrators include in their pictures and that we adults may overlook. A first-grade boy noticed, for example, that the tiny book on a hassock in the crowded room in Shulevitz's *Oh, What A Noise!* had the book's title printed on its spine. Others found the mushrooms growing under the Strawberry Snatcher's feet in Bang's *The Grey Lady and the Strawberry Snatcher* or the tiny mouse in Spier's *Gobble Growl Grunt*. The rewards of looking carefully at illustrations to find what one teacher called "secrets" may in turn have helped children to become more sensitive to the artistic qualities in picture books.

Indeed, as I observed children at different grade levels engaged in responding to picture books in so many different ways, I found that they developed more critical thinking not only about cognitive factors but also about aesthetic factors and that this awareness varied with the age of the child. The differences in stylistic awareness may have been tied to factors of cognitive development, as Applebee (1978) has suggested.

One change that I noted at different ages related to the children's awareness of the artist behind the book. Some younger children were confused about who created the pictures. Some thought that machines made the pictures rather than an artist who created an original work that was then photographed and printed by machines. Other young children were unsure about variations in individual styles or the stylistic choices made by artists in the process of illustration. Often their attention to stylistic qualities was idiosyncratic. One first grader argued that *Mother, Mother, I Want Another* (Polushkin) was illustrated by the same artist who did *I Saw a Ship A Sailing* (Domanska). When pressed to explain why he thought two books that differed greatly in style were by the same artist, he explained, "the words." Both books had been printed in Abbott Old Style, a distinctive type face. The boy had, in fact, overgeneralized from the form of the printed letters to the entire art work. Older children, however, seemed to know that a real person created the pictures and that this person made choices that affected their own reaction to the book.

The differences in stylistic awareness among the ages also extended to the elements of art that are the artist's means of expression. All children seemed familiar with elements like lines, shapes, and colors although they did not always have the correct nomenclature. Kindergarteners and first and second graders talked about squiggly lines, twisty lines, or construction paper shapes (those with sharp edges). Many of these youngsters confused bright colors (bright in intensity) with light colors (light in value) and used the term *light* to indicate brightness, while several referred to black-and-white illustrations as colored. Children of all ages referred to the element of texture by using terms like *rough* or *smooth*. And although even the older children rarely used the term *value*, they seemed to be aware of the presence of this element by talking about "dark" pictures or an artist's use of "sunlight."

Children in grades three through five talked about an artist's role in evoking emotional responses through the elements of art, and they commented on technical choices relating to book production. A fourth grader stated of Galdone's *Hansel and Gretel*, "The lines sorta make it look detailed and the detail makes it look scary." Looking at Marushi's *Hiroshima No Pika*, a third grader remarked, "The pictures look sad. They don't have a certain shape to them." Other older children mentioned such technical choices as endpapers, page layout, and choice of original media. A fourth-grade boy examined the rust-colored endpapers as he opened Zwerger's version of *Hansel and Gretel*: "They look reddish brown like somebody's put something there and just forgot about it and never got it up again. They put it in the forest and left it there forever." Many of the third, fourth, and fifth graders who looked at the Zwerger book speculated about what seems to be an abrupt cut-off of several of the illustrations, leaving large areas of white at the edge of the page:

Mark: This page has white over there and these pages he just paints right to the end.

I doubt it's blanked out or anything.

Kristin: He probably did it on purpose.

Interviewer: Why?

Kristin: Well he might have said in the end of the thing you know when they copy the pages . . .

Mark: And he might have wanted you to see them [the characters] instead of . . .

Interviewer: So he was kind of spotlighting the people?

Mark: Like there was nothing else out there.

A fourth grader seemed to recognize the emotive power of the artist's choices as she compared illustrations in Paterson's *The Crane Wife* to those in another version of the folktale, Matsutani's *The Crane Maiden*:

> *Heather:* In *The Crane Wife* the paper used is rice paper and the painting is done by taking soft light shades of watered ink and brushing it on with light strokes. In the *Crane Maiden* the artist chose simple shapes with watercolor and the color sort of blue.
>
> *Interviewer:* Which one do you like better?
>
> *Heather: The Crane Maiden* is too blocklike, like it's all straight, made up of squares. *The Crane Wife* is made up of circles. It fits the story better because it's a smooth story and a ball rolls and a square won't.

Her remarks indicate how children seem to grow in understanding the meaning-making power of visual art.

Furthermore, the books that engendered the deepest responses among children were not ones that we might have predicted from looking at the results of many of the preference studies cited earlier. Among other findings, these had suggested that children preferred illustrations in color rather than in black and white, illustrations with familiar everyday content rather than the unusual or fantastic, and illustrations executed in representational style rather than abstract color. Yet books like Van Allsburg's *Jumanji* or Kennedy's *Song of the Horse*, Sendak's *Outside Over There* and Bang's *The Grey Lady and the Strawberry Snatcher* accounted for the longest-lasting and most complex responses on the part of many of the children (Kiefer, 1985). As a result of their experiences with these books they talked, questioned, argued, inferred. They sought out other works by the illustrators. They created art and wrote stories and poetry. They created classroom displays and produced dramas. Their responses to these particular books indicate that perhaps books that are puzzling rather than pretty may be the ones that shape children's deepest aesthetic understandings. When I asked first and second graders how they felt about black-and-white illustrations, Steve replied. "Pictures don't have to be in color. . . . It's harder when it's in black and white. It takes more time and you don't just whip through the book." He pointed to the cover of *Jumanji* and explained that the monkeys hiding in the closet would have been easy to see if the book had been in color. But, he explained, "You like to take time." Older children also seemed to agree that an important criterion for a picture book was not that it was "easy for you to find things" but that it "makes you think more." Certainly it is this type of outcome that educators, publishers, and librarians would wish for children.

Conclusion

Marantz has argued that the art in picture books ought to be viewed as "more than some ancillary decoration or visual relief for a literary effort" (1977, p. 149). Picture books "are not literature (i.e., word dominated things) but rather a form of visual art" (p. 150). Although a book illustrator must be guided by the necessity of interpreting a narrative or a concept, in the best picture books the illustrator creates an art form that involves as much as it informs, and transforms as much as it tells. The request of so many of these children for picture books that make them "think more" is, I believe, a reflection of the power of the *art* in picture books as much as their verbal text. Moreover, the children's simple words would seem to be a profound reflection of the theory of aesthetics so beautifully articulated by Langer (1953):

> The exhilaration of a direct aesthetic experience indicates the depth of human mentality to which that experience goes. What it [the work of art] does to us is to formulate our conceptions of feeling and our conceptions of visual, factual, and audible reality together. It gives us *forms of imagination* and *forms of feeling* inseparably; that is to say it clarifies and organizes intuition itself. That is why it has the force of a revelation, and inspires a feeling of deep intellectual satisfaction. (p. 397)

Although it is difficult to generalize the responses of the children I have observed to all situations, the variety of children's responses to picture books described here show what is *possible* rather than probable when children have the time and opportunity to interact with picture books. Practical recommendations that grow out of these observations are tied to the contexts in which these responses occurred. To provide for the deepest and richest response to picture books, publishers must understand the unique nature of the picture book as an art object and must recognize and support the unique role of the individual illustrator in discovering a "tacit personal illuminating contact with the symbols of feeling" (Langer, 1953, p. 401). Moreover, the framework for the children's responses I have described would not, I believe, hold together were it not for such crucial factors as adults who give children access to books and time to respond to books in a community of readers (Hepler and Hickman, 1982).

Teachers and librarians who wish to explore the meaning-making potential of picture books with children will want to begin by building good classroom, school, and municipal library collections. Such collections should include a variety of different styles and genres of picture books. With librarians as partners and advisors, teachers should plan to use picture books across the curriculum with all ages, not just in the primary grades. Collaborating with the school art teacher to help children deepen their understanding of a variety of art forms both in and out of museums may also help children deepen their critical awareness. But more important may be the mutual exploration of picture books by adults and children within the school walls. Here children do not need art experts so much as they need adults who enjoy picture books and read them regularly, several times a day. Children also need time to talk about picture books, with the teacher or librarian in large group settings, or more informally in small discussion groups, or with a friend. They need time to choose books that interest or intrigue them, time to read, and the time and encouragement to respond to books through a variety of means other than talk, especially through art, writing, and creative dramatics. In contexts such as these, children will certainly come to be literate. But perhaps more important, they can move beyond mere preferences for books and deepen their understanding of the rich worlds of images and ideas found between the covers of picture books.

References

Applebee, A. N. 1978. *The Child's Concept of Story*. Chicago: University of Chicago Press.

Bader, B. 1976. *American Picture Books: From Noah's Ark to the Beast Within*. New York: Macmillan.

Halliday, M. A. K. 1975. *Learning How to Mean: Explorations in the Development of Language*. London: Longman Group Ltd.

Harker, J. O. 1988. "Contrasting the Content of Two Story Reading Lessons: A Propositional Analysis." In J. Green and J. Harker, Eds., *Multiple Perspective Analysis of Classroom Discourse*. Norwood, N.J.: Ablex.

Heath, S. 1983. *Ways With Words: Language, Life, and Work in Communities and Classrooms*. Cambridge: Cambridge University Press.

Hepler, S., and J. Hickman. 1982. "'The Book Was Okay. I Love You': Social Aspects of Response to Literature." *Theory Into Practice* 21: 278–283.

Hickman, J. 1981. "A New Perspective on Response to Literature." *Research in the Teaching of English* 15: 343–354.

Kiefer, B. 1982. "The Response of Primary Children to Picture Books." Doctoral dissertation: The Ohio State University.

———. 1985. "Looking Beyond Picture Book Preferences." *The Horn Book Magazine* 61: 705–713.

———. 1986. "The Child and the Picture Book: Creating Live Circuits." *Children's Literature Association Quarterly* 11: 63–68.

———. 1988. "Picture Books as Contexts for Literary, Aesthetic and Real World Understandings." *Language Arts* 65: 260–271.

Langer, S. K. 1953. *Feeling and Form*. New York: Charles Scribner & Sons.

Levin, J. 1981. "On Functions of Pictures in Prose." In F. Pirozollo and M. Wittrock, Eds., *Neuropsychological and Cognitive Processes in Reading*. New York: Academic Press.

Marantz, K. 1977. "The Picture Book as Art Object: A Call for Balanced Reviewing." *Wilson Library Bulletin*, 148–151.

Martin, H. 1931. *Children's Preferences in Book Illustrations*. Cleveland: Western Reserve University Bulletin.

Purves, A., and R. Beach. 1972. *Literature and the Reader: Research in Response to Literature, Reading Interests, and the Teaching of Literature*. Urbana, Ill.: National Council of Teachers of English.

Rosenblatt, L. 1976. *Literature as Exploration*. 3d ed. New York: Noble and Noble.

———. 1978. *The Reader, the Text and the Poem: The Transactional Theory of the Literary Work*. Carbondale: Southern Illinois University Press.

Rudisill, M. 1952. "Children's Preferences for Color versus Other Qualities in Illustrations." *Elementary School Journal* 52: 444–451.

Samuels, S. J. 1967. "Attentional Process in Reading: The Effect of Pictures on the Acquisition of Reading Responses." *Journal of Educational Psychology* 58: 337–342.

———. 1970. "Effects of Pictures on Learning to Read: Comprehension and Attitudes." *Review of Educational Research* 40: 397–408.

Schallert, D. L. 1980. "The Role of Illustrations in Reading Comprehension." In R. Spiro, B. C. Bruce, and W. F. Brewer, Eds., *Theoretical Issues in Reading Comprehension: Perspectives from Cognitive Psychology, Linguistics, Artificial Intelligence, and Education*. Hillsdale, N.J.: Lawrence Erlbaum.

Smerdon, G. 1976. "Children's Preferences in Illustration." *Children's Literature in Education* 20: 97–131.

Yaden, D., L. Smolkin, and A. Conlon. 1989. "Preschoolers' Questions About Pictures, Print Convention, and Story Text During Reading Aloud at Home." *Reading Research Quarterly* 24: 188–213.

Children's Books

Ben and the Porcupine by C. Carrick. Illustrated by D. Carrick. New York: Clarion, 1981.

The Bremen Town Musicians by the Grimm Bros. Illustrated by D. Diamond. New York: Delacorte, 1981.

The Bremen Town Musicians by the Grimm Bros. Illustrated by I. Plume. New York: Doubleday, 1980.

The Bremen Town Musicians by the Grimm Bros. Translated by E. Shubb. Illustrated by J. Domanska. New York: Greenwillow, 1980.

The Crane Maiden by M. Matsutani. Illustrated by C. Iwasaki. New York: Parents Magazine Press, 1968.

The Crane Wife by S. Yagawa. Translated by C. Paterson. Illustrated by S. Akaba. New York: Wm. Morrow, 1981.

Dawn by U. Shulevitz. New York: Farrar Straus & Giroux, 1974.

The Garden of Abdul Gasazi by C. Van Allsburg. Boston: Houghton Mifflin, 1980.

Gobble, Growl, Grunt by P. Spier. New York: Random House, 1978.

The Grey Lady and the Strawberry Snatcher by M. Bang. New York: Four Winds, 1980.

Hansel and Gretel by the Grimm Bros. Illustrated by A. Browne. London: Julia MacRae Books, 1981.

Hansel and Gretel by P. Galdone. New York: McGraw Hill, 1976.

Hansel and Gretel by the Grimm Bros. Translated by E. Crawford. Illustrated by L. Zwerger. New York: Morrow, 1979.

Hansel and Gretel retold by R. Lesser. Illustrated by P. Zelinsky. New York: Dodd Mead, 1984.

Hiroshima No Pika by T. Marushi. New York: Lothrop, Lee and Shepard, 1980.

I Saw A Ship A Sailing by J. Domanska. New York: Macmillan, 1971.

Jumanji by C. Van Allsburg. Boston: Houghton Mifflin, 1981.

Mother Mother I Want Another by M. Polushkin. New York: Crown, 1978.

Oh, What A Noise! by U. Shulevitz. New York: Macmillan, 1971.

Outside Over There by M. Sendak. New York: Harper and Row, 1981.

Song of the Horse by R. Kennedy. Illustrated by M. Sewall. New York: E. P. Dutton, 1981.

We Be Warm Till Springtime Come by L. Chaffin. Illustrated by L. Bloom. New York: Macmillan, 1980.

What Do You See? by J. Domanska. New York: Collier Macmillan, 1974.

9

Which Book Will Win the Caldecott?

Carol A. Doll

In 1937, the American Library Association (ALA) inaugurated the Caldecott Medal, which was established by Frederick G. Melcher. A committee of fifteen members of ALA's Association for Library Service to Children (ALSC) selects the winner. This committee changes each year. The Caldecott Medal is "awarded annually to the artist of the most distinguished American picture book for children published in the United States during the preceding year" (statement adopted by the ALSC Board, January 1978; revised midwinter 1987). Over the years, the Caldecott Medal has become one of the most prestigious awards in the field of children's literature. The announcement of the latest winner is eagerly awaited each January.

Bette J. Peltola does a very nice job of reporting the function and mechanics of ALSC's Caldecott Committee. Fifty-four years after the founding of the Caldecott Medal, the goals of this award are still valid: "To honor distinguished illustration for children, to promote interest in quality picture books for children, and to encourage talented artists to create picture books for children" (Peltola, 1988, p. 156). The success and popularity of medal winners, as reflected in the wide availability of these titles in libraries and media centers, indicates that ALA has succeeded, to some degree, in meeting at least the first two goals.

The Caldecott winners and the work of the Caldecott Committee have been discussed and written about extensively by library professionals. Many areas now have "mock Caldecott" committees which select a distinguished picture book and later compare their choice to the actual Caldecott winner. It is not unusual to hear people wonder about why a particular title was or was not chosen. (This is an interesting but futile exercise, since the Caldecott Committee deliberations are confidential.)

For librarians and media specialists, one national public forum for the discussion of newly published books for children is the system of reviews published in the professional literature. Various journals and reviewing services regularly examine new books, evaluate those books, and then print their reviews. This study will evaluate reviews of children's picture books that later won the Caldecott Medal and try to answer this question: Is it possible, based on contemporary reviews, to predict which title will be awarded the Caldecott?

The Methodology

In order to gather data to answer this question, Caldecott Medal winners and reviewing sources were identified. It was decided to limit the study to the last twenty-five Caldecott winners. Twenty-five years is surely long enough to identify a pattern, and, because the main interest is in future Caldecott Medal winners, the older titles and reviews could be eliminated from the scope of this study.

There are many sources of reviews of children's books, such as the professional literatures of library science, English, or education. And materials are produced for the publishing industry or for the general public. Because the Caldecott Medal is under the auspices of the American Library Association, this initial study is limited to reviews produced for or used by librarians and media specialists. Specifically, reviews of the twenty-five Caldecott Medal winners were taken from these seven publications: *Booklist, Bulletin of the Center for Children's Books* (BCCB), *Horn Book, Kirkus Reviews, New York Times Book Review, Publishers Weekly,* and *School Library Journal.* These titles were selected because they are often mentioned in the published articles that discuss or report research about reviews of children's materials (see Busbin and Steinfirst, 1989; Stewig, 1980; Weber, 1979; and Witucke, 1980, 1982). Using these same reviewing sources allows this study to build on and extend earlier research findings.

Once the seven publications were identified, *Book Review Index* was used to identify reviews of the pertinent titles. Then copies of those reviews were made and analyzed. As all reviews used in this study were published *before* the Caldecott Medal winners were announced, the reviewers were not influenced by the decisions of the Caldecott Committees.

Data Analysis

Weber examined seven reviewing sources of children's and young adult books in 1977. After a discussion of the characteristics and policies of each source, Weber presented data on the number of titles reviewed in one or more than one source.

Weber's data indicate what percentage of total titles available were actually reviewed by each of the seven sources investigated (table 1). Similar percentages were calculated for each of the twenty-five Caldecott titles in this

TABLE 1
Percent of Titles Reviewed

	Total Number Books Considered[1] (n=3915)	Caldecott Books (n=25)
Booklist	51.70	100
BCCB	18.44	100
Horn Book	12.18	88
Kirkus	30.32	84
New York Times Book Review	9.73	80
Publisher's Weekly	13.54	96
School Library Journal	58.49	100

[1] From Weber's data, 1979, p. 133.

study. As can be seen, a higher percentage of future Caldecott Medal winners were reviewed than were titles in general. Since Weber examined reviews of all titles published in 1977 and this study examined all Caldecott winners since 1967, both sets of reviews analyzed are populations, not samples. Therefore, the differences observed in table 1 are real differences. So, more reviews of future Caldecott winners are published than reviews for children's books in general.

Weber also determined how many of the seven sources reviewed individual titles (table 2). The data indicate that 93 percent of titles are reviewed four times or fewer; of these, 55 percent were reviewed only once. Conversely, all of the Caldecott titles were reviewed more than four times, and 60 percent were reviewed by all seven sources. Because both data sets represent populations, these are true differences. So, it is possible to say that more Caldecott titles than general books were reviewed by five, six, or seven of the reviewing sources studied. For comparative purposes, table 2 also gives percentages for each category.

TABLE 2
Reviews of Individual Titles

Number of Journals Reviewing	Number of Titles Reviewed Weber[1]	Caldecott	Percent of Titles Reviewed Weber[1]	Caldecott
7	35	15	.89	60
6	83	8	2.12	32
5	154	2	3.93	8
4	261	0	6.67	0
3	429	0	10.96	0
2	814	0	20.79	0
1	2139	0	54.64	0
	3915	25		

[1] From Weber, 1979, p. 133.

In terms of the number of titles reviewed and the number of reviews per title, Caldecott winners have better coverage than children's books overall. So, those who read and watch reviews and who wonder about the next Caldecott winner should pay attention to titles they read about several times.

Virginia Witucke examined the performance of juvenile book reviews in five journals. First, titles published in 1972, 1973, and 1974 were used. This study was replicated for titles published in 1978, 1979, and 1980. Primary focus of this research was on thirty titles selected randomly from books on ALA's Notable Children's Books for the pertinent years. Witucke examined the reviews in several ways, including number of reviews, length, and critical themes.

Like Weber, Witucke examined the number of titles reviewed by the five different sources examined (table 3). Like Weber, Witucke found that more of the Caldecott winners were reviewed than juvenile book titles in general. (Also, when Witucke examined all reviews for the total book output, the data set represents a population.) *School Library Journal* reviewed a very high percentage of all titles published (from 88 to 97 percent). For this reason, there is less difference between the coverage of Caldecott titles and the coverage of general titles in *School Library Journal*. Further examination of the

TABLE 3
Percent of Titles Reviewed

	Total Book Output 1972-4[1] (n=7, 160)	Total Book Output 1978-80[2] (n=8509)	Notable Book Sample 1972-4[1] (n=30)	Notable Book Sample 1978-80[2] (n=30)	Caldecott Books (n=25)
Booklist	40	42	93	87	100
BCCB	32	30	97	67	100
Hornbook	17	16	77	80	88
New York Times Book Review	13	11	57	53	80
School Library Journal	97	88	93	97	100

[1] From Witucke 1980, pp. 154–55.
[2] From Witucke 1982, pp. 49, 51.

data shows that the Notable Children's Books also are widely reviewed. (In the case of Notable Books, Witucke's data set represents a sample, since thirty titles were randomly selected from the larger group of all Notable titles for those years.) Examination of these data shows that more Caldecott books were reviewed than general juvenile titles in *Booklist, Bulletin of the Center for Children's Books, Horn Book*, and *New York Times Book Review* (table 3). However, there is less difference between the number of Notable Books reviewed and the number of Caldecott books reviewed. Given that the data from the Caldecott titles represent a population, further statistical analysis is appropriate where the number of titles reviewed is less than 100 percent (table 4). In general, results in tables 3 and 4 tend to show that books that receive the recognition as Caldecott or Notable books tend to be reviewed more widely than other titles.

Wituke also calculated the average length of reviews of Notable Children's Books. Ideally, longer reviews should give more information about the book, and perhaps be more evaluative than descriptive. When compared to the average length of reviews of Caldecott winners, the raw data show that the Notable Book reviews are shorter (table 5). Statistical analysis shows that half these differences are not significant and half are significant. So, sometimes both types of award books received about the same length of coverage in these five sources, and sometimes the Caldecott titles received longer reviews.

TABLE 4
Calculated z Values Comparing Frequency of Caldecott Reviews to Witucke's Data

	Notable Book Sample 1972-4[1]	Notable Book Sample 1978-80[2]
Horn Book	-1.4317[3]	-1.0445[3]
New York Times Book Review	-2.987[4]	-3.4020[4]

[1] From Witucke, 1980.
[2] From Witucke, 1982.
[3] Not significant.
[4] Significant at $p < .01$.

TABLE 5
Average Length of Reviews

	Notable Books Sample 1972-4[1]		Notable Books Sample 1978-80[2]		Caldecott Books	
	mean	standard deviation	mean	standard deviation	mean	standard deviation
Booklist	113.43[4]	43.26	148.15[4]	34.94	203.76	193.11
BCCB	127.72	42.91	133.45	39.60	136.36	45.78
Horn Book	178.65	78.05	173.12	44.86	188.27	46.99
New York Times Book Reivew	228.44[3]	179.27	233.12[4]	121.62	309.32	248.08
School Library Journal	134.86[4]	43.27	172.45	65.35	189.68	70.58

[1] Witucke, 1980, p. 157.
[2] Witucke, 1982, p. 52.
[3] Difference between this mean and that of Caldecott books significant at $p < .05$.
[4] Difference between this mean and that of Caldecott books significant at $p < .001$.
Unless noted above, difference between means is not significant.

Witucke briefly discusses the concept of a critical theme, "defined as evaluative, subjective comments. A statement such as 'well-written, fast-moving story' would be counted as having two critical themes" (Witucke, 1980, p. 157). As she states, part of the function of book reviews is to evaluate the books critically. The concept of critical themes was developed to try to analyze

TABLE 6
Average Number of Critical Themes Per Review

	Notable Books Sample 1972-4[1]		Notable Books 1978-80[2]	Caldecott Books	
	mean	standard deviation	mean	mean	standard deviation
Booklist	4.89	2.59	7.92	5.2	3.87
BCCB	5.24	2.01	6.95	5.16	2.20
Hornbook	6.30[3]	2.16	6.29	4.86	1.42
New York Times Book Review	6.65	6.54	7.25	6.82	4.61
School Library Journal	5.64	3.25	7.13	5.36	2.67

[1] From Witucke, 1980, p. 158.
[2] From Witucke, 1982, p. 52. Insufficient data reported for statistical analysis.
[3] Difference between this mean and that of Caldecott books significant at $p < .001$.
Unless noted as above, difference between means is not significant.

this aspect of reviews. Using Witucke's description, an attempt was made to count the critical themes in reviews of the Caldecott winners (table 6). Raw data seem to indicate some differences between the number of critical themes in reviews of Notable Books and of Caldecott winners. Where statistical analysis is possible, only one of the differences is significant. Further research needs to be done in this area, but at this time there is not enough evidence to support a hypothesis of a significantly higher number of critical themes in reviews for either type of book.

So, comparison of Caldecott reviews with Witucke's work shows that Caldecott titles were reviewed more often than children's books in general. When compared to Notable Book titles, Caldecott titles receive longer reviews in *Booklist* and in the *New York Times Book Review*. But there is no difference in the number of reviews or critical themes between Notable Books and Caldecott winners. This would seem to indicate that, for whatever reasons, award books seem to be reviewed more often than general titles, and seem to be treated in much the same way by reviewers.

Concerned by what he perceived to be poor review coverage of the pictorial elements of picture books, John Stewig randomly selected fifty reviews of picture books from four commonly used review sources. Then he calculated the percentage of each review "describing any aspects of the art of the book" (Stewig, p. 83) (table 7). A similar analysis was done on the reviews of the Caldecott winners in this study. The raw data seem to indicate that a higher

TABLE 7
Number of Reviews with Indicated Percentage Given to Illustration

		0-15%	16-30%	31-45%	46-60%	61-75%	Over 75%	χ^2
Booklist	Stewig[1]	19	22	6	2	1	1	
	Caldecott	5	8	9	2	1	0	7.4161^2
BCCB	Stewig[1]	31	16	2	1	0	0	
	Caldecott	5	10	4	5	0	1	18.0755^4
Hornbook	Stewig[1]	11	24	6	7	2	0	
	Caldecott	2	5	6	5	4	0	9.1782^3
School Library Journal	Stewig[1]	26	13	7	1	2	1	
	Caldecott	5	7	9	2	1	1	8.9353^3

[1] From Stewig, p. 84.
[2] Not significant.
[3] Significant at $p < .05$.
[4] Significant at $p < .001$.

percentage of Caldecott book reviews is devoted to illustration than are reviews of picture books in general. The Chi Square test indicates that, except for *Booklist*, these differences are significant. (Cells were combined to increase frequencies so that the Chi Square calculations were possible.)

Therefore, results support the conclusion that, in general, reviews of Caldecott winners probably do devote more space to discussing the artistic aspects of the book than do reviews of picture books in general. Since the Caldecott Medal is awarded for the quality of illustrations, this is a hopeful sign.

Busbin and Steinfirst worked to develop an instrument to use for content analysis of reviews of children's picture books. Based on this instrument, they evaluated a total of 1,075 reviews in five reviewing sources. This researcher attempted to use their instrument to evaluate the Caldecott book reviews. Interested researchers are advised to read their article for a full discussion of their material. Results are reported as proportions. Further statistical analysis is not possible until work is done to ensure that this researcher used Busbin and Steinfirst's content analysis instrument in the same way they did and that the results of both experiments are truly comparable.

One area Busbin and Steinfirst examined was whether or not the reviewer identified the style of art used in the book (table 8). As their results showed, only a very small proportion of the reviews actually mention this. Analysis

TABLE 8
Proportion of Reviews Identifying Styles of Art

	Booklist B&S[1] (n=223)	Booklist Cald. (n=25)	BCCB B&S[1] (n=231)	BCCB Cald. (n=25)	Horn Book B&S[1] (n=99)	Horn Book Cald. (n=22)	School Library Journal B&S[1] (n=491)	School Library Journal Cald. (n=25)
Representational/ Realistic	.03	-	.02	.04	.02	-	.05	.12
Abstract	.004	-	-	-	.01	.04	.002	.12
Expressionism	-	-	-	-	-	-	-	-
Cubism	.01	-	.004	-	-	-	-	-
Surrealism	.009	.12	-	-	.01	.04	.004	-
Impressionism	.01	-	-	.04	-	.04	.004	-
Folk/Native	.01	-	.01	-	.02	.14	.03	.08
Cartoon	.08	-	.05	.04	.08	-	.15	.08
Photography	.03	-	.02	-	.03	-	.02	-
Other	.03	.16	.01	.08	.06	.09	.008	.08

[1] Busbin and Steinfirst, p. 261.

of the Caldecott Medal winners shows that this same pattern continues. In some areas, the Caldecott winners have a higher score than the general reviews; in other areas, the Caldecott winners had no score.

Busbin and Steinfirst also examined their reviews for mention of elements of technique, such as color, line, or shape (table 9). Except for color and composition, these scores also tend to be quite low. In most cases, scores for the Caldecott winners are higher than scores for general picture books. Without additional research it is not possible to determine whether these differences are statistically significant, if they are due to chance or sampling error, or if this researcher made mistakes in applying the content analysis instrument.

In the next section of their study, Busbin and Steinfirst determined whether or not reviewers identified the media used by the illustrator (table 10). In this case, there seems to be closer agreement between their data and that from reviews of the Caldecott winners. Without further research to allow statistical analysis, no other conclusions can be reached. However, it is possible to say that mention of artists' techniques, except for those pertaining to painting, is alarmingly low.

The next area examined was whether or not the reviews commented on the relationship between art and text (table 11). In this case, scores for

TABLE 9
Proportion of Reviews Identifying Elements of Art Technique

	Booklist		BCCB		Horn Book		School Library Journal	
	B&S[1] (n=23)	Cald. (n=25)	B&S[1] (n=231)	Cald. (n=25)	B&S[1] (n=99)	Cald. (n=22)	B&S[1] (n=491)	Cald. (n=25)
Color	.72	.88	.41	.88	.73	.82	.60	.80
Line	.17	-	.11	.04	.14	.09	.07	.04
Shape	.03	.20	.01	.16	.08	.09	.01	.04
Perspective	.05	.08	.02	-	.04	.14	.03	.12
Texture	.11	-	.10	.08	.10	.04	.02	.04
Detail	.19	.24	.11	.32	.34	.23	.20	.24
Composition	.19	.52	.19	.64	.19	.64	.27	.32

[1] Busbin and Steinfirst, p. 262.

TABLE 10
Proportion of Reviews Identifying Media Used in Illustrations

	Booklist		BCCB		Horn Book		School Library Journal	
	B&S[1] (n=23)	Cald. (n=25)	B&S[1] (n=231)	Cald. (n=25)	B&S[1] (n=99)	Cald. (n=22)	B&S[1] (n=491)	Cald. (n=25)
Painterly	.42	.48	.33	.44	.43	.27	.43	.40
Graphic	-	.04	-	.08	.01	.09	.002	.12
Multi-Media	.004	-	-	-	-	-	.004	-
Collage	-	.04	.004	.04	-	-	.002	.08
Photography	.004	-	.004	-	-	-	.01	-

[1] Busbin and Steinfirst, p. 263.

TABLE 11
Proportion of Reviews Commenting on Art in Relationship to the Text

	Booklist		BCCB		Horn Book		School Library Journal	
	B&S[1] (n=223)	Cald. (n=25)	B&S[1] (n=231)	Cald. (n=25)	B&S[1] (n=99)	Cald. (n=22)	B&S[1] (n=431)	Cald. (n=25)
Extend	.05	.16	.06	.12	.10	.27	.08	.04
Clarify	.02	-	.004	-	.02	-	.02	-
Interpret	.02	.04	.008	.04	-	-	.02	.08
Complement	.07	.40	.008	.24	.20	.27	.14	.28
Set Mood	.08	.40	.02	.20	.13	.23	.04	.08
Portray Character	.05	.32	-	.16	.07	.41	.01	.32
Clarify Setting	-	.28	.008	.15	.06	.23	.004	.28

[1] Busbin and Steinfirst, p. 264.

Caldecott winners seem to be consistently higher than scores for general picture books. In numerous cases, the discrepancy in scores is rather large. It is possible that the reviews of Caldecott books do discuss this relationship between book and text better than the other reviews. It is also possible that this researcher had more difficulty with the content analysis of this aspect of the reviews. Given the greater similarity in results on other areas analyzed, the second possible explanation is considered to be more probable.

This same argument should be applied to the last two areas of investigation: whether or not the review compared the book to other titles (table 12) and the percentage of the reviews that discussed illustration (table 13).

Overall, Busbin and Steinfirst deserve recognition for their rigorous approach to the content analysis of reviews of children's picture books. The data do show that such reviews are lacking in useful critical information about the illustrations in children's books. And this study finds little evidence, within the limitations discussed, to show that Caldecott winners fare better than general picture books in these areas.

Conclusions

This study compared reviews of twenty-five Caldecott winners published before the award was announced to research about reviews of children's

TABLE 12
Proportion of Reviews that Compared Title to Work By:

| | Booklist | | BCCB | | Horn Book | | School Library Journal | |
| | B&S[1] | Cald. | B&S[1] | Cald. | B&S[1] | Cald. | B&S[1] | Cald. |
	(n=223)	(n=25)	(n=231)	(n=25)	(n=99)	(n=22)	(n=431)	(n=25)
Same Illustrator	.06	.24	.03	.16	.03	.36	.07	.12
Other Illustrator	.04	-	.009	-	.02	.04	.08	.08

[1] Busbin and Steinfirst, p. 265.

TABLE 13
Percentage of Reviews Devoted to Illustration

| Booklist | | BCCB | | Horn Book | | School Library Journal | |
B&S[1]	Caldecott	B&S[1]	Caldecott	B&S[1]	Caldecott	B&S[1]	Caldecott
.024	.2923	.018	.302112	.030	.391927	.224	.3269

[1] Busbin and Steinfirst, p. 265.

books by Weber, Witucke, Stewig, and Busbin and Steinfirst. There is no evidence that the reviews treat the Caldecott winners differently from general books in terms of critical themes, or the artistic elements investigated by Busbin and Steinfirst.

In three areas, however, there are differences. First, *Booklist* and the *New York Times Book Review* do seem to give longer reviews of the Caldecott titles than of Notable Books. But there is no evidence that reviewers take this opportunity to be more critical or discuss the illustrations in more depth than is done for Caldecott titles in other reviewing sources. Second, comparisons to data from Stewig's work on illustration show that reviews of Caldecott books do devote significantly more space to discussing illustration than do reviews of picture books generally. Hopefully this is because reviewers recognize some elements of the artist's work that deserve recognition. Although there are no empirical data to support this hope, the majority of the reviewers (86 percent) wrote positively about the quality of the illustrations (table 14). This could indicate that both reviewers and the Caldecott Committees are identifying good illustrations in these Caldecott winners.

Third, Caldecott winners were reviewed more frequently and more widely than general children's books. With the exception of *School Library Journal*, which comes close to reviewing all children's books published, the reviewing sources are selective about titles they choose to include. Some, such as *Booklist* and *Horn Book*, have historically reviewed recommended titles primarily. However, wide coverage is given to Caldecott winners, *even before the award*

TABLE 14
Reviewers' Comments On Illustrations in Caldecott Reviews

Positive	139
Neutral	12
Negative	3
Mixed	7
Total	161

is announced. This could indicate that reviewers see something significant enough in these picture books to justify a review in even the more restrictive reviewing sources.

Is it possible to predict the next Caldecott winner? Not with certainty. After all, evidence indicates other award titles, such as ALA's Notable Children's Books, also generate wide coverage. But, chances are very high that the next Caldecott Medal will be awarded to the illustrator of a book that is widely reviewed by reviewers who do discuss the illustrations.

References

Busbin, O. M., and S. Steinfirst. 1989. "Criticism of Artwork in Children's Picture Books: A Content Analysis." *Journal of Youth Services in Libraries* 2: 256–266.

Peltola, B. J. 1988. "Choosing the Caldecott Medal Winners." *Journal of Youth Services in Libraries* 1: 153–159.

Stewig, J. W. 1980. "Picture Books: What Do the Reviews Really Review." *Top of the News* 37: 83–84.

Weber, R. 1979. "The Reviewing of Children's and Young Adult Books in 1977." *Top of the News* 36: 131–137.

Witucke, V. 1980. "A Comparative Analysis of Juvenile Book Review Media." *School Media Quarterly* (Spring): 153–160.

Witucke, V. 1982. "The Performance of Juvenile Book Review Media." *Serials Review* (Spring): 49–55.

APPENDIX

Twenty-five Caldecott Medal Winners Used in This Study

(The Caldecott Medal is awarded in January of the year following publication, so the 1967 winner was published in 1966.)

1967   *Sam, Bangs and Moonshine* by Evaline Ness. Holt, Rinehart and Winston.
1968   *Drummer Hoff* by Barbara Emberley. Illustrated by Ed Emberley. Prentice-Hall.
1969   *The Fool of the World and the Flying Ship* by Arthur Ransome. Illustrated by Uri Shulevitz. Farrar, Straus.
1970   *Sylvester and the Magic Pebble* by William Steig. Windmill/Simon and Schuster.
1971   *A Story, A Story* by Gail E. Haley. Atheneum.
1972   *One Fine Day* by Nonny Hogrogian. Macmillan.
1973   *The Funny Little Woman* by Arlene Mosel. Illustrated by Blair Lent. Dutton.
1974   *Duffy and the Devil* by Harve Zemach. Illustrated by Margot Zemach. Farrar, Straus.
1975   *Arrow to the Sun*. Adapted and illustrated by Gerald McDermott. Viking.
1976   *Why Mosquitoes Buzz in People's Ears* by Verna Aardema. Illustrated by Leo and Diane Dillon. Dial.
1977   *Ashanti to Zulu: African Traditions* by Margaret Musgrove. Illustrated by Leo and Diane Dillon. Dial.
1978   *Noah's Ark* by Peter Spier. Doubleday.
1979   *The Girl Who Loved Wild Horses* by Paul Goble. Bradbury.
1980   *Ox-Cart Man* by Donald Hall. Illustrated by Barbara Cooney. Viking.
1981   *Fables* by Arnold Lobel. Harper and Row.
1982   *Jumanji* by Chris Van Allsburg. Houghton Mifflin.
1983   *Shadow* by Blaise Cedrars. Illustrated by Marcia Brown. Scribner's.
1984   *The Glorious Flight: Across the Channel with Louis Bleriot, July 25, 1909* by Alice and Martin Provensen. Viking.
1985   *Saint George and the Dragon* adapted by Margaret Hodges. Illustrated by Trina Schart Hyman. Little, Brown.
1986   *Polar Express* by Chris Van Allsburg. Houghton Mifflin.
1987   *Hey, Al* by Arthur Yorinks. Illustrated by Richard Egielski. Farrar, Straus and Giroux.
1988   *Owl Moon* by Jane Yolen. Illustrated by John Schoenherr. Philomel.
1989   *Song and Dance Man* by Karen Ackerman. Illustrated by Stephen Gammell. Knopf.
1990   *Lon Po Po: A Red Riding Hood Story from China*. Illustrated by Ed Young. Philomel.
1991   *Black and White* by David Macauley. Houghton Mifflin.

10

Fantasy: Inner Journeys for Today's Child

Susan Lehr

Since Curdy and the Princess foiled a goblin takeover in 1872, fantasy has yanked children from everyday reality into what Tolkien has called believable secondary worlds. Hobbits and unpredictable wardrobes appeared in the middle of the twentieth century, and by the time L'Engle was effectively wrinkling time and catapulting Meg across deep space in 1962, fantasy for children was firmly established in all of its wonderful diversity.

The 1960s and '70s brought us misguided male heroes like Ged, a wizard of Earthsea, but they also brought us Taran, the assistant pig keeper in *The Book of Three*, rabbit wars in *Watership Down*, Winnie's decision regarding immortality in *Tuck Everlasting*, and Abel's struggle to stay alive to return to civilized mouse society in *Abel's Island*. The 1980s offered the female victim Tehanu, Vesper Holly, a take-charge woman, and a sensitive male called Gom Gobblechuck. They also brought us Cluny the Scourge, one of the vilest of villains.

In a parallel fashion, picture book fantasy was evolving from the turn of the century when Beatrix Potter first sketched water-colored gardens in which Peter nibbled lettuces, carrots, and radishes. Today we have tub people coming alive not unlike velveteen rabbits or Lionni's wind-up mouse. We have the genius of Van Allsburg with rhino stampedes in the living room and his mysteries surrounding Jack Frost and the enigmatic Mr. Burdick.

What is this diverse genre we call fantasy? I will take a look at current fantasy in five broad categories: (1) high fantasy, (2) time-slip fantasy, (3) animal fantasy, (4) realistic fantasy, and (5) picture-book fantasy. What are the current trends and issues in fantasy? What are some of the ways that teachers are using the fantasy genre in the classroom as a part of literature-based programs?

High Fantasy

J. R. R. Tolkien and C. S. Lewis generated this subgenre in fantasy when *The Hobbit* and *The Lion, the Witch and the Wardrobe* were published in 1937 and 1950 in Great Britain. Tolkien was heavily influenced by George MacDonald's work in the late 1800s; however, no one had created a secondary world with such energy and thorough abandon before the appearance of Bilbo's and Frodo's Middle Earth. I mention this bit of history because Tolkien defined the high fantasy genre. Many of the books published since then have been highly imitative. Lewis wrote independently but was also influenced through his friendship with Tolkien. L'Engle, LeGuin, McKillip, Cooper, Chetwin, Jacques, Yolen, and Alexander represent the best of those who have carried on this tradition of fantasy. When it is well done, its characteristics include common heroes any of us might have the capacity to become, and a believable other world, a secondary world into which we can easily slip. Frequently, helpful companions compose a loyal crew. Gandalf was a wizard, whereas Sam Gamgee was a gardener. Magic in fantasy must adhere to the basic rules of the secondary world. If the magic is whimsical or contrived, the reader never connects. Quests are common and basically outline the struggles of the hero. The struggle itself is usually classic in the sense that good battles against evil and is typically victorious, at least for a time. Evil is real, and the hero's side usually pays a price. No tidy solutions; no easy fixes: what Jane Yolen calls tough magic.

Current high fantasy includes a variety of well-crafted novels for children, novels that reflect today's culture. One of the most notable series of books to come out is a trilogy by the English author Brian Jacques, with at least two more adventures to follow. *Redwall* is the first and strongest of this series of books. I believe two factors contribute to this strength. First, the "good guys" are real and highly likable characters with whom children can easily identify. Matthias is young, naive, inexperienced, and fairly clumsy. We first meet him as he stumbles and spills nuts all over the floor of Redwall Abbey. He is any child reader, male or female, who vicariously knows that (1) he too is awkward at times and (2) she too could defeat Cluny the Scourge who is ready to descend on the Abbey. Second, Jacques creates a brilliantly believable bad guy and does so effectively by alternating chapters between Cluny and Matthias. Cluny is a Portuguese water rat, some say, with a whiplike tail. His scars tell his story. He is evil. He is complex. We don't like him, but we love seeing him close up from the safety of an armchair. Jacques grew up near the waterfront docks of Liverpool and worked as a longshoreman. He's met Cluny, I'm sure. Jacques' cast is woven with detail and a complexity of emotion and thought. The author pulls us in and keeps us there for 351 pages. One teacher read this book aloud to a class of sixth graders thoroughly caught in Jacques' spell. Another had several fifth graders immersed in independent reading. I've also seen this book in adult science fiction/fantasy corners in bookstores, and it sits on adult bookshelves as well. It has the appeal of *Watership Down* because it is written with the same attention to detail. This book will find an audience that spans several age groups. There are not many high fantasy books published with this care, depth, and precision.

Another effective newcomer is Grace Chetwin. Gom Gobblechuck first appeared in oral stories told to Chetwin's children at bedtime. Perhaps this is why he is so fleshed out as a real character. Like Matthias, he is naive and must learn the ways of the world quickly. What both books share are real struggles and the gradual growth of the main character. Unfortunately they are both males. One could wish for more gender variety when it comes to high fantasy, not merely women struggling to make it in men's worlds, but women who have other evils to battle.

Gom's eventual quest is to find his mother, who left a mysterious rune threaded about his neck when she disappeared on the day of his birth. Book One explores the close relationship between Gom and his father, and the emptiness left by his mother's disappearance. A simple life is shattered gradually when Gom has his first encounter with an evil magician. No Sauron here. Small bits of evil, greed, deceit, attempted murder. The balance of the universe does not hang by threads, for Gom is not yet ready to reweave them. Chetwin lets Gom grow slowly, richly, with integrity, and the reader can identify with him.

So far there are four books about Gom. I could wish for more stories like Gom's by other authors who are willing to take the time to weave intricate characters. As Chetwin travels about the country talking to classrooms of children I hear that Gom is on hold, but that more stories will emerge. In the last book, Gom met a feisty female about whom I sense we will hear more.

Another device used by authors of high fantasy involves connecting characters from this world to other worlds. This is the most difficult type of fantasy to pull off successfully for several reasons. First, if characters leap into other worlds too unbelievably, we as readers never quite leap with them. Second, if they show too little or too much surprise or annoyance upon entering another world, we as readers are merely annoyed. Third, if speech or magic is too contrived and at times uneven, we ask the wrong questions and shut the book.

Hilgartner's *Colors in the Dreamweaver's Loom* is uneven with regard to our initial entry into her secondary world. The heroine wanders off the interstate in Vermont and wakes up in the land of the Orathi. She spends several weeks in a house learning a language, comes out nearly fluent, meets the villagers on market day and is on a quest the next. She is not happy about her circumstances, but she has just lost her father and has no substantial ties to our world. I found it a bit thin but kept reading. Once all that was behind, Hilgartner's story took on a wonderful life.

Her main characters are outcasts from their respective backgrounds and are highly believable and likable. Tsan (Alexandra) can read minds, and her struggle at coping with this gift enriches the plot. The reader gets a double exposure with regard to seeing behind the words that are heard. "'I am so pleased the Orathi have come to parley with us,' he said though under the words his thoughts ran, *Miscalculation: never thought they would. Wish they'd stayed home. Much easier"* (Hilgartner, p. 90). This provides delightful twists for the reader.

The book ends abruptly, which is usually jolting, but in this case when Alexandra lands back in the present, in an airport, longing to return to the forest dwellers, the reader wants to know more and is willing to wait for Book Two. Fantasy is typically self-contained, but Hilgartner has created a cliffhanger. I'll wait for Tsan's return, knowing that Hilgartner will get her out of that airport and back to Windsmeet where she belongs. Tsan is a strong and believable female protagonist.

A gap in children's high fantasy is being filled by authors like Hilgartner, Robin McKinley, Meredith Pierce, Tamora Pierce, and Ursula LeGuin's newest wizard of Earthsea, *Tehanu*. Tehanu reflects all of the complexity of women's issues. Tehanu was abused severely and abandoned in a campfire. The wizard, Goha, found her, healed her, and raised her as her own daughter. By the book's end we realize that not all quests cover traditional miles. Sometimes quests are mere reflections of struggles and mirrors on society. Through Tehanu, LeGuin suggests a new kind of wizardry to hold the fabric of the lands together: women must now wield the magic, because men's wizardry has failed on certain levels and is now dysfunctional. Powerful messages.

Meredith Pierce has redefined old images connected with vampires and helpless females. Both are present in her trilogy, but it is Aeriel, a woman, who quests to free a male vampire.

Tamora Pierce, in a similar fashion, reflects images of women breaking out of stereotyped roles, a recurring theme in female fantasy authors' works. Alanna binds her chest, cuts her hair, and trains as a warrior in male guise. This mirrors women breaking out of traditional roles, first in the guise of the mores of men and then in newly defined and newly respected roles as active participants in society, no longer bound by society's strictures. Mere reflections or wishful thinking?

Robin McKinley's voice is refreshing amid the pleas for equality; her maid Marian in *The Outlaws of Sherwood* is the real brains and brawn in Robin's merry band of men. What a delightful spoof on all of us! Her female hero in *The Blue Sword* doesn't take a back seat to men, nor do any of her women. They may clean, they may cook, but they never grovel.

Adventures often include people of color once one reaches a new land, but aside from Virginia Hamilton's series in the 1970s, *Justice and Her Brothers*, and Patricia Wrightson's trilogy beginning with *The Ice is Coming*, which chronicles the battle between the aborigine Wirrun and the ancient spirits who are disrupting the land, few series exist today which originate in the experiences of people with a multiethnic base.

For adults, Orson Scott Card has rather effectively explored the Native American perspective and experiences in his Hatrack series. Jamake Highwater's historical fiction has a distinct blend of nature, fantasy, and spirit world in the Native American tradition, but who makes the leap exploring economic and racial problems in modern society? Hilgartner's Tsan is lonely, but nonetheless from a privileged background.

Clare Cooper does so in *Shadow Warrior*, which is similar to what George MacDonald did 120 years ago in *The Princess and the Goblin*. Cooper, not surprisingly, shows more sympathy to her goblins than did MacDonald. Most of his drowned; Cooper's challenge goblin stereotypes and stretch perspectives of readers with regard to stereotypes of other races. The strength of her book is the relationship and dialogue between the princess and the goblin warrior.

High fantasy is a powerful vehicle for exploring systems of all kinds. Whether evil is composed of stereotypes, prejudice, or the destruction of a way of life, a prevalent theme involves the struggle between that which is considered good and that which would annihilate or subjugate others. By stepping back from our real world and entering into secondary worlds, authors can effectively and honestly explore issues. And, more important, they can offer us fresh visions of what could be if enough Frodos, Lucys, Tehanus, Geds, Tarans and Alannas were willing to leave the comfort of their armchairs and instigate change.

Time Slip Fantasy

A second broad category of fantasy comes from the real world and invites the reader to go back in time. No one has done this more effectively than Jane Yolen in *The Devil's Arithmetic*. One example will suffice to explore this category. Yolen has created a believable character in the modern era who is Jewish and, more important, is fed up with old rituals and rememberings that have no relevance for her life. The reader is easily hooked. During the seder dinner when Hannah opens the door of an apartment in New York to invite Elijah in, she finds instead that she has time warped back into 1942 Poland. As Hannah goes through all of the motions of Chaya, whom she has replaced, the reader becomes deeply involved in "remembering." As the horror of the Nazi experience intensifies, Hannah becomes Chaya and the modern era becomes a dream. Her experiences in the concentration camp teach us what the devil's arithmetic is. As the reader marches with Chaya to the final confrontation with the ovens, we too have forgotten Hannah. This is a powerful device for luring readers into historical fiction. Janet Lunn did so effectively with *The Root Cellar* and Belinda Hurmence did so with *A Girl Called Boy*, both placed in the Civil War, both told from the unique perspective of a modern child going back in time to view the conflicts through different eyes.

More and more authors are linking readers to experiences of the past by blending elements of the fantastic with today's world. Teachers use these books effectively as they integrate literature into their social studies programs and bring young readers directly into history. An integrated classroom will tie the themes of exemplary literature into the reading, writing, and social studies programs. Books like these lend themselves to be used in a variety of ways. Children create time lines of book events juxtaposed against historical events, they write diary entries based on characters' perspectives, they create authentic newspapers which characterize the history of the book and the era, they create artistic responses to scenes in books, poems dedicated to characters, series of letters to characters, think links, box dancing poems which explore character. They enter into rich discussions with other children and teachers about how characters felt as they left the safety of our era and went back into perilous times. They explore the reality of history firsthand and see the horror of battles, gas ovens, segregation, discrimination. Textbooks can never convey the personal response that a book like *The Devil's Arithmetic* emits.

Realistic or Humorous Fantasy

Roald Dahl, although controversial with adults, almost perfected this genre in the eyes of children. Some of his books go too far for me personally, but *Matilda* achieves a wonderful wit and humor. His *Matilda* ostensibly occurs in our time, our world, but there ends the similarity. Matilda reads novels at four. She babysits for herself as a toddler. She cracks the code for getting to and using the library, and this is just her introduction. She is neglected, and when verbally abused she determines to get even with each of her parents' lapses of niceness. Dahl has always delivered humor, sometimes crass, usually vulgar, but in Matilda, her father, and the formidable Ms. Trunchbull, the principal at Crunchem School, the reader finds nonstop gags that delight and amuse. Fantasy and humor link quite naturally. To do this effectively is not so easy. There is a thin line between ludicrously acceptable and ludicrously obnoxious. In *Matilda* the reader delights in all of it. Some of it could happen. Sometimes we wish it would.

Another noteworthy trend is the 1991 Newbery Award book, *Maniac Magee* by Jerry Spinelli. Not exactly a fantasy, not exactly real either, Maniac is a legend. He is a tall tale character for the 1990s. Paul Bunyan chopped down trees and made lakes with his feet. Maniac builds bridges between the races, between the generations. He's an orphan. He's a runner. He doesn't exist. He runs everywhere, and boundaries between neighborhoods don't stop him. This book isn't realistic fiction, nor is it fantasy. It's a legend come to life. Books like this hold strong messages for readers, but they are primarily to be savored for their innovative ways of using narrative language to invite readers to experience life from a variety of perspectives.

Vesper Holly has been Lloyd Alexander's latest contribution to the fantasy world beginning with *The Illyrian Adventure*. His Prydain series of high fantasy is still widely read by students. With Vesper he has given us a Victorian heroine who travels all over the world with her wonderful sidekick and guardian Brinnie, battling evil in the form of the wickedly notorious Helvitius. He's a fiend, and Vesper is worthy of all of their encounters. Their adventures always start off in unlikely fashion. Vesper asks Brinnie if it's ever too late to return a library book. Brinnie pompously and predictably says never. So begins an adventure to the other side of the globe to return a library book. The books are somewhat redundant and patterned, but they are lively reads, and I would not be sorry to see a fifth book.

A newer title by Patricia Wrede is strictly tongue-in-cheek. *Dealing with Dragons* offers a female hero with spunk and humor. Cimorene has been raised resistingly as a proper princess. She breaks all previous molds as she runs away from an unwanted marriage and decides to become princess to the most demanding and precise dragon Kazul. A variety of bumbling and intrusive princes attempt to rescue her, but she sends them away in annoyance. There's some evil afoot as well, but Wrede's strength lies in her humorous depictions of misguided males and their conversations with Cimorene.

This genre of lighter fare in fantasy is important. I believe it pulls reluctant readers into wanting to become independent readers. Strong themes are couched in humorous adventures that kids relate to enthusiastically, and when done well, as I believe these titles are, they make the reader laugh and clamor for more. You never convinced a child to become an active fluent reader by telling her that it was intrinsically good for her and that she would be a better person for the experience. Make a child laugh and enjoy the experience, however, and she'll be back for more.

Animal Fantasy

Charlotte's Web set a particular standard for thinking, feeling animals in the 1960s. Dick King-Smith, from England, has most notably carried on with this tradition in recent decades, and he is still writing. King-Smith likes pigs. His pigs talk, fly, herd sheep, and watch television. I like reading about his pigs. They don't have the arrogance of *Animal Farm* pigs; rather, they share with Wilbur a certain innocence about life in the barnyard. Animal fantasy like this was made for reading aloud. Enjoyment is paramount, but King-Smith also has important underlying messages about the uniqueness of being who you are, striving for goals, and believing in yourself. He does this with humor and narrative that captivates with titles like *Pigs Might Fly, Babe the Gallant Pig, Ace the Very Important Pig*. His nonpig titles, *Noah's Brother* and *Tumbleweed*, are equally amusing and tell the true story of the flood from the perspective of Noah's brother and about a bumbling knight turned arrogant after he picks up helpful animal companions. King-Smith exemplifies the type of fantasy that has high appeal for children, is custom made for reading aloud to classes after a noisy lunch and play period, and endures over time.

Picture-Book Fantasy

The same rules of believability apply to picture-book fantasy. When authors become cute, they become trite. I see dozens and dozens of whambangled wizzers and pumpkin-sweet mice stories in any given publishing year. In a first-grade classroom where many current titles are housed, the contrived and cutesy fantasy books sit on the shelves after only one brief reading. Children do not go back to them for seconds. They want episodes and characters of substance. That's why Lionni's earlier books remain so popular. In a brief bit of time you meet Alexander or Frederick or Tico or Swimmy and you want to meet them again and again.

Today's fantasy includes *The Tub People* by Pam Conrad. Toys that have secret lives work well with children. Remember those little wooden people who fit snugly on fingers? These are tub people. When one disappears down the drain hole, one sees a family in mourning. One studies Egielski's characters closely, and at the end of the book a happy reunion causes the briefest of smiles to appear on their wooden faces. Clearly, effective fantasy worlds can be as near as one's bathtub.

The advent of D. and A. Woods' work has been a boon for fantasy. "King Bidgood's in the bathtub and he won't get out. Oh, who knows what to do?" In this highly repetitive pattern of verses, the Woodses have created another tub fantasy. King Bidgood holds court in the tub all day. The effective concept, catchy refrain and ending, coupled with lushly detailed pictures, make this book come alive. Unbelievably believable and funny.

Audrey Woods' *Elbert's Bad Word* is equally effective as a common childhood experience rears its ugly head. The bad word has a life and personality of its own that Woods captures convincingly in her illustrations. Taking the familiar and creating a new twist or perspective, which Conrad and the Woodses have done, is one trend in picture books.

Dreams are another avenue for exploration as illustrators create *Free Fall* fantasies that are wordless invitations of an oral and written nature. As David Weisner's young boy fades into sleep we see the green checks of his bedspread gradually becoming the green squares of a field. A motif on each page fades into the frame of the next as castles and chess pieces grow in size. Books like these ignite the imagination. Children pore over details, looking for clues, following story line, building oral skills while telling the story. His latest book, *Tuesday*, is a nightmare of frogs flying through the night into the living room of the reader. One shudders with anticipation to think about the possibilities for Wednesday!

Along the same lines is the 1991 Caldecott Award book by David Macaulay, *Black and White*. Four stories occur simultaneously on each page in different frames. The stories overlap and run in and out of each other. Cows crossing a track in one story delay a train in another. A marvelous interweave of story in black, white, green, and blue. Innovative. Fresh approaches. The ability to pull older readers into new worlds, new ways of looking.

Chris Van Allsburg teases his readers in similar fashion. *The Stranger* remains unidentified. *The Polar Express* recharges the reader's batteries. *Two Bad Ants* gives innovative perspectives. *The Mysteries of Harris Burdick* creates a fantasy in the introduction which heightens with each picture and caption.

These stories invite the reader to have responses somewhat akin to befuddled wonder. Stories like *Just a Dream* are less effective because they seem contrived with strong-arm messages. Magic works best out of the pulpit.

Jon Agee teases about the pomposity of art, any art, with *The Incredible Painting of Felix Clousseau*. Like Van Allsburg, his double entendre emerges on the last page when our artist hero returns to his own picture, having wreaked havoc in Paris with art that came to life.

In a different vein is N. Willard's *The High Rise Glorious Skittle Skat Roarious Sky Pie Angel Food Cake*. Her story is as exuberant as her title suggests! Moms are hard to buy for, but once when Mom was seven there was this most wonderful birthday cake which she'll never forget, an angel food cake with one secret ingredient that grandma never revealed. Her daughter sets out to discover this recipe and does so in a most amusing fashion. The angels who later appear are a wonderful pastiche of color and feathers and quilted wings. What an engaging story coupled with Richard Watson's brilliantly colored pictures! Longer stories that are neither simple picture books, nor lengthier novels, like Antonia Barber's *The Mousehole Cat* and Willard's *High Rise. . .* provide readers with substantial stories that are shorter reads.

Picture-book fantasy that has a strong story line, a twist that surprises, and illustrations that enhance pull us in quickly and grip us to the last page. As Maurice Sendak has said, we become trapped in the book. Books like these are effective with older children. Older readers delight in the twists and surprises of Van Allsburg's and Macaulay's work. As writing continues to remain a strong part of the daily elementary school curriculum, books like these are exemplary models for young writers.

Conclusion

Fantasy is a genre in which the imagination parallels the play worlds children enter. Reader response is critical. No passive readers are allowed. Authors and illustrators who invite the reader into the game, into the action, and ask something of the reader are highly successful. This includes well-crafted short stories enhanced by illustrations, imaginative scenarios for younger children that are rooted in the familiar, and wordless picture books that invite oral storytelling. Books that link children of today with children of yesterday help bridge the gap of time and distance and invite children to explore history through the lens of a modern hero's (both male and female) perspective.

Children find the appeal of humor with animal characters and real-life characters irresistible. These characters are often vulnerable and likable, but the antics and escapades in which they land are often hilarious. They may poke gentle fun at some of our customs and habits, but they generally make us chuckle at our assumptions.

Books that create secondary worlds and explore strong themes of morality with real struggles, real dilemmas, and real depictions of evil provide frameworks for children to grow as individuals and make choices about how they will live. Even as Meg successfully confronted It on Camazotz in 1962, so do today's heroes confront tyrants and dictators in other worlds. "Dare to reach out and touch the face of the unknown" (Yolen, p. 72). Imaginary worlds are places where children can leave video games and television behind to battle or befriend dragons, to explore tough magic eyeball to eyeball.

Children's Books Cited

High Fantasy

Chetwin, G. *Gom on Windy Mountain*. Lothrop, Lee & Shepard, 1986.
————. *The Riddle and the Rune*. Bradbury, 1987.
————. *The Crystal Stair*. Bradbury, 1988.
————. *The Starstone*. 1989.
————. *Collidescope*. Bradbury, 1990.
Cooper, C. *The Shadow Warrior*. Atheneum, 1990.
Hilgartner, B. *Colors in the Dreamweaver's Loom*. Houghton Mifflin, 1989.
Jacques, B. *Redwall*. Philomel, 1986.
————. *Mossflower*. Philomel, 1989.
————. *Mattimeo*. Philomel, 1990.
LeGuin, U. *Tehanu*. Atheneum, 1990.
McKinley, R. *The Outlaws of Sherwood*. Greenwillow, 1988.
————. *The Blue Sword*. Greenwillow, 1982.
Pierce, M. *Darkangel*. Little, Brown, & Co., 1982.
————. *A Gathering of Gargoyles*. Little, Brown, & Co., 1984.
————. *The Pearl of the Soul of the World*. Little, Brown, & Co., 1990.
Pierce, T. *Alanna: The First Adventure*. Atheneum, 1983.
————. *The Woman Who Rides Like a Man*. Atheneum, 1986.
————. *Lioness Rampant*. Atheneum, 1988.

Time Slip Fantasy

Hurmence, B. *A Girl Called Boy*. Clarion, 1982.
Lunn, J. *The Root Cellar*. Scribner, 1983.
Yolen, J. *The Devil's Arthmetic*. Viking Kestrel, 1988.

Realistic/Humorous Fantasy

Alexander, L. *The Illyrian Adventure*. Dutton, 1986.
————. *The Jedera Adventure*. Dutton, 1989.
————. *The Philadelphia Experiment*. Dutton, 1990.
Dahl, R. *Matilda*. Viking, Penguin, 1988.
Spinelli, J. *Maniac Magee*. Little, Brown, & Co., 1990.
Wrede, P. *Dealing with Dragons*. Harcourt, Brace, Jovanovich, 1990.

Animal Fantasy

King-Smith, D. *Ace the Very Important Pig*. Crown, 1990.
———. *Pigs Might Fly*. Viking, 1982.
———. *Babe the Gallant Pig*. Dell, 1983.
———. *Noah's Brother*. Gollancz, 1986.
———. *Tumbleweed*. Gollancz, 1987.

Picture-Book Fantasy

Agee, J. *The Incredible Paintings of Felix Clousseau*. Farrar, Straus & Giroux, 1988.
Barber, A. *The Mousehole Cat*. Ill. by Nicola Bayley. Macmillan, 1990.
Conrad, P. *The Tub People*. Harper & Row, 1989.
Macaulay, D. *Black and White*. Houghton Mifflin, 1990.
Van Allsburg, C. *The Stranger*. Houghton Mifflin, 1986.
———. *The Polar Express*. Houghton Mifflin, 1985.
———. *Two Bad Ants*. Houghton Mifflin, 1989.
———. *Just a Dream*. Houghton Mifflin, 1990.
———. *The Mysteries of Harris Burdick*. Houghton Mifflin, 1984.
Weisner, D. *Free Fall*. Lothrop, Lee & Shepard, 1988.
———. *Tuesday*. Lothrop, Lee & Shepard, 1991.
Willard, N. *The High Rise Glorious Skittle Skat Roarious Sky Pie Angel Food Cake*. Harcourt, Brace, Jovanovich, 1990.
Woods, D. & A. *King Bidgood's in the Bathtub*. Harcourt, Brace, Jovanovich.
———. *Elbert's Bad Word*. Harcourt, Brace, Jovanovich, 1988.

Classic Fantasy

Adams, R. *Watership Down*. Macmillan, 1974.
Babbitt, N. *Tuck Everlasting*. Farrar, Straus, 1975.
Hamilton, V. *Justice and Her Brothers*. Greenwillow, 1978.
———. *The Magical Adventures of Pretty Pearl*. Harper, 1983.
Highwater, J. *Legend Days*. Harper, 1984.
Kingsley, C. *The Water Babies*. Platt & Munk, 1863.
L'Engle, M. *A Wrinkle in Time*. Farrar, Straus, 1962.
Lewis, C. S. *The Lion, the Witch and the Wardrobe*. Collins, 1950.
Lionni, L. *Frederick*. Pantheon, 1967.
MacDonald, G. *The Princess and the Goblins*. Garland, 1872.
Potter, B. *Peter Rabbit*. Warne, 1902.
Steig, W. *Abel's Island*. Farrar, Straus, 1976.
Tolkien, J. R. R. *The Hobbit*. Allen & Unwin, 1937.
White, E. B. *Charlotte's Web*. Harper, 1952.
Williams, M. *The Veleveteen Rabbit*. Doubleday, 1922.
Wrightson, P. *The Ice Is Coming*. Atheneum, 1977.

II
Young Adult Literature

11

Critics and Kids

Ken Donelson

Adult literature has rarely had to justify itself. Some Victorian and early twentieth century moralists disliked the novel, but critics usually ignored them and the reading public paid no attention at all. Children's literature has rarely had to justify itself to anyone. But adolescent literature (as English teachers call it—librarians usually call it young adult, or YA literature) has never been without its loud and righteous critics.

Adolescent literature has a long heritage, going back at least to Louisa May Alcott and her still readable books and Horatio Alger and his still unreadable books. There were many series writers of dubious quality but unquestioned popularity like Harry Castlemon and Oliver Optic. Later, in this century, we had writers as good as Ralph Henry Barbour and Mabel Robinson. And in the 1940s and 1950s we had superb writers, some of them still read, like John Tunis and his sports novels (most of them currently being reissued), Maureen Daly and her apparently eternal *Seventeenth Summer*, and Mary Stolz and her wonderful girls' stories, but the criticism persisted. The *Louisville Courier-Journal* for 17 June 1951, under the headline, "Trash for Teen-Agers: Or Escape from Thackeray The Brontës and The Incomparable Jane," lashed out at the secret sin of some kids, apparently for finding a few books they enjoyed.

> The blame for the vulgarity, the dull conformity and the tastelessness of much in American life cannot be laid altogether at the doors of radio, television and the movies as long as book publishers hawk these books for young people. Flabby in content, mediocre in style, narrowly directed at the most trivial of adolescent interests, they pander to the vast debilitation of taste, to intolerance for the demanding, rewarding and ennobling exercise which serious reading can be. . . . Like a diet of cheap candies, they vitiate the appetite for sturdier

foods—for that bracing, ennobling and refining experience, immersion in the great stream of the English classics.[1]

In other words, kids in Louisville apparently weren't reading the right books, namely books an editorial writer thought they ought to read, great books he read when young (or now realized he should have read when young).

And in 1965, two nasty criticisms appeared, the first by a prominent *New York Times Book Review* editor which began

> If I were asked for a list of symptoms pointed to what is wrong with American education and American culture, or to the causes for the prolongation of American adolescence, I should place high on the list the multiplication of books designed for readers in their teens. . . . The teen-ager book, it seems to me, is a phenomenon which belongs properly only to a society of morons.[2]

That year a prestigious report by the College Entrance Examination Board hit at adolescent books.

> Claims are frequently advanced for the use of so-called "junior books," a "literature of adolescence," on the ground that they ease the young readers into a frame of mind in which he will be ready to tackle something stronger, harder, more adult. For classes in remedial reading a resort to such books may be necessary, but to make them a considerable part of the curriculum for most students is to subvert the purposes for which literature is included in the first place. *In the high school years the aim should be not to find the students' level so much as to raise it, and such books rarely elevate.* (emphasis mine)[3]

Luckily for adolescent literature—and for young readers—the report had little national effect.

Some criticism was legitimate. A set of taboos—never published but known by librarians, teachers, writers, and publishers—to protect the innocence of the young and to ensure that reality seldom intruded into adolescent books pervaded the field. Good writers—the John Tunises and the Mary Stolzs and the Maureen Dalys—worked their way around the taboos. Most writers gave in to them.

The no-nos included these: no sex (especially no homosexuality), no pregnancy (unless it served as an object lesson and even then only for a minor character), no profanity (certainly no obscenity), no divorce, no deaths (except for object lesson minor characters), no school dropouts (save for object lessons), no alcohol or tobacco or drugs (save as object lessons), and no alienation of young people or generation gaps or the ambivalent cruelty/compassion of young people (again, save for using any of this as object lessons).

With these exceptions, too much of adolescent literature focused solely on problems like acne, teenage dating (especially the prom), making the pep squad or the team, being in the popular crowd, and surviving parents. These are still problems for lots of kids, but most adolescent novels prior to 1967 ignored real issues (then *and* now) like death, drugs, alcohol, gangs, sex and love, early marriage, racial prejudice, suicide, abortion, violence, mental illness, and more. Parents then, and some foolish and ignorant ones now, laugh at kids' problems and pontificate, "These are the happiest years of your life." But kids know that the key factor in their lives is survival—physical and emotional. That hardly means that kids' lives are perpetually tragic, only that life is usually puzzling and sometimes scary, just as it is for adults.

Then came 1967, and adolescent literature hasn't been the same since. Two books made the difference—S.E. Hinton's *The Outsiders* (Viking) and Robert Lipsyte's *The Contender* (Harper and Row). Hinton (who turned out to be a woman, thus confusing and alarming young boys for years to come) wrote some personal experiences about the socs (upper-class kids) and the greasers (lower class) and their warfare and Ponyboy who's tough and sensitive and one of the nicest and most honest young person that kids had met in a book. *The Contender* was by a sportswriter who, like John Tunis, knew that locker rooms stink with sweat and defeat and even with the glory of winning. Lipsyte's story of Alfred Brooks, a black kid seeking a way out of where he lived who thought he'd found it in boxing, stuck with readers. And in 1969, Paul Zindel's *The Pigman* (Harper and Row), with its screwed-up dual narrators and its story of death and redemption caught on and is in print today (as are Hinton's and Lipsyte's books). Not bad in a world where adult bestsellers are usually out of print within a very few years.

In 1974 Robert Cormier's *The Chocolate War* (Pantheon), the first of what most critics of adolescent literature call the classics of the field, was published. There's been no stopping since. Junk is still being produced and sold, as it is in all other fields of human endeavor, but where a Hinton or Lipyste or Zindell or Cormier was an exception, there are a number of first-rate writers, all competing for kids' attention. For better or worse (and some would vote for the latter) taboos in adolescent literature are now almost as rare as taboos in adult literature.

But critics of the field are still easily found. In 1985, a New York City high school English teacher had trouble finding works that her students would enjoy and benefit from. So the teacher chose *The Pigman*, and the kids understood it, and they loved it. One student wrote,

Teachers all over the world should give their students such books to read. It makes them understand about responsibility, about growing up, and not always thinking about themselves. It also shows us how to deal with death. I am glad you gave us this book to read.

And what did the teacher's supervisor say? She "reluctantly said, 'O.K., but I hope you choose more difficult books afterward.'"[4]

Criticism today often seems irrational and defensive, almost as if the books threatened English teachers (and a very few librarians) and their worlds. These are the ten most common protestations.

1. "No one around here knows anything about it. If it was really worth knowing, we'd have heard about it." (A better justification for ignorance would be hard to find. Learning about what's new, and knowing about it before tossing it out is a goodly part of every English teachers' job.)

2. "Adolescent literature has no heritage and no respectability." (Same response as #1.)

3. "We teach only the greatest of literature and that automatically eliminates adolescent literature from our consideration. Why should we demean ourselves or our students—and their parents—by stooping to something inferior?" (Most of us teach or use literature with students, and students seem to be largely ignored in this argument. Who, incidentally, chose this "greatest" literature? Who decided it ought to be taught to these kids at this time in their lives? Lots of English teachers sincerely believe that one of the purposes of literature is to find pleasure. Not the only purpose, just one of the most important. This response leaves more unanswered than answered.)

4. "We can't afford thirty or forty copies of something we don't know. That's why we don't use adolescent books." (But advocates of adolescent books don't necessarily order multiple copies, and some never do. Often, individual titles are more helpful than a class set.)

5. "Kids have to grow up and take themselves and their work seriously. I do. We expect them to. That takes care of adolescent books as far as this school is concerned." (Most teachers take their work and their kids and their literature seriously, in one sense at least. So what else is new?)

6. "Adolescent literature has no permanence. Something is popular today, and something else is popular tomorrow. Great literature is timeless and unchanging. How can we be expected to keep track of ephemera?" (What a wonderful defense for reading nothing new. New books come out all the time, adult as well as adolescent. A few last. Most don't. *The Outsiders*, *The Contender*, *The Pigman*, and *The Chocolate War* have lasted longer than most publishers would have guessed. I'd put money on the likelihood that almost anything by Cormier, Katherine Paterson, Leon Garfield, Alan Garner, Robin McKinley, or several others will last for at least a dozen years more, maybe much longer. Discussing an author's likelihood of entering the literary pantheon is fun so long as no one takes it too seriously. We ought to remember that at one time Joachim Raff's now virtually forgotten music was almost as highly regarded as the work of Johannes Brahms.)

7. "Why have kids spent time in class reading something they can easily read on their own? Shouldn't class time be spent on books that are challenging, books kids won't find on their own, books that will make kids stretch intellectually?" (What about the rare kids who've found and enjoy Shakespeare? Should we stop them from reading what they found on their own, as I did. Some kids may not find those books as challenging as Garner's *The Owl Service* (Walck, 1967),

Cormier's *After the First Death* (Pantheon, 1979), Robin McKinley's *Beauty* (Harper and Row, 1978), or Walter Wangerin, Jr's *The Book of the Dun Cow* (Harper, Row, 1978), a demanding theological thriller. Besides, what's so challenging about three commonly read classics, John Steinbeck's *The Pearl*, George Eliot's *Silas Marner*, or Ernest Hemingway's *The Old Man and the Sea*? Are they really difficult and worth stretching for? The painful truth for all of us English teachers is that lots of students don't find reading enjoyable. While it's true that those kids may not find *Silas Marner*, they may also not find *The Pigman* or *The Owl Service*. And those two, among many more, may come closer to reaching those kids.)

8. "Isn't adolescent literature formula literature?" (Yes, sometimes, just as most adult books follow formulas. Formula is a dirty word—archetype is more impressive. And most teachers will be impressed when they hear a scholar talk about the grand inevitability in Dostoevsky's *Crime and Punishment*. They may not be so impressed when someone talks about the lamentable predictability in Nancy Drew books.)

9. "Isn't adolescent literature silly and simple-minded stuff about dating and trivia like that?" (See below.)

10. "Isn't it mostly about depressing problems—like suicide, death, abortion, pregnancy? Hasn't it been censored a lot?"

Those last three almost mutually exclusive objections are common. Two defenders of adolescent literature, one in 1975 and one in 1989, answer the charges:

> For years librarians and others have criticized junior novels saying they are written to a formula; they all have pat, sweetness and light resolutions that instill false conceptions of life; they fail to deal with fundamental problems of personal and societal adjustments that are of immediate concern to young adults, etc., etc. But, they would continue, teenage fiction does serve a purpose. It is good transitional material for the younger readers; it helps them to move on to the adult books. And, besides, it's all we've got.

> Then juvenile authors and editors began giving us such books as *Go Ask Alice; Run Softly, Run Fast; Admission to the Feast; Run Shelley, Run; The Chocolate War*. I could go on and on naming both fiction and nonfiction.

> And what happened? All too many of these same people who had been asking for an honest story about serious teenage problems began protesting: language like *that* in a book for young people? Are rape, abortion, homosexuality, unwed mothers, suicide, drugs, unsympathetic portrayal of parents, and violence appropriate for junior novels? Are young people ready for such explicit realism? Would you want your daughter to read one?[5]

> The young adult novel [is] often maligned by critics. I want to deal with only one of the charges often expressed by the ultra conservatives, namely, that young adult novels are not uplifting. Why, oh why, cry these critics, do the

authors have to deal with such depressing subjects. Why can't we go back to the good old days?

As one who has spent six decades on this planet, let me tell you an important fact: *there were no good old days.* Every problem confronted in a young adult novel today not only existed during my childhood and adolescence, but was known to most of us. There were drunks in families, there were wife abusers, there were child molesters, divorce, certainly death and dying, mental illness, premarital pregnancy, and, yes, abortions if you were among the elite. In high school, one of my classmates went home one day to find his father had hung himself in the garage; a couple of weeks later he went home to find his mother had done the same thing.[6]

Adolescent literature has a continuing appeal to many young people. Why? Adolescent novels are brief, certainly shorter than most other modern novels or classics. They're usually easier to read than adult novels or classics because they're about young people facing real issues and problems that young people face (and that's often not true with classics or modern adult literature). They're often popular because adults forbid or demean them. Robert C. Small, Jr. added another reason, not one English teachers should be proud of.[7] The goal of most literature programs is to make the English teacher the designated expert reader and designated expert translator of books to lowly students who have no role at all, other than receiving the holy word of truth from the teacher, copying it in a notebook, and then regurgitating it at test time. When students read adolescent books, *they* are the *experts,* and they may need to translate to the teachers. Some people find that an uncomfortable role for teachers.

Adolescent literature has a place on library shelves and in the English curriculum. It can be used for common reading by an entire class. Certainly, *The Outsiders, The Pigman,* and *The Contender* have been widely read and taught anywhere from seventh through eleventh grade, depending on the class and the teacher. *The Owl Service* is a demanding book that could be used in the upper two years in high school. A teacher looking for a first-rate historical novel magnificently written could hardly do better than Leon Garfield's *The Sound of Coaches* (Viking, 1974). Margaret Mahy's *Memory* (McElderry, 1988) hits hard at current issues, a brother who feels responsible for his sister's death and longing to forget, an Alzheimer's victim who wants to remember and cannot. Robert Newton Peck's *A Day No Pigs Would Die* (Knopf, 1973), a great favorite of many readers, tells a simple story of life and love and death. Katherine Patterson's *Bridge to Terabithia* (Crowell, 1977) lies somewhere in that blurry area between children's and adolescent books, but never mind, the story of death and transfiguration is wondrous for anyone as are two of her fine books for older students, *Jacob Have I Loved* (Crowell, 1980) and *Lyddie* (Lodestar, 1991).

For teachers who rarely use long books for common reading or for anyone who needs supplementary materials for units or free reading or anything at all, adolescent books are a godsend. Of course, using them demands that English teachers know authors and books, not all of them but more than a smattering, so they can get books and authors into the hands of the particular kids who can best use them. These ten authors only hint at the range of good books out there:

Judy Blume's *Tiger Eyes* (Bradburg, 1981), a young girl and her family go west to find peace after the father is killed.

Bruce Clements' *The Treasure of Plunderell Manor* (Farrar, Straus, and Giroux, 1987), a delightful historical/adventure/romance about nasty relatives and a lost treasure.

Brock Cole's *Celine* (Farrar, Straus and Giroux, 1989), an extraordinarily rich book about the most fascinating heroine in modern adolescent fiction, funny and moving and complex.

Harry Mazer's *The Island Keeper* (Delacorte, 1981), a young girl lives alone on a small island and finds herself; *The Last Mission* (Delacorte, 1981), the youthful protagonist's airplane is shot down near the end of WW II.

Gary Paulsen's *The Island* (Orchard, 1988), a young boy, an island, nature, and more, by one of the most popular writers today.

Sandra Scoppettone's *Happy Endings Are All Alike* (Harper and Row, 1978), a homosexual love affair, a voyeur, and a rape.

Rosemary Sutcliff's *The Eagle of the Ninth* (Walck, 1954), a boy in Roman Britain whose father has disappeared tries to regain the family's honor. Her most recent book is *The Shining Company* (Farrar, Straus, and Giroux, 1990).

Mildred Taylor's *Roll of Thunder, Hear My Cry* (Dial, 1976), a Southern black family find dignity.

Robert Westall's *The Machine Gunners* (Greenwillow, 1976), how war affects young people.

Robb White's *Deathwatch* (Doubleday, 1972), maybe the most perfect adventure novels with a boy facing an insane expert hunter and death.

In growing up, adolescent literature has developed a body of texts and scholarly criticism. Speaking immodestly, Alleen Nilsen and Ken Donelson's historical and critical text, *Literature for Today's Young Adults*, 4th ed. (Harper/Collins, 1993), serves admirably as an introduction to the field. Arthea J. S. Reed's *Reaching Adolescents: The Young Adult Book and the School* (Holt, Rinehart and Winston) is reputedly due out in a second edition within the year. While Robert E. Probst's *Response and Analysis: Teaching Literature in Junior Senior High School* is not largely concerned with adolescent literature, it is brilliant work (as is everything that Probst writes) and it serves as a theoretical and pedogical base for using adolescent literature. Two recent texts on teaching literature have chapters on adolescent books and are, in any case, worth knowing: Richard Beach and James Marshall's *Teaching Literature in the Secondary School* (San Diego: Harcourt, Brace, Jovanovich, 1991) and John S. Simmons and H. Edward Deluzain's *Teaching*

Literature in Middle and Secondary Grades (Boston: Allyn and Bacon, 1992). Dwight L. Burton's *Literature Study in the High Schools*, 3rd ed. (New York: Holt, 1970) was the book that introduced many English teachers to adolescent literature.

Of the histories of adolescent literature, the most helpful are John Cech's *American Writers for Children, 1900–1960. Dictionary of Literary Biography*, vol. 22 (Detroit: Gale Research, 1983); Mary Cadogan and Patricia Craig's *You're a Brick, Angela! A New Look at Girls' Fiction from 1839 to 1975* (London: Gollancz, 1976); Glenn E. Estes' *American Writers for Children before 1900: Dictionary of Literary Biography*. vol. 42 (Detroit: Gale Research, 1985); Christine Kloet's *After Alice: A Hundred Years of Children's Reading in Britain* (London: Library Association, 1977); Cornelia Meigs' *A Critical History of Children's Literature*. rev ed. (New York: Macmillan, 1969); John Rowe Townsend's *25 years of British Children's Books* (London: National Book League, 1977); and Townsend's *Written for Children: An Outline of English-Language Children's Literature*, 3rd ed. (Philadephia: Lippincott, 1988).

The best resources for recent work are Betty Carter and Richard F. Abrahamson's *Nonfiction for Young Adults: From Delight to Wisdom* (Phoenix: Oryx Press, 1990); Aidan Chambers' *Reluctant Reader* (London: Pergamon Press, 1969); *Children's Literature Review* (Detroit: Gale Research, 1976– , a continuing and invaluable series); Shelia Egoff's *Thursday's Child: Trends and Patterns in Contemporary Children's Literature* (Chicago: American Library Association, 1981); and Glenn E. Estes' *American Writers for Children Since 1960: Fiction Dictionary of Literary Biography*. Vol. 52 (Detroit: Gale Research, 1986).

Of the many books and reference tools on authors of adolescent books, these are the most useful: Tracy Chevalier's *Twentieth Century Children's Writers*, 3rd ed. (New York: St. Martins, 1989); Anne Commire's *Something about the Author* (Detroit: Gale Research, 1971– , a continuing series which can be read with profit by upper grammar school kids and college graduate students); Donald R. Gallo's *Author's Insights: Turning Teenagers into Readers and Writers* (Portsmouth, NH; Boynton/Cook Heinemann, 1992); Gallo's *Speaking for Ourselves: Autobiographical Sketches by Notable Authors of Books for Young Adults* (Urbana, Ill.: National Council of Teachers of English, 1990); David Rees' *The Marble in the Water: Essays on Contemporary Writers of Fiction for Children and Young Adults* (Boston: Horn Book, 1980); Rees' *Painted Desert, Green Shade: Essays on Contemporary Writers of Fiction for Children and Young Adults* (Boston: Horn Book, 1984); Rees's *What Do Draculas Do? Essays on Contemporary Writers of Fiction for Children and Young Adults* (Metuchen, N.J.: Scarecrow Press, 1990); John Rowe Townsend's *A Sense of Story: Essays on Contemporary Writers for Children* (Philadelphia: Lippincott, 1971); and Justin Wintle and Emma Fisher's *The Pied Pipers: Interviews with the influential Creators of Children's Literature* (New York: Paddington, 1974).

The Twayne series on young adult authors has produced a dozen books on individual authors such as Patricia Campbell's *Presenting Robert Cormier* (1985, rev. ed. 1989), Alleen Nilsen's *Presenting M. E. Kerr* (1986), Sally Holmes Holktze's *Presenting Norma Fox Mazer* (1987), Jack Forman's *Presenting Paul Zindel* (1988),

Donald Gallo's *Presenting Richard Peck* (1989), Maryann N. Weidt's *Presenting Judy Blume* (1990), and Rudine Sims' *Presenting Walter Dean Myers* (1991).

The best journals for material on adolescent books are these:

The ALAN Review. Lelia Christenbury and Robert Small, editors, Office of the Dean, College of Education and Human Development Radford University, Radford, VA 24142. Four issues per year, $15.00, order from William Subick, ALAN/NCTE, 1111 Kenyon Road, Urbana, IL 61801. The only journal devoted to adolescent literature.

Booklist. Bill Ott, editor. Twice monthly except for monthly issues in July and August, $60.00 per year. Published by the American Library Association, 50 E. Huron St., Chicago, IL 60601.

Children's Literature in Education. Anita Moss, editor, University of North Carolina at Charlotte, UNCC Station, Charlotte, NC 28223. Four issues per year, $23.00. Published by Human Science Press 233 Spring St., New York, NY 10013–1578.

Journal of Youth Services in Libraries. Donald Kenney, Editor, Library, Virginia Tech, P.O. Box 9001, Blacksburg, Virginia 24062–9001. Four issues a year, $20.00. Published by the Association for Library Service to Children and the Young Adult Service Association.

School Library Journal. Lillian N. Gerhardt, editor, 249 W. 17th St., New York, NY 10011. Monthly issues, $63.00 per year, order from P.O. Box 1978, Marion, OH 43305–1978.

Voice of Youth Advocates. Dorothy Broderick, editor. Six issues a year, $32.50 a year. Order from Scarecrow Press, Department YOYA, 52 Liberty St., P. O. Box 4167, Metuchen, NJ 08840.

Wilson Library Bulletin. Mary Jo Godwin, editor. $50.00 for ten issues. Order from H. W. Wilson Co., 950 University Avenue, Bronx, NY 10452. *Wilson* has little about adolescent literature except for a great column, "The Teenage perplex," begun by Patty Cambell and now written by Cathi Dunn MacRae.

NOTES

1. *The Louisville Courier-Journal*, June 17, 1951, quoted in Stephen Dunning, "Junior Book Roundup." *English Journal* 53 (December 1964): 702–703.
2. J. Donald Adams, *Speaking of Books—and Life* (New York: Holt, Rinehart and Winston, 1965), 250–251.
3. *Freedom and Discipline in English: Report of the Commission on English* (New York: College Entrance Examination Board, 1965), p. 49.
4. Else Weinstein, "High School Teacher." "Education Life" supplement, *New York Times.* 6 November 1988, 19.
5. Elaine Simpson, "Reason, Not Emotion." *Top of the News* 31 (April 1975): 302.
6. Dorothy Broderick, "Serving Young Adults: Why We Do What We Do." *Voice of Youth Advocates* 12 (October 1989): 204.
7. Robert C. Small, Jr., "Teaching the Junior Novel." *English Journal* 61 (February 1972): 222.

12

Young Adult Literature and the Test of Time

Ted Hipple

It is a commonplace in literary studies to suggest that one of the standards by which classic literature is so identified is that the novel or play or poem has "stood the test of time." In essence, this criterion holds that a work cannot be a classic unless and until it has been read by generations of readers beyond the time of its writing. Thus, Twain's *Adventures of Huckleberry Finn* easily makes the list, as does most of Dickens and Hardy and Jane Austen and virtually all of Shakespeare. Curiously, a book does not necessarily have to be read in its own time—just in succeeding times; witness *Moby Dick,* not a popular novel when Melville first published it but eminently so after its first few decades of sparse readership.

Certain limitations are, in effect, mandated by a strict adherence to this criterion. One is that no book written in the last thirty years (the period demographers agree represents an adult "generation") can be a classic during that time; it has to be successful in a later generation. We're left with speculation, then, about current literature and whether it will survive the temporal cut. Take, for argument's sake, six enormously popular novels of the 1980s and ask which you think will be read by the next generation, those readers of the first decade of the twenty-first century: *Beloved* by Toni Morrison, *Cold Sassy Tree* by Olive A. Burns, *Prince of Tides* by Pat Conroy, *Bonfire of the Vanities* by Tom Wolfe, *Cider House Rules* by John Irving, and *Presumed Innocent* by Scott Turow. My own hunch is that the first three might still be read, emphasis on "might," but that the last three will not survive and achieve classic status.

Classics are helped in their survival over time by, certainly, their own quality, but also by extraneous yet related events, such as being the subject of literary scholarship, for example, or being used in high school and college literature studies. Again with reference to using adult fiction, the Morrison,

Burns, and Conroy novels have been written about somewhat widely and all are used in school classes much more—I think—than the other three titles mentioned. Hence, my hunch of the previous paragraph.

What all of this has to do with young adult literature—particularly adolescent novels—may seem obscure, but I think a valid link can be developed. I should like to argue that young adult literature, in order to be considered classic, must also stand the test of time and be read by succeeding generations, but we must redefine terms when that literature is under consideration.

Take "young adult." In popular parlance the term refers to someone between, as they say, puberty and adultery, or at least someone in the teen years, say twixt twelve and twenty. Yet even these boundaries are soft. Parents speak worriedly of their eleven-year-old who is, they say, going on twenty-five and, later, with equal worry about their twenty-three-year-old who "hasn't quite found himself." But when the term is used with literature, "young adult" is much more narrowly described: we are usually referring to someone between eleven or twelve years of age and fifteen or sixteen, in other words, someone within about a four- or five-year span. (This is, I hasten to add, not indicative that YA literature is not read by persons outside this age range; it is, of course, by youngsters of nine or ten and oldsters of eighteen or fifty-three enjoying a Judy Blume novel or one by Sue Ellen Bridgers.)

Given, then, an age range of about five years for an author to aim for, we can, I believe, argue that a "generation" for a young adult novel is but that four or five years. If a book, say a young adult novel, is read over several of these generations, these five-year spans, then it merits the label "classic." It has stood the test of time. Robert Cormier's *Chocolate War*, for example, published in 1974, is still widely popular, some eighteen years later, about four generations later. No one ought to dispute its being considered a classic in its field.

But it is far from alone. In December 1989 I published the results of a small survey in the *English Journal*, one in which I had asked scholars in the field of adolescent literature and English teachers and educators (including a number of past officers of ALAN, the Assembly on Literature for Adolescents of the National Council of Teachers of English), to identify the ten adolescent novels they hoped all English teachers had read. Fifty-six people responded, and their top six were as follows (with the year of publication and the number selecting each title in parentheses):

> *The Chocolate War* by Robert Cormier (1974–39)
> *The Outsiders* by S. E. Hinton (1967–19)
> *The Pigman* by Paul Zindel (1968–19)
> *Home before Dark* by Sue Ellen Bridgers (1976–17)
> *A Day No Pigs Would Die* by Robert N. Peck (1972–17)
> *All Together Now* by Sue Ellen Bridgers (1979–11)

What is important to note is that these books are all classics—by my definition. They have stood the test of time, have been read by succeeding generations beyond that approximately four-year generation that read them when they were first published. Both *The Outsiders* and *The Pigman* have, in fact, gone through almost six generations of young adult readers, a record that matches, say, Twain's *Adventures of Huckleberry Finn,* which was published about six adult generations ago. Clearly they are classics. It is significant, too, to recall that these were not the only young adult books published when they came out; there were many others, which have failed to capture the attention of subsequent generations and, thus, no longer merit the label "classic." In this regard you might recall Ann Head's *Mr. and Mrs. BoJo Jones,* almost as popular in the late 1960s, I believe, as the Hinton and Zindel novels, but now much less commonly read. Like today's *Bonfire of the Vanities* it had its moments, but it is not a classic.

But why these six books? Why Hinton and Zindel and Cormier and not Head or many of the other writers whose books of a couple of decades ago—five young adult generations—have failed to reach classic status? Just as with adult literature, we need, I think, to look at the books themselves and then at the help they get from scholarship about them and from their appearance in school and college literature classes.

I'm assuming that most of my readers are familiar with these six novels, and thus there is no need to retell their stories, all of which, I would argue, compel us onward. We want to turn the pages to find out what is going to happen next. Whether it's Stella's confrontation with Rodney Biggers in *Home Before Dark* or Haven Peck's death in *A Day No Pigs Would Die,* we must know about it. But let's go beyond the excellence of the stories to focus attention on three literary elements: character, theme, and writing.

First, character. All six of these novels possess well-drawn, fully fleshed-out characters, people of depth who ring true. This statement is particularly germane in regard to their youthful protagonists. Who can forget Casey, who "came unwillingly" to her grandparents' small town for a summer in *All Together Now* or the mentally retarded Dwayne in that same novel? Or the evil Archie and his henchman Obie in *The Chocolate War,* aided and abetted by the equally evil Brother Leon? Or Ponyboy and Johnny in *The Outsiders?*

These characters become real people, as much as do the characters of classics in adult literature, Ma Joad and Preacher Casey in *The Grapes of Wrath* and Pip and Estella and Miss Havisham in *Great Expectations.* When Casey lies near death at the end of *All Together Now,* readers do not fear that a character in a book may die, but sorrow over someone they have come to know, to love. In *The Chocolate War* Jerry's daring to disturb the universe, departing thereby from Eliot's J. Alfred Prufrock, is thrilling, even as we sense he may pay a terrible physical and mental price for his boldness; and when he does, we suffer with him. The poverty Robert Peck grows up with becomes our poverty. We anguish with John and Lorraine at the pigman's death and share their uncertainty about the degree of their involvement in its cause.

Fine novels, those already classics or destined to become so, not only have exemplary central characters, they have minor characters of substance as well.

Cormier has populated *The Chocolate War* with bit players like Obie and Goober and Jerry's passive father, and all of them are carefully and distinctly drawn. Bridgers places in her novels a whole raft of characters, including some much older than her teenaged central characters, and none of them are unidimensional; they are fleshed out. Even the Bore, John's father in *The Pigman*, takes on the temperament and the behavior of a father at his wits' end about a son he cannot and will not try to understand. *The Outsiders* offers us the juvenile delinquent we somehow like, Dally.

In addition to their adroitly portrayed characters, classic novels have important themes that they explore intelligently, a statement true for Bridgers and for Balzac, for Cormier and for Conrad. (The juxtaposition of these authors is not to imply that Bridgers is a Balzac, Cormier a Conrad, but that all of them, in their respective fields, have written novels that deserve to be called "classic.") The themes of adolescence differ, of course, from those of adulthood, but they are just as significant, as telling in the lives of the young people for whom the novels are intended. One of the great themes of young adult literature—the loss of innocence—is, interestingly, central to each of these six novels. In *The Chocolate War* Jerry matures in a hurry when he encounters the malevolence of Archie and Brother Leon. Only fourteen at the novel's beginning, Ponyboy ages considerably in the relatively few days covered in *The Outsiders;* the death of friends reminds him of the truth of the Frost poem he likes so much: "Nothing Gold Can Stay." In Mr. Pignati's death, John and Lorraine discover that behavior has consequences. Try though they might, they cannot escape some sense of guilt for what occurred. Both of Bridger's heroines—Stella in *Home Before Dark* and Casey in *All Together Now*—move from innocence to experience, to use the terms of Romantic poet William Blake. Stella has to come to grips with her mother's death, her father's relatively quick remarriage, and her own ambivalence about Maggie, her new stepmother. Casey tries to take on a whole town as it considers whether to send Dwayne to a mental institution. Robert Peck faces the death of his father with a grown-up's dignity, a mandate Haven Peck provided his son: you are now the head of this family; care for it. These are, in other words, novels about rites of passage, those experiences all adolescents undergo in their inevitable journey to adulthood.

Other themes important to young adults come into play and may be examined in these six novels. All of the novels deal in significant ways with relationships, and with different kinds of relationships. In each there is to some degree an exploration of the central character's relationship with self. For instance, Jerry's questions about disturbing the universe receive an answer that he, at the end of the book, regrets. Though home before dark, Stella must determine where that home is, with her father and his new bride or by herself in the little cottage on the Willis homestead. Hinton actually has Ponyboy write *The Outsiders* as his way of maintaining his sanity about the events that occurred.

Relationships with parents and other family members are examined in these six novels, particularly in *A Day No Pigs Would Die* and in Bridgers's two novels. Peck's book touchingly but unsentimentally looks at Robert and his father and their family, all of it set amid poverty that might defeat people of less determination. Casey, separated from her mother and father for the summer, lives with her grandparents and finds wisdom there. Stella learns from an aunt that life can be more than following the crops.

Relationships with others outside the family merit study in these six books, too, as many of the characters encounter people very different from themselves. Stella meets people with a solid foundation—a home, a job, school, a future; she had not experienced these kinds of things in her migrant world life, where a bed was the rear end of the station wagon and matters like education and medical care were more the result of convenience than of design. Jerry runs into evil incarnate. Ponyboy learns that the socs from the rich side of town enjoy the same sunset he likes.

All six of these novels use language well, a trait they share with adult classic novels, those of Twain and Hawthorne, for example. The following passages suggest the richness of the writing one can find in these books.

From *The Chocolate War* comes this passage when all involved now know that Jerry's refusal to sell the chocolates was simply a Vigils' assignment, one now ended. But no one, least of all Jerry's friend Goober, is prepared for Jerry's continuing refusal; it comes as Brother Leon is calling the roll and recording the number of boxes of chocolates each boy sold:

Then Brother Leon called out "Parmentier." And there was tension in the air. Parmentier could have called out any number and it wouldn't have mattered, it wouldn't have created any impact at all. Because the next name was Renault.

"Three," Parmentier called out.

"Right," Brother Leon answered, making the check against the name. Looking up, he called "Renault."

The pause. The damned pause.

"No!"

The Goober felt as if his eyes were the lens for a television camera in one of those documentaries. He swung around in Jerry's direction and saw his friend's face, white, mouth half-open, his arms dangling at his sides. An then he swiveled to look at Brother Leon and saw the shock on the teacher's face, his mouth forming an oval of astonishment. It seemed almost as if Jerry and the teacher were reflections in a mirror.

Finally Brother Leon looked down.

"Renault," he said again, his voice like a whip.

"No. I'm not going to sell the chocolates."

Cities fell. Earth opened. Planets tilted. Stars plummeted. And the awful silence.

In *The Outsiders* some socs have grabbed Ponyboy and Johnny near a park fountain and are holding Ponyboy (the narrator) under the water:

> The next thing I knew I was lying on the pavement beside the fountain, coughing water and gasping. I lay there weakly, breathing in air and spitting out water. The wind blasted through my soaked sweatshirt and dripping hair. My teeth chattered unceasingly and I couldn't stop them. I finally pushed myself up and leaned back against the fountain, the water running down my face. Then I saw Johnny.
>
> He was sitting next to me, one elbow on his knee, and staring straight ahead. He was a strange greenish-white, and his eyes were huger than I'd ever seen them.
>
> "I killed him," he said slowly. "I killed that boy."

The Pigman, John and Lorraine's story of their relationship with Mr. Pignati, begins with their taking an oath to be truthful:

> Being of sound mind and body on this 15th day of April in our sophomore year at Franklin High School, let it be known that Lorraine Jensen and John Conlan have decided to record the facts, and only the facts, about our experiences with Mr. Angelo Pignati.
>
> Miss Reillen, the Cricket, is watching us at every moment because she is the librarian at Franklin High and thinks we're using her typewriter to copy a book report for our retarded English teacher.
>
> The truth and nothing but the truth, until this memorial epic is finished, So Help Us God!

Bridgers's first novel *Home Before Dark* echoes with images from the tobacco farming that is so important in North Carolina, where Sue Ellen Bridgers was reared. In this passage Stella's young friend Toby Brown is wishing he could be the one to explore with Stella what going to a tobacco auction was like:

> Toby could tell Stella how it felt to step on mice and feel the soft infant bodies rolling under his feet until the floor was bloody and raw. Or how the sky looked on nights when he lay in a tobacco truck under the stars, not because Newton needed him to watch the barns but because he wanted the feeling of being completely alone, just Toby Brown and the barn owls and the old cat sleeping at his feet and so many stars the sky seemed on fire.

At the end of *A Day No Pigs Would Die,* Haven Peck is buried in an orchard near the family homestead. His son Robert, having done the chores, having eaten supper, having helped his mother, now goes for a final visit to his father's resting place:

I don't know why I walked out toward the orchard. All the work there
was done. But I guess I had to give a goodnight to Papa, and be alone with
him. The bugs were out and their singing was all around me. Almost like
a choir. I got to the fresh grave, all neatly mounded and pounded. Somewhere down under all that Vermont clay was my father, Haven Peck.
Buried deep in the land he sweated so hard on and longed to own so
much. Now it owned him.

"Goodnight, Papa," I said. "We had thirteen good years."

That was all I could say, so I just turned and walked away from a patch
of grassless land.

The second of Bridgers's novels to make the list, *All Together Now*, features in
prominent roles—almost parental roles—Casey's grandparents, Jane and Ben,
whose love for each other is revealed in their every action and in this reflection
from Jane:

Jane knew she was still in love with Ben. *In love*. That was what she meant,
although she'd have a hard time saying it, even to him. It was so much
easier just to say she loved him. After all, she had spent years loving him,
taking care of him. Her dedication to him and their sons had consumed
her, energized her, probably even aged her, but she was still in love with
him, could feel giddy when she looked out from the church choir to see
him looking back at her.

Other attributes that suggest why these novels merit classic status, have
stood the test of time, could be discussed—their vivid use of setting, for example, or the tension of the stories they tell—but these will suffice. Recall,
though, my earlier assertion that classics cannot meet this time-standard without help, particularly scholarly attention and classroom use in schools and
colleges.

The scholarship in adolescent literature is relatively recent, but it is growing
almost as much as and as quickly as the field itself. There are now books about
adolescent literature, and these sell well; witness the fact that *Literature for
Today's Young Adults* by Ken Donelson and Alleen Pace Nilsen is now in its
third edition. Other books focusing on young adult literature have enjoyed
critical and commercial acclaim: *A Guide to Young Adult Literature* by Ruth
Cline and William McBride, *Reaching Adolescents* by Arthea J. S. Reed, *Adolescent
Literature: Response and Analysis* by Robert E. Probst. Critical biographies have
recently been introduced to the world of young adult scholarship and, of the
five authors whose novels are the centerpiece of this essay, four have been the
subject of works in the Twayne Young Adult Authors Series: *Presenting Robert
Cormier* (by Patricia J. Campbell), *Presenting S. E. Hinton* (by Jay Daly), *Presenting Paul Zindel* (by Jack J. Forman), and *Presenting Sue Ellen Bridgers* (by Ted
Hipple). Numerous other authors have been and will be "presented" in this

Twayne series. Publishers have produced teaching guides for several of these novels, and Bantam Doubleday Dell commissioned a 40-page guide on the total body of Zindel's work (by Ted Hipple).

Theme issues of journals, like the very one you are now reading, focus on young adult literature. Several journals are wholly devoted to adolescent literature, with thoughtful and scholarly articles appearing in each issue, along with reviews of new books. In past issues of *The ALAN Review,* published by the Assembly on Literature for Adolescents of the National Council of Teachers of English, and *Signal,* a similar publication produced by a special interest group in the International Reading Association, one can often find articles about these six books. Each year, in conjunction with the NCTE convention, ALAN holds a workshop for two days, with 300 participants (the maximum possible) always in attendance. All five of these authors have been featured speakers, with Cormier, Zindel, and Bridgers having made many appearances. Dissertations have been written on these authors (for example, Pamela S. Carroll's study of Bridgers), and on aspects within the field. In sum, scholarship on young adult literature in general—and on these six novels and their authors in particular—is alive and well.

And the books are being used in schools and colleges, all six of them. Just as the whole field of young adult literature has grown, so also has the study of that literature on college campuses. Time was, and not so long ago, that a smallish unit in an English methods course might be devoted to young adult literature; students preparing to be English teachers might have one activity within the course that permitted them to use an adolescent novel. Now it is the rare campus that does not have a young adult literature course, sometimes more than one, undergraduate and graduate, often with multiple sections enrolling not only English and English education majors but library science students and those from psychology and social work and, finally, simply those who want to read good books. And what good books do they read? You guessed it—these six, among them the most commonly adopted texts in such courses at colleges all over the country.

These books make appearances in the secondary schools, too. The largest-selling paperback young adult novel is *The Outsiders,* followed in sales by *The Pigman.* Many of these sales, of course, are at bookstores, one copy at a time. But many, many more are from classroom sets purchased for junior and senior high school use. These two novels particularly, but the others as well, frequently appear in classrooms as readings in common. More and more secondary school teachers are recognizing the value of these titles and are replacing the unread adult classics of yesteryear with these more relevant and more-likely-to-be-read young adult classics. These teachers want readers, and they know that the *that* of student reading is, ultimately, more important than the *what* if lifelong reading is the goal. The high school student who reads Zindel or Bridgers today may read Dickens or Faulkner tomorrow; at the least he or she is likely to read something. The first objective of such teachers is to encourage a love of reading.

In summary, then, the rules governing what a classic is in young adult literature are changing as fast as the field is changing. Given a generation of adolescents that lasts but four or five years, a number of books have already com-
manded the attention of almost six generations, with no end in sight to their
readership and to the scholarship about them. It is likely that more and more
young adult works will be added to their number.

References

Campbell, Patricia J. *Presenting Robert Cormier.* Boston: Twayne Publishers, 1987.

Carroll, Pamela Sissi. "Sue Ellen Bridgers's Southern Literature for Young Adults," Dissertation, Auburn
University, 1988.

Cline, Ruth, and William McBride. *A Guide to Literature for Young Adults.* Glenview, Ill.: Scott, Foresman and
Company, 1983.

Daly, Jay. *Presenting S. E. Hinton.* Boston: Twayne Publishers, 1988.

Donelson, Ken, and Alleen Pace Nilsen. *Literature for Today's Young Adults,* 3d ed. Glenview, Ill.: Scott,
Foresman and Company, 1989.

Forman, Jack J. *Presenting Paul Zindel.* Boston: Twayne Publishers, 1987.

Hipple, Ted. "Have You Read? Parts 2 and 3." *English Journal* 78 (December 1988): 79.

———. *Presenting Sue Ellen Bridgers.* Boston: Twayne Publishers, 1990.

———. *A Teacher's Guide to the Novels of Paul Zindel.* New York: Bantam Doubleday Dell, 1988.

Probst, Robert E. *Adolescent Literature: Response and Analysis.* Columbus: Charles E. Merrill Publishing Company, 1984.

Reed, Arthea J. S. *Reaching Adolescents: The Young Adult Book and the School.* New York: Holt, Rinehart and
Winston, 1985.

13

Leading Them to Books—For Life

Diane P. Tuccillo

There was another visitor here today. I hadn't seen Tim for a year, since his last visit from California, where he is stationed with the Marines. I was surprised to hear of his "vacation" in the Persian Gulf, and glad to know he is fine. Tim, twenty-two now, had grown taller and had slimmed down. Yet, as I looked at him I could still see the quiet, concise talker with the infectious smile, much shorter and rounder, who had first come to Mesa Public Library to join our Young Adult Advisory Council and to participate in fantasy role-playing games eight years ago. Now, every time he comes to Arizona to visit his family, we in the YA Room are included in his visit, to catch up on things and to share information about books. After all, as Tim told me, we are his second family, his home away from home. At Mesa Public Library, we've learned that kids who feel this way about their library keep coming back, into adulthood. How to get them to do that is important for librarians to know.

The key, we've learned, is to help teenagers to appreciate and use books on their own. An old Chinese proverb says, "Give a man a fish, and you feed him for a day. Teach him to fish, and you feed him for a lifetime." The wisdom in this proverb can be applied to many things, and one of those things is books and reading. Kids can be given books, and can have books read to them, and can be handed reading assignments, but until they learn the personal value and enjoyment of books and reading, they will most likely enter adulthood without becoming continual readers and library supporters. Those kids who *do* learn the importance and pleasure of books, who come to and get involved in the library *on their own,* will become lifelong readers and learners.

In 1985, *Library Journal* published an excellent article by Barbara Will Razzano called "Creating the Library Habit." The article documents a positive pattern of adult library usage stemming from usage that began in childhood and adolescence. Most important, it discusses a pyramid effect of library usage passed down to the children of those adults. To my great delight, I am witnessing this process right now. Former teen library users who are now adults still use the library regularly. Some, like Tim, stop by when visiting from a distance. Others who live locally still come to the library often. Those who have families are not only continuing to read themselves but are bringing in their children for story times, for other special programs, and to find books.

One couple, Sandy and Kenny, were teens when they became library regulars in the 1970s. Their interest in books came directly from the influence of Christy Tyson, who began the YA department at Mesa Public in 1977. Sandy was even one of the charter members of our Young Adult Advisory Council (YAAC), a teen book review and library volunteer group. Now, Sandy, Kenny, and their three children come often to the library to find books for the whole family. Many times, if I'm not too busy, I spend time with the eldest, little Kenny, who is just starting kindergarten. He shows me his books, makes me little drawings, and chatters away about *everything.* He loves coming to story times and finding books, especially about dinosaurs. Already a serious library user in his own right, he is a prime example of what Barbara Razzano was talking about. When he's ready, he'll know the YA Room will be here for him, as it was for his mother and father. I have high hopes that he, and his brother and sister, will be bringing *their* children to the library one day.

All this teaches something about YA literature: the literature that is published for teens as well as the literature "adopted" from other areas is at the heart of developing lifelong readers. The way to this "heart" is in providing a book collection for teens and a place in the library they can call their own. This requires support from administrators and the community. In Mesa there are approximately 24,000 young adults in junior and senior high school. Last year, the collection in our YA Room totaled 35,000 books and had a circulation of 158,000, an average of 13,166 books or 38 percent of the collection per month. These encouraging circulation figures show that when the books are provided, young adults will really use their library. When they see that their community's administrators truly care about YA books and teen reading by supporting well-planned, adequate collections for them, it helps them to learn these books must be something special.

It is not necessarily easy to get and keep this support. YA librarians must promote their books and services regularly. It is important to be outspoken in the community about teen reading and to get information about YA literature into print. Parents, teachers, and counselors need to know the YA collection is there, and bibliographies and newsletters can help to share the wealth. A review column printed in the local newspaper or a press release advertising programs can get kids into the library and ultimately looking for books. The YA librarian needs to be a youth advocate, getting involved with other community leaders serving teens. But most of all, the YA librarian needs to be familiar with YA literature and the professional resources that help connect teens to that literature.

A number of professional resources address the needs of teen readers, and most include useful bibliographies. They are a great help in understanding and appreciating young adult literature and promoting it to its intended audience. *New Directions for Young Adult Services* by Ellen V. Libretto describes in careful detail what library service to teens is all about. Another guide to teen library service is Amelia Munson's *An Ample Field.* Though published in 1950, its advice on attracting teens to the library and getting them involved in reading is still relevant today. Certain books that teach about young adult literature itself and serve as excellent guides for library collection development and maintenance can aid in teen reader advisory. These include Robert G. Carlsen's *Books and the Teenage Reader: A Guide for Teachers, Librarians, and Parents;* Ellen V. Libretto's *High/Low Handbook: Encouraging Literacy in the 1990s;* Arthea Reed's *Reaching Adolescents: The Young Adult Book and the School;* Robert E. Probst's *Adolescent Literature: Response and Analysis;* Ken Donelson and Alleen Nilsen's *Literature for Today's Young Adults;* Ruth Cline and William McBride's *Guide to Literature for Young Adults;* and Sister Mary Elizabeth Gallagher's *Young Adult Literature: Issues and Perspectives.* Besides giving librarians information on YA literature, these books are valuable resources for teachers, parents, and others interested in teen reading.

Once a librarian feels confident that he or she understands YA literature and how to effectively let teens know about it, it will be time to try a book talk. A book talk is a presentation designed to introduce both already avid and prospective readers to a number of books, telling just enough about each to entice them without revealing the endings. Book talks provide a vital connection between teens and their literature, luring them to the library in the process.

Three related books that serve as an excellent resource for learning book-talking techniques, teach how to use those techniques with teen (or any age) audiences, and show how to prepare individual "book talks" are Joni Bodart's *Booktalk: Booktalking and School Visiting for Young Adult Audiences, Booktalk! 2: Booktalking for All Ages and Audiences,* and *Booktalk! 3: More Booktalks for All Ages and Audiences. Wilson Library Bulletin* also publishes Bodart's "The Booktalker," a newsletter supplement to that journal giving book-talking ideas and samples.

At Mesa Public Library, we do book talks for sixth graders, for junior high and high school students, for special education students, and for accelerated learning students. Meeting the informational and recreational reading needs of all readers, regardless of level, is an important step in encouraging reading and lifelong library use. Book talks are a channel for spreading the word about books and libraries to teens who might never consider their value.

Becoming familiar with the professional resources mentioned and employing their advice would be a great starting place for anyone serious about beginning or improving service to teens, whether in school or public library settings. Of course, in addition a number of journals review YA books and publish research, bibliographies, and articles on YA literature, reading, and both school and public library use. *Voice of Youth Advocates, Kliatt Young Adult Paperback Book Guide, The Horn Book, School Library Journal,* and *The Book Report* are among the best known. A steady diet of the information and reviews found in these journals can keep a librarian who serves teens up-to-date on issues, new titles, and program ideas.

School and public library cooperation is another great path to encouraging teen reading. Junior and senior high school students with a knowledgeable school librarian and teachers who promote reading seem more likely to use the public library on their own and to use and support their school library. These school librarians and teachers advertise the public library to students and provide special programs, like book talks and storytelling, either on their own, by inviting the public librarian in, or both. (Yes, in case you are wondering, storytelling for teens can be a surprisingly successful option for promoting reading.)

Besides developing special book collections for teens, in many cases the public library has information, resources, and services that can benefit school librarians and teachers who take advantage of them. Often, public libraries have bibliographies available for reprinting, will provide library orientations, book talks, or storytelling in the classroom, and offer student library tours when arranged as a field trip.

All this takes us back to the subject at hand: helping teenagers to become lifelong readers and library supporters. Librarians can do everything "right," like following the advice in professional resources, developing a well-rounded YA book collection, and planning programs, without much teen response. The key to success is in finding out *what the teenagers themselves think about books and reading.* Librarians must know what teenagers in their own community like and dislike. In Mesa, for example, Michael Jackson was never much of a hero. Oh, he had his brief claim to fame when the album "Thriller" was first released. We had twenty copies of a biography on him that circulated like hotcakes for a few months. Then, for some reason, it became uncool to like Michael Jackson. His concert tour—a sellout elsewhere—was canceled locally owing to lack of ticket sales. We withdrew most of those well-worn twenty copies instead of replacing them, keeping two for the "closet" Jackson fans who still wanted them. The teens *told* us they didn't like Michael Jackson any more. They laughed at the number of Jackson biographies sitting on the shelf, untouched. We listened to what the kids were telling us, and we responded. On the other hand, our teenagers told us they love science fiction and fantasy, and we developed an outstanding collection for them. We subscribed to *LOCUS* magazine to find the latest SF releases and bought in quantity the ones highest in demand. Books on martial arts, the "Sunfire" historical romances, and Gary Paulsen's books were also bought in quantity because of their popularity. Examples like these can be found in many areas of our YA collection. Librarians need to listen to their clientele to keep YA collections current and exciting, two qualities especially attractive to teens.

On that note, libraries, especially school libraries and public ones with YA services, would do well to organize a support group of teenagers who love books. Members of such a group can gather regularly to review books and serve as library volunteers. Their input and recommendations become extremely valuable for the library in learning firsthand what teens enjoy and do not enjoy reading.

At Mesa Public Library, YAAC serves in this capacity. They review books at meetings and publish a newsletter of reviews called "Open Shelf," to encourage teen reading. They help as volunteers in the YA Room, and their visibility often proves inviting to teens who may feel too shy to stop by. They even, at times, participate in peer reader advisory, sharing book suggestions with fellow teens in search of something good to read or who need to satisfy a class assignment. Peer reader advisory can be a wonderful way to get young adults into books and reading.

I think of Eric when the possibilities of peer reader advisory come to mind. When Eric was twelve, he decided the kids in YAAC were neat and he wanted to become part of their group. Until he met our YAAC volunteers, Eric had read only one whole novel—*The Hobbit*, by J. R. R. Tolkien. He came to the first few YAAC meetings and reviewed the same book each time. Eventually, he picked up on the reading suggestions of the other YAAC members and began trying some of the books they mentioned. Soon, Eric was checking out many books each month, and he became one of the best and most reliable reviewers on the council. His grades in school improved; he said all that reading and writing for YAAC was paying off.

About a year after Eric joined YAAC, he came in to get some books to take on a camping trip with his father. At that time, our circulation limit per library card was thirty books. Eric walked out of the library balancing a stack that tall (almost as tall as he was), to take along with him. And he read all the books, too, though not all on that particular trip. Eric is now in his early twenties, and college is keeping him busy so we don't see much of him these days. But he is a prime example of what peer reader advisory is all about. In the course of his YAAC membership, Eric's excellent reviews turned a number of other teenagers on to reading, just as his fellow YAAC members did for him when he was twelve.

YAAC (or any kind of library or book club) is just one outlet of expression for teenagers in the avenue of books and reading. Libraries need to be aware of other ways teens can be encouraged to participate in the fun of reading—and writing—on their own. I mention writing because the art of writing holds an important connection to reading: one cannot exist without the other, and teens need to see this connection. There are a few ways library activities can help.

Besides writing reviews, teens can put together their own literary creations and have copies available in and distributed through their library. Here at

Mesa Public Library, we annually publish *E.T.* magazine, which includes science fiction and fantasy art and writing by local teens. Teens also serve on the editorial staff. Copies of *E.T.* are published at our city print shop and sold to benefit our Friends of the Library fund. But programs to develop interest in reading and writing do not need to be so large in scale. Small publications work well, too, and so do writing programs and contests.

Many publishers, companies, and organizations sponsor writing contests for teenagers. For example, Avon Flare sponsors an annual young adult novel competition. Poetry, short stories, and essays can also earn everything from monetary awards to publication to scholarships. Librarians can keep an eye out for notices about these special writing competitions, or better yet purchase Mary Ellen Snodgrass's *Contests for Students,* and get themselves on mailing lists for announcements. Posters and brochures received can be placed prominently in an area serving teenagers. Sometimes the library may be the only place teens learn of such contests. The contests not only give teens a chance at winning prizes but, more important, encourage them to get involved in reading and writing on their own. They give teens a personal connection to the value of literacy.

Another wonderful way for teens to make that personal connection is by seeing and hearing real live authors. People of all ages enjoy meeting the creators of their favorite books, but somehow teenagers are especially impressed by them. The idea that a published author who understands what teens are feeling is actually there talking to them makes them feel special and makes that author's writing come more alive. When Gloria Miklowitz came to meet our teens two years ago, we hardly had one of her books on the shelf for months. Every YAAC meeting included another Miklowitz book review. Members passed books around among themselves and made recommendations to one another. There is nothing like an author visit to get kids interested in books. One useful resource in arranging such visits is *How to Capture Live Authors and Bring Them to Your Schools* by David Melton, information which can be adapted to library programs.

What about the teenager who seems uninterested in reading but who, due to parental or school assignment pressure, is still searching for a book? Librarians need to know how to approach reluctant readers in particular, for the right questions and the right books could change that reluctant reader's perspective; the wrong approach could unwittingly reinforce it. Steering these kids to a book they will finish and enjoy is a challenge. The key is a friendly smile and a casual attitude, careful listening, and knowing when to back out. These reluctant readers don't need more pressure from a librarian!

Librarians who know the technique of "aisle annotating" are at an advantage with unwilling readers, for they can quickly and very briefly present the interesting aspects of a number of books, keeping the attention of those skeptical teens they are trying to reach. I like to think of aisle annotating as giving a mini-book talk right there in the library stacks. Then, the reluctant reader can take the books mentioned to a table and look through them to decide which one to try. I say books—plural—because librarians need to remember that multiple titles should always be recommended, even to avid readers. That way, the teens can decide what to read, giving them a feeling of power in the process. This feeling of power can help teens feel more positive about the act of reading. With a selection of titles, chances are there will be at least one a reluctant reader will agree to try. If only one book is shown, and it "misses," a reader's interest may be lost entirely. It is also important (and very hard) for librarians not to gush over books they think are wonderful. A positive word or two in describing the story and remaining somewhat objective will help a teenager decide independently, without feeling obligated to read the *librarian's* favorite.

In connecting teen readers and books, librarians need to see adolescent literature as something more than just the books published and promoted as "YA." We need to see the entire picture of what kids *are* reading and *want* to read. This means awareness of adult and juvenile titles teens also enjoy. Adult authors such as Anne Rice or Jean Auel are popular among teen readers, but interestingly enough some teens like a children's book every once in a while as well. It is not uncommon at one of our YAAC meetings to hear a review of a Stephen King book followed, perhaps, by a review of Norman Juster's *The Phantom Tollbooth*. Many of our teens still enjoy the Hardy Boys and Nancy Drew books. Even picture books, seen from a new, "mature" perspective, are interesting and fun at times, and teens who have young siblings sometimes enjoy sharing favorites. At the same time, it is important for librarians to remember that teens who like to read need the inspiration of outstanding new as well as classic titles. Sometimes these young adults can lose interest if they are not encouraged to read widely and expand their horizons. It certainly helps for a YA librarian to be a well-rounded reader in *all* areas to meet these varying needs.

Behind-the-scenes involvement can help, too. Librarians need to let publishers know how we feel about adolescent reading and the needs of our clientele. Bantam/Doubleday/Dell has made great strides in this area by developing its Library Advisory Board. Librarians from throughout the nation meet and communicate regularly with this publishing group to give feedback, share ideas, and recommend changes. Kate Havris, YA Librarian at Mesa Public Library, served on this advisory board for three years, and she noticed frequent results of the board's advice in items being published. Many other publishers are also listening to what librarians are saying.

More attention still needs to be paid to the old bugaboo, book jacket artwork. Publishers have a responsibility to provide books that are not only well written but that have covers that will appeal to kids. Many covers on YA books are attractive. It's just that, with some, the reader begins to see that the person on the cover does not match the character described inside! Then there are the downright *awful* covers that completely turn kids away from a book. It never ceases to amaze me that some publishers will approve an unattractive cover that will inhibit sales of an otherwise promising book before it even has a chance.

I think Sonia Levitin's *Smile Like a Plastic Daisy* is a good example. It is an excellent book and makes some great points about justice and women's rights. But—no matter how many kids I mention the book to—one look at that terrible cover and they hand it back. When the book came out in paperback with a completely different, nice-looking cover, lo and behold, all the paperback copies were checked out constantly! We glued and taped and kept those copies around as long as possible, because when they finally bit the dust, they were irreplaceable. The book was out of print in paperback. Now, the lone hardback with the ugly cover sits on the shelf, in mint condition because no one reads it. I am almost tempted to break the binding so I can send it out to be rebound. It would be easier to convince a teenager to read it with the generic class A binding than with the cover it has now. Other examples come to mind, though covers do seem to be improving. Still, even the occasional cover with characters who look ten when inside the book they are sixteen, or the boring nondescript covers, or the unappealing abstract covers that make the characters look like aliens from another world (and these are not SF books) can detract from an otherwise good story. An interesting look at how and why these covers are produced the way they are appears in a recent *Publishers Weekly* article, "Covers that Catch the Eye."

Publishers need to know what teachers and librarians think so they can make appropriate changes, bring a book back into print, *keep* it in print, or aim to produce a new book on a hot topic. Better yet, they need to listen to the kids themselves, perhaps by developing teen panels functioning like the Bantam/ Doubleday/Dell Library Advisory Board. Publishers are vital allies in the all-important mission of developing lifelong readers.

Making the library and books mean something valuable to teens as they reach full adulthood needs to be a major aim of all youth-serving librarians. It is ours at Mesa Public Library, and I get constant assurances that what we're doing to meet that goal is working. One came in a letter I just received from a young woman who had been a YAAC member and had moved to West Virginia over a year ago. Her letter was filled with news of all the exciting highlights of her teenage life but also with descriptions of books she had recently read. Her concluding sentiment is a fitting end to this article as well: "Hope your life is full of books!" Librarians, teachers, publishers, and authors can work as a team in promoting positive teen reading experiences. By helping young people to see how interesting and gratifying reading can be, we are giving them a gift—a *lifetime* filled with books.

Books Mentioned

Bodart, Joni. *Booktalk!: Booktalking and School Visiting for Young Adult Audiences.* New York: H. W. Wilson, 1980.

_____. *Booktalk! 2: Booktalking for All Ages and Audiences.* New York: H. W. Wilson, 1985.

_____. *Booktalk! 3: More Booktalks for All Ages and Audiences.* New York: H. W. Wilson, 1988.

Carlsen, Robert G. *Books and the Teenage Reader: A Guide for Teachers, Librarians, and Parents.* 2d ed. New York: Harper & Row, 1980.

Cline, Ruth, and William McBride. *Guide to Literature for Young Adults: Background, Selection and Use.* Glenview, Ill.: Scott, Foresman, 1983.

Donelson, Kenneth L., and Alleen Pace Nilsen. *Literature for Today's Young Adults.* Glenview, Ill.: Scott, Foresman, 1989.

Gallagher, Mary Elizabeth. *Young Adult Literature: Issues and Perspectives.* Harverford, Pa.: Catholic Library Association, 1988.

Juster, Norton. *The Phantom Tollbooth.* New York: Random House, 1961.

Levitin, Sonia. *Smile Like a Plastic Daisy.* New York: Atheneum, 1984.

Libretto, Ellen V., ed. *High/Low Handbook: Encouraging Literacy in the 1990s.* 3d ed. New York: Bowker, 1990.

_____. *New Directions for Young Adult Services.* New York: Bowker, 1983.

Melton, David. *How to Capture Live Authors and Bring Them to Your Schools: Practical and Innovative Ways to Schedule Authors for Author-In-Residence Programs, Children's Literature Festivals, and Young Authors' Days.* Kansas City, Mo.: Landmark Editions, 1986.

Munson, Amelia H. *An Ample Field.* Chicago: American Library Association, 1950.

Probst, Robert E. *Adolescent Literature: Response and Analysis.* Columbus: Merrill, 1984.

Reed, Arthea J. S. *Reaching Adolescents: The Young Adult Book and the School.* New York: Holt, Rinehart, and Winston, 1985.

Snodgrass, Mary Ellen, ed. *Contests for Students.* Detroit: Gale Research, 1991.

Tolkien, J. R. R. *The Hobbit.* New York: Ballantine, 1937.

Articles

Feldman, Beth. "Covers that Catch the Eye." *Publishers Weekly* 238 (November 1, 1991): 46–48.

Razzano, Barbara Will. "Creating the Library Habit." *Library Journal* 110 (February 15, 1985): 111–114.

Journals

The Book Report. Columbus: Linworth Publishing, 1982–.

Horn Book Magazine. Boston: Horn Book, Inc., 1945–.

Kliatt Young Adult Paperback Book Guide. Newton, Mass.: Kliatt Young Adult Paperback Book Guide, 1978–.

LOCUS. San Francisco: Locus Publications, 1968–.

School Library Journal. New York: Bowker, 1961–.

Voice of Youth Advocates. Metuchen, N.J.: Scarecrow Press, 1978–.

Wilson Library Bulletin. New York: H. W. Wilson, 1939–.

14

Enhancing Literary Understandings Through Young Adult Fiction

Maia Pank Mertz

Over the last two decades, as young adult literature has grown in sophistication, so has its acceptance as a literary form. Given the efforts of publishers, educational organizations such as the National Council of Teachers of English's Assembly on Literature for Adolescents (ALAN), International Reading Association's SIGNAL, as well as teacher education programs which include courses on young adult literature, teachers no longer need to feel guilty about using adolescent literature as part of the regular English curriculum. Although it is true that these books are still too frequently relegated to the "reading" rather than "literature" classes, there is no reason that this practice should continue, given the literary quality of many young adult novels.

Ironically, those of us who advocate the use of these books are partly to blame for these works being viewed as belonging primarily in classes for less able students. As an instance, my own earlier essays regarding these works have emphasized their thematic and developmental appropriateness for adolescents rather than their literary qualities (Mertz 1975, Mertz and Mertz 1976, Mertz 1978, Mertz and England 1983). Many young adult novels have been lauded for introducing young readers to current cultural issues and problems such as racial tensions, the dissolution of the traditional family, drugs, teen pregnancy, and a plethora of other social ills. Even discussions of historical fiction, science fiction and fantasy, and romance have emphasized how the themes or issues in these novels are appropriate for study by adolescent readers. What has not received as much attention in professional journals is how these works can be used to enhance students' literary understandings. Therefore, discussions of young adult novels that emphasize their literary and artistic merit would add to the already excellent analyses of these works in terms of their thematic and developmental appropriateness.

I would be remiss not to note some excellent essays, written some time ago, that did emphasize the literary aspects of young adult novels. Almost two decades ago, Al Muller, in "The Adolescent Novel in the Classroom," provided examples of novels that could be used to teach concepts such as flashbacks, interior monologues, in medias res, point of view, symbolism, irony, integral use of literary allusions, integral use of setting, subplots, journalistic writing, extended dramatic monologue, extended metaphor, and parallelism (*Media and Methods*, April 1974). Similarly, in "The Adolescent Novel as a Working Model," Robert C. Small compiled a list of novels that would be particularly helpful in teaching concepts such as plot, characterization, setting, use of dialogue, and viewpoint. He also provides examples of activities that can be used to enhance students' understanding of these concepts (ALAN, 1977). In a later essay by Small, "The Y.A. Novel in the Composition Program (Part II)," he also provides examples of adolescent novels that can be used to illustrate various literary concepts (*English Journal*, October 1979). Currently, the most comprehensive discussion of the uses of young adult literature to teach literary concepts is found in "Literary Aspects of Young Adult Books," in Kenneth L. Donelson and Alleen Pace Nilsen's *Literature for Today's Young Adults* (3d ed., 1989).

Even though some essays have drawn attention to the value of young adult novels in teaching literary concepts, it is clear to me, after teaching prospective English teachers for twenty years, that this aspect of young adult literature needs much more emphasis. Even college students find it easier to talk about plot, theme, or characterization than about allusions, symbolism, style, or structure in literary works. This is not a condemnation of college students; rather, it is an attempt to reconsider the emphases many of us in teacher education have made in our teaching of young adult novels. I am not questioning the current attention on student interaction and student response to literary works, nor am I suggesting that we eliminate such emphases. Rather, I am encouraging the addition of teaching about how writers are able to achieve such transactions and responses with students. What better means to get young readers to think about literary techniques and strategies than through the works that engage them as readers?

"Transition" Literature

One of the most frequently cited justifications for young adult literature concerns its role as "transition" literature between children's and adult fiction. One of the earliest discussions of the purposes of young adult novels—then referred to as "junior novels"—is found in Dwight Burton's *Literature Study in the High Schools* (3d ed., 1970), the book that introduced me to literature for adolescents. Burton states that "the major function of literature written expressly for adolescents is to provide a vital transition in the literary education"

(239). Burton provides an example of how "junior novels" can "prepare the young reader to comprehend mature works in later years":

> If in the junior high school the pupil is able to discern the simple symbolic treatment of the theme of good versus evil in something like Annixter's *Swiftwater*—in one exciting scene a boy fights with a wolverine—he is making important preparation for reading later, say, the novels of Thomas Hardy, or Nathaniel Hawthorne. (239)

Although Burton's example seems unrealistically hopeful, given the reading interests and abilities of too many of today's adolescents, the point he makes needs to be reconsidered in today's educational climate. Getting students to read and to enjoy what they read is important, but that is only part of what we must accomplish in literature study. We must begin to emphasize to a much greater degree than we have thus far the literary elements of good adolescent fiction in order to help young adults become more sophisticated readers. In our efforts to engage nonreaders, entertain poor readers, and assure response from all readers, too many teachers have overlooked the possibilities young adult novels present for literary study. To teach literary concepts only through traditional literature—those works found in the anthologies—is to miss a great opportunity to teach adolescents about the wonderful ways in which good writers have created the fictive worlds that they, the young readers, find so easy to understand and enjoy.

To illustrate the kind of analyses that I think would help young readers gain insights into the art of literature, I have selected two young adult novels that throughout my years as a teacher educator have helped prospective English teachers appreciate the complexities of good young adult literature. One of the novels is straightforward and simple, Paul Zindel's *The Pigman;* the other novel, Robert Cormier's *I am the Cheese*, is difficult both structurally and thematically. It is a book that even college students find challenging as well as disturbing. Their appreciation of *I am the Cheese* as literature usually is achieved only through a thorough analysis of its literary elements, an analysis that is best achieved when we as a class attempt to discern how Cormier achieves his effects on the reader.

The Pigman

Because I approach my courses in young adult literature chronologically, *The Pigman* is one of the first contemporary novels that we study. Because the book was published in 1968, many of my students read this work in school or on their own when they were adolescents. (Not surprisingly, most of those students who were in the college "track" in their school are not familiar with young adult novels unless they discovered them on their own.) Students who studied the book in school remember only the basic story and the names of the two main characters. Some recall not wanting to read the book because the title sounded boring. Many also express their disappointment at the novel's conclusion, for recent editions of the book contain a promotional blurb on the back that implies Mr. Pignati's "secret" is so unusual that some readers antici-pate there will be a dead body in Mr. Pignati's basement! This is the context in which we begin to look at *The Pigman* as a work of literature.

Some students overlook "The Oath" at the beginning of the book and begin reading at chapter 1. Having done that, they miss a key element in how Zindel establishes the *tone* for the novel. The oath functions in at least two ways: it gets the reader to anticipate humor in the book, and it also establishes the "reality" of the main characters, John and Lorraine, for their signatures are at the end of the oath. It is an opening that captures the attention of readers at all levels.

The Oath

Being of sound mind and body on this 15th day of April in our sophomore year at Franklin High School, let it be know that Lorraine Jensen and John Conlan have decided to record the facts, and only the facts, about our experiences with Mr. Angelo Pignati.

Miss Reillen, the Cricket, is watching us at every moment because she is the librarian at Franklin High and thinks we're using her typewriter to copy a book report for our retarded English teacher.

The truth and nothing but the truth, until this memorial epic is finished, So Help Us God!

The "truth" of this "epic" is affirmed by John and Lorraine's signatures.

Few of my college students associate this beginning with the opening of *The Adventures of Huckleberry Finn*, where the narrator, Huck, introduces himself and the novel.

You don't know about me, without you have read a book by the name of "The Adventures of Tom Sawyer," but that ain't no matter. That book was made by Mr. Mark Twain, and he told the truth, mainly. There was things which he stretched, but mainly he told the truth. That is nothing. I never seen anybody but lied, one time or another, without it was Aunt Polly, or the widow, or maybe Mary. Aunt Polly—Tom's Aunt Polly, she is—and Mary, and the Widow Douglas, is all told about in that book—which is mostly a true book; with some stretchers, as I said before.

In both novels, the narrators establish that "truth" will be told. We anticipate humor from what the narrators tell us, but both works will provide the reader with not only humor, but with insights about the human experience, about human relationships, and about the culture in which the protagonists live. (Another excellent example where the opening paragraphs successfully establish the tone of the novel is John Knowles's *A Separate Peace*. The descriptions of the school and the repetition of the word *fear* anticipate the serious issues that will be addressed in the work.)

As these examples illustrate, *tone* is one of the literary concepts that we can help young readers understand. Using the opening of *The Pigman* as an initial introduction to the concept, followed by examples from throughout the novel, the novice reader has a relatively simple introduction to the elements that compose tone. For example, because Zindel uses two narrators, John and Lorraine, the reader can look for differences in the tone used by these two adolescents in their respective chapters. Throughout the novel, readers' feelings alternate between laughter and empathy for two fascinating but troubled adolescents. As the novel develops, the growth and development of the characters are reflected in subtle differences in tone. Although the novel opens with an oath that is humorous, the ending is somber:

> Our life would be what we make of it—nothing more, nothing less.
> Baboons.
> Baboons.
> They build their own cages, we could almost hear the Pigman whisper, as he took his children with him. (159)

After reading the novel, many young readers also see the parallel between the opening oath and the oath individuals swear in a court of law. Given the events of the story, it is understandable how the "oath" can foreshadow both the humorous and serious aspects of life. A challenge for adolescent readers would be to try to discover the points throughout the novel where the tone shifts. This kind of analysis would help adolescents understand how writers, through the use of particular words, in unique ways, can elicit certain kinds of responses from readers.

In addition to discussions concerning tone, *The Pigman* is also particularly appropriate for dealing with the concept of *point of view*. Because of the alternation of chapters—John and Lorraine take turns giving their version of the events that occur—young readers can easily see how point of view functions. Although both characters tell their stories from a first-person point of view, the variations in the retelling of identical events reveal the importance of who tells the story and how the story is told. Contrasting the chapters can show the limitations of one character's perspective. Clearly, one of the keys to the success of the novel with young readers is the author's ability to bring to life both John and Lorraine. We know them through their own words, their views of life and of each other, and their internal as well as external struggles. Reading their chapters is like reading their diaries, and we are drawn into their lives. As informed readers, we need to understand how Zindel achieves this effect. Looking at his use of point of view provides insights into how he is able to manipulate the reader to achieve the desired response.

In addition to discussing tone and point of view, Zindel's novel is also extremely effective for teaching concepts such as *characterization, motif, symbolism,*
and *foreshadowing.* The study of characterization is integrally related to point of
view in this novel. Given the novel's structure—the alternating chapters—it is
easy to get to know both characters. John and Lorraine talk about themselves,
each other, and other characters and events in the story. How they perceive
the world, and how others perceive them, is presented through the alternating
chapters. As many of my college students have noted, they feel as though they
know John and Lorraine very well because of all that the author reveals about
them through this technique.

Although the novel is relatively short, the two main characters establish
themselves as distinct individuals. John's chapter opens the novel with these
words:

> Now, I don't like school, which you might say is one of the factors that got
> us involved with this old guy we nicknamed the Pigman. Actually, I hate
> school, but then again most of the time I hate everything.
>
>   I used to really hate school when I first started at Franklin High. I hated
> it so much the first year they called me the Bathroom Bomber. Other kids
> got elected G.O. President and class secretary and lab-squad captain, but I
> got elected the Bathroom Bomber. They called me that because I used to
> set off bombs in the bathroom. I set off twenty-three bombs before I didn't
> feel like doing it anymore. (7)

Most readers understand John, for he represents the type of adolescent that
many know or remember from their own school days. He is a basically nice
kid, a misfit who got into trouble a great deal. By having John admit his dislike
of school, Zindel draws in even the most uninterested reader.

Our understanding of John is enhanced by Lorraine's description and analysis of him.

> He's six feet tall already, with sort of longish brown hair and blue eyes.
> He has these gigantic eyes that look right through you, especially if he's in
> the middle of one of his fantastic everyday lies. And he drinks and smokes
> more than any boy I ever heard of. The analysts would call his family the
> source problem or say he drinks and smokes to assert his independence. I
> tried to explain to him how dangerous it was, particularly smoking, and
> even went to the trouble of finding a case history similar to his in a book
> by Sigmund Freud. I almost had him convinced that smoking was an
> infantile, destructive activity when he pointed out a picture of Freud smok-
> ing a cigar on the book's cover. (14)

Lorraine's penchant for psychological analysis lends insight into her character as well as John's. Throughout the novel, Lorraine and John attempt to

understand each other as well as themselves. Zindel's characterization of his two main characters succeeds because he is able to develop believable adolescents. The relative simplicity of this novel enables teachers to help young readers easily understand and appreciate Zindel's craft.

Although *The Pigman* is particularly valuable in teaching the concepts of tone, point of view, and characterization, it can also be used to discuss *motif, symbolism,* and *foreshadowing.* "Games" constitute a motif in the novel. John and Lorraine meet Mr. Pignati though a phone game; in chapter 4 there is an illustration of a memorization game; chapter 6 has the snake game or quiz; and in chapter 10 they play the assassin game. Additionally, there is the "game" they played with Mr. Pignati as they "were zooming right from the porch through the living room and dining room down the hall into the room with the pigs" (108). The game, however, ends in disaster because Mr. Pignati "started to double over . . . and fell to the bottom of the stairs" (p. 109). Zindel's message about "games" is relatively easy to grasp; some games are innocent, but some result in disaster. Part of growing up is knowing which games to play. Perhaps most important, Zindel tries to get the young reader to think about the consequences of actions, whether bombing bathrooms or entering and interfering in the life of another person.

The most obvious example of symbolism in the novel deals with animal imagery: pigs (the name Pignati and his collection of pigs), monkeys, and baboons. The animal imagery is particularly appropriate, for John, Lorraine, and Mr. Pignati often visit the zoo where Mr. Pignati spends time with Bobo, the baboon. Zindel draws parallels between the animals and his main characters. For example, Lorraine describes the three of them as "three little monkeys" as they leave Beekman's toy department. "The Pigman, John, and me— three funny little monkeys" (88). Norton's destruction of the pigs during the party foreshadows Mr. Pignati's death, as does the death of Bobo near the conclusion of the novel. Also, as noted earlier, the novel concludes with a parallel between the animals in the zoo and humans who "build their own cages."

There is clearly more to be discovered in this novel—the theme of maturation, the dangers of "trespassing" into others' lives, adolescents' acceptance of parents growing older, and the desire for independence, among other issues. But it is counterproductive to try to "teach" too much from any one literary work. I think we lose the interest of the reader if we do not limit our analyses of any one novel to just a few literary elements. I have often told my students that if they can help their pupils understand just one new literary concept with each work that they study, they will be moving their novice readers on to greater literary understandings. Perhaps the best statement concerning the dangers of "overteaching" a literary work came from one of my college students years ago—I wish I could recall his name. After an extended discussion of why most adolescents dislike poetry, the young man, who considered himself to be a poet, said, "All my English teachers taught me how to take a poem apart, but no one ever taught me how to put it back together." Good, meaningful analysis concerning the literary elements of fiction should aid students in "putting it back together" in ways that enhance their understanding and appreciation of the work. If it does not, then we are not helping their literary understandings; instead, we are simply leaving them with fragments of literary works.

I am the Cheese

I am the Cheese is consistently one of the most difficult novels for my college students, yet also one of their favorite works for analysis. Cormier's novel is particularly appropriate for dealing with two concepts that inexperienced readers seem to find particularly elusive: *style* and *structure*. Because a number of essays have analyzed Cormier's work, and this novel in particular, I will try to avoid repeating what has been stated elsewhere. The most recent study of Cormier is Patricia J. Campbell's *Presenting Robert Cormier* (1990), one of the books in the Laurel-Leaf Library of Young Adult Authors. In her chapter on *I am the Cheese*, Campbell states that the "triple strands that are braided together to make the story, the three alternating levels on which the narrative progresses, are an intricate but internally consistent device" (85). According to Campbell, these are the three levels of narrative:

> The bike ride is told in first-person present tense. The tapes, as dialogue, have neither person nor tense (but we assume they are happening in the present), and the revelation of Adam's past that grows out of these tapes proceeds chronologically and is in third-person past tense. (85)

Structurally, then, there are three levels of story, and three points of view. As Campbell notes, this is extremely confusing when the novel is read for the first time. Only in subsequent readings does it become possible to see the relationships that exist among the various levels of story. Campbell describes the novel as a mosaic. My students compare it to a jigsaw puzzle, a puzzle that is extremely difficult to put together because the pieces are so varied. In fact, one student noted that even when the last piece is in place, the "picture" is still not clear. But good novels, like good puzzles, became easier to "put together" the more we work with them.

Although the internal structure of the novel is complex, the external structure—the juxtaposition of the "tapes" with the bike journey and the past—provides a means to start discussions of structure. After reading the first two chapters, readers can begin to understand how the writer is using the different levels and points of view to move the story forward. What emerges, then, is a structure or form that is integral to the story. In effect, form and content merge. The way the story is told is essential to the content of the story. A clear example of how the structure relates to the story is that the opening lines of the novel are repeated at the end. The story is cyclical. Like Adam's interrogations, it begins anew.

If structure is the overall form of the story, the design that the author has used, *style* constitutes the manner of expression that the writer has chosen to tell the story. Young readers seem to understand the term best when it is simply described as *how* the writer tells the story. Consistently, Cormier's style captures the pace and intensity of the events in the story. For example, the opening is extremely powerful.

> I am riding the bicycle and I am on Route 31 in Monument, Massachu-setts, on my way to Rutterburg, Vermont, and I'm pedaling furiously because this is an old-fashioned bike, no speeds, no fenders, only the warped tires and the brakes that don't always work and the handlebars with cracked rubber grips to steer with. A plain bike—the kind my father rode as a kid years ago. It's cold as I pedal along, the wind like a snake slithering up my sleeves and into my jacket and my pants legs, too. But I keep pedaling, I keep pedaling. (11)

The first sentence parallels the "furious" pace of the boy pedaling the bike. There is an urgency in the tone, an urgency that couches something overtly evil—"like a snake slithering up my sleeves." The alliteration of that phrase—when read out loud it sounds ominously like hissing—presents even to the most inexperienced reader a sense of foreboding. Throughout the novel, Cormier is able to capture the mood of a scene by his powerful use of language. For example, he conveys the cold, clinical, almost mechanistic tone of the taped interviews through brief, abrupt dialogue.

> A: It's hazy—just a series of impressions.
> T: Let the impressions come.
>   (5-second interval)
> A: That night—
> T: Tell me about that night. (16)

These clinical interviews are juxtaposed against vivid descriptions of Adam in the clinic: "He was in bed and the sheets were twisted around him and his body was hot, his eyes like raw onions, head aching. He cried out once or twice, softly, tentatively" (17). Early in the novel the inhumanity toward Adam becomes apparent.

Throughout the novel, Cormier is able to enhance our knowledge of *what* happens by his vivid descriptions. One of the most memorable is the descrip-tion of the car accident.

> Into them. Into his father, his mother, himself. The car smashing, shatter-ing. A flash of steel, sun glinting, and he felt himself, crazily, moving

through the air, no feeling, no pain, no sense of flight, but actually in the air, not flying but moving as if in slow motion, everything slowed down, tumbling now and twisting and in the tumbling and the twisting he saw his mother die. Instantly. (206)

The one-word sentence, "Instantly," punctuates the almost dreamlike slow motion of the accident itself. It is final. As he says at the end of this passage, "He looked at his mother, her head at the wrong angle, a rag doll tossed away" (208). His mother's lifeless body is like a child's toy—limp, with eyes that are "sightless, vacant." The horror of the accident is conveyed by altering the pace of the description and by evoking parallels that all readers can understand. By comparing the dead mother to a rag doll, Cormier assures a strong emotional response from readers.

Although the novel is complex both structurally and thematically, it has some very simple and obvious literary elements that are worthwhile noting. The use of names, for instance, is relatively easy for students to analyze. The name "Grey," for example, embodies the ambiguities of good and evil; he also represents the unknown, the "grey" areas of life. "Adam" is the symbol of innocence because of the biblical allusion and also because children traditionally represent innocence in fiction. "Farmer," the name given Adam's family to replace their real name, Delmonte, also evokes purity. Throughout the American literary tradition, the country, embodied in the farmer, has epitomized innocence because to work with the earth is to be in contact with God.

The analyses that this novel has received since its publication attest to its power and sophistication. Adults as well as adolescents are challenged by its structure, style, and theme. It speaks to readers of all ages about the loss of innocence and the pervasive nature of evil in current society. But only through an analysis of its literary elements is it possible for young readers to understand why it is a powerful work.

Young adult fiction will continue to grow and mature in the coming years. As my discussion of *The Pigman* and *I am the Cheese* has revealed, there is more to good young adult novels than just an entertaining story. Although some young adult novels, like formula fiction, are best used for diversion, the substantive ones can help young readers expand their knowledge of literature and the literary elements that undergird all good fiction. Unless we help adolescent readers understand how writers achieve their effects, we are keeping them from understanding the power of language to evoke thought and feelings. Perhaps with more discussions of the literary aspects of young adult fiction, those who are still skeptics about this form of literature will realize that it is an important part of today's diverse literary landscape.

References

Burton, Dwight L. 1970. *Literature Study in the High Schools,* 3d ed. New York: Holt, Rinehart and Winston.

Campell, Patricia J. 1990. *Presenting Robert Cormier.* New York: Dell.

Cormier, Robert. 1977. *I am the Cheese.* New York: Dell.

Donelson, Kenneth L., and Alleen Pace Nilsen. 1989. *Literature for Today's Young Adults,* 3d ed. Glenview, Ill.: Scott, Foresman.

Knowles, John. 1960. *A Separate Peace.* New York: Bantam,

Mertz, Maia Pank, 1975. "Understanding the Adolescent Reader," *Theory Into Practice* 14, 3 (June): 55–58.

_____, 1978. "The 'New Realism': Traditional Cultural Values in Recent Young Adult Fiction," *Phi Delta Kappan* (October): 101–05.

Mertz, Maia Pank, and Robert J. Mertz, 1976. "Adolescents Against Society Institutional Values in *The Magician* and *The Chocolate War*," *Focus: Teaching English Language Arts* 3, 2 (Winter): 27–35.

Mertz, Maia Pank, and David England, 1983. "The Legitimacy of American Adolescent Fiction," *School Library Journal* (October): 119–23.

Mueller, Al. 1974. "The Adolescent Novel in the Classroom." *Media and Methods* (April): 32–33.

Small, Robert C. 1977. "The Adolescent Novel as a Working Model." *ALAN,* pp. 4, 2 (Winter): 4–6.

_____, 1979. "The Y.A. Novel in the Composition Program (Part II)." *English Journal* (October): 75–77.

Zindel, Paul. 1968. *The Pigman.* New York: Dell.

15

Reviewing Young Adult Books: The VOYA Editor Speaks Out

Dorothy M. Broderick

Basically, there are three types of review media. The first, best personified by *Booklist*, employs a full-time staff of in-house reviewers; the second type, such as the *New York Times Book Review*, employs an editor who selects outside reviewers who are paid for the reviews; and finally, there are the periodicals with a paid editor but whose reviewers are all unpaid volunteers. *Voice of Youth Advocates* falls into the third category.

There is one important point to keep in mind when reading what follows: *VOYA* began as the work of two dedicated youth librarians; it was not conceived by some corporate structure. It began as a personal periodical and remains so to this day. I make all decisions about content; there is no editorial board, no advisory committee, no harassment from its corporate owner, Scarecrow Press.

There is both joy and frustration when dealing with volunteers whether as teacher aides or as reviewers. Since there is a strong tendency to emphasize the problems of a review periodical, I begin with the joys.

An Editor's Joys

At any given time, *VOYA* has close to two hundred reviewers. This is a huge extended family for me. When the Oakland-San Francisco earthquake struck, I worried about six people, only one of whom I've ever met personally. Were they okay; were their libraries and schools okay. Fortunately, the answer was yes, although one library required considerable repairs. When a tornado blazes through Indiana, barely missing a town where a reviewer resides, I worry about whether she was in its path. Worrying about other people's welfare may not strike some as a joy, but since I live almost the life of a hermit, caring about other people reminds me that I am connected to a bigger world than the narrow physical one I inhabit. There is an even more personal sense of caring that occurs. In my years as editor, I have "lost" two reviewers to drunk drivers who left them quadriplegic; one reviewer had her home broken into and was raped; others marry, become pregnant, and divorce. Spouses suffer heart attacks or strokes; elderly parents die; and friends acquire AIDS. Wonderful people like Elaine Martindell die long before their time. Many Americans view school and public librarians as somehow a class apart from society. If these people could occupy my chair for just a few months they would know that each and every one of us is vulnerable to the violence and disasters that permeate society. Understanding that reality just might lessen the tendency of politicians and social critics to discuss life in terms of "them" and "us."

Beyond these cosmic concerns, there is constant joy in reading a totally felicitous phrase by a reviewer that leaps from the page. There is joy in seeing reviewers become active in the American Library Association and become leaders within the Young Adult Library Services Division. There is joy in watching authors of articles as well as reviewers gain the self-confidence to write books. When Kim Sands is voted Maine's Teacher of the Year, and Lola Teubert is granted Indiana's Librarian of the Year award, I burst with pride to have them among our reviewers.

Beyond the joys offered by the reviewers is the joy of dealing with an exciting literature. Although it can be fashionable to denigrate young adult literature, the fact is that careful reading of the books could alert a society to as-yet-undiscovered societal problems. Fran Arrick was years ahead of the weekly magazines and daily newspapers when she wrote *Tunnel Vision*, a book about teenage suicide. Now we have scholarly studies of the phenomenon. S. E. Hinton's *The Outsiders* remains a perennial favorite because class-based gang warfare continues, even if the major groups change from white against white to Hispanic versus blacks or blacks versus Jews.

I began by outlining just a few of the joys that accrue to a review editor because without them, the annoyances and frustrations could make the job unbearable. Just as a person can love a child while seeing the flaws in the child's personality, so a review editor can care about reviewers while ranting and raging about some of their characteristics.

Frustrations Abound

A primary frustration is the number of youth librarians who do not read adult books and really don't want to. The only major exception to this are the science fiction, fantasy, and horror fans. Since the goal of young adult services is to serve as a bridge from children's books to adult books, librarians without a solid adult literature background have no ability to lead the young across the bridge. Sad to say, many of them don't even understand when I draw the analogy to Thornton Wilder's *The Bridge of San Luis Rey* because they have never read the book.

I am not talking just about adult books they could recommend to young adults. There are adult titles such as Shelby Steele's *The Content of Our Character* and Stephen Carter's *Reflections of an Affirmative Action Baby* that affect social policy in the United States and need to be part of the public dialogue. I may be a physical hermit, working alone as I do in my enclosed sun porch, but I fear there are too many people in our country who are intellectual hermits, even when the issues have great impact on the future of their jobs.

Part of this problem of ignoring adult books stems from a misguided (to me) emphasis on giving kids what they want, which is, as Richard Peck has said succinctly, "another book just like the last one only different." I have no problem with the concept of giving young people what they want. In fact, when Mary K. Chelton and I began *VOYA*, its underlying principle was that librarians working with adolescents should recognize that these young people have a basic right to read what they want to read, not what we wish they would read. This philosophy mandates a collection that includes books featuring Nancy Drew for younger teens and series such as The Babysitters Club as well as photo essays on serial killers for older teens. However, saying that does not remove from the librarian the responsibility to do all she or he can to expand the horizons of the young people being served. We cannot want what we do not know. It is the role of librarians to expand our "wants" list. To do that, librarians must have their own expanded lists of interests.

Beyond having an interest in current events, I love the few reviewers who actually seem to know something about what happened before the current year. For example, when I receive a review on Bataan in World War II and the reviewer does not tell us whether it deals with the infamous "Bataan Death March," I reject the review. Similarly, when Corregidor is the topic and the review doesn't tell us it was from this tiny island that MacArthur made his famous "I shall return" promise, I reject it. I have no way of knowing whether the material is in the book and the librarian doesn't know it is important, or whether the author should receive a small slap on the wrist for not including the information. If the book is truly significant, by which I mean by a well-known author and/or not part of the numerous all-of-a-kind series, I query the reviewer. Otherwise, the review simply gets tossed.

Saving reviewers from themselves requires an editor to walk a fine line. For example, one review damned a book with faint praise because all the characters were adults, observing in the process that teens don't relate to adult characters. That sentence set me thinking about such books as *One Flew Over the Cuckoo's Nest* and dozens of others. I deleted the sentence and explained to the reviewer why I deleted it. If it started me down that path, other readers might be inclined to do the same, and thus the overall thrust of the review would be lost in the resulting static.

Sometimes I do let reviewers hang themselves. I published a review of an Australian book in which the reviewer complained about strange Australian words such as "shearing," that the author did not explain! Other reviewers complain about "British" words in important titles. I let them complain, and I'll tell you why. I hope most of *VOYA's* subscribers are bright enough to understand how silly these objections are. American young people who read can't be that dumb!

I lived for almost six years in Canada. Canadian young people read books from the Commonwealth countries and the United States. Words such as harbor are spelled harbour in some books. The slang comes from all the English-speaking countries. No one in Canada complains that the "strange" vocabulary will deter reading enjoyment. Only in America!

Librarians are normal human beings. They miss deadlines; they fail to read instructions; they tell us too much about a book or too little. They drop a new name into the third paragraph without telling us who this character is.

Worst of all, from an editor's viewpoint, they have their share of prejudices. That's okay; we all do. The problem for the editor is in knowing what these prejudices are so the reviewer and the book match. No one who is basically homophobic should be asked to evaluate a nonjudgmental book on homosexuality. A pro-choice person should not be asked to evaluate a book that focuses on abortion as murder. A right-wing Republican should not be given Gary Trudeau's Doonesbury books for review!

For me, it is an article of faith that every book deserves to be read by someone basically in tune with its premises. To aid in that process, our reviewer interest forms do ask some very personal questions. We want to know how potential reviewers view themselves on the political and religious spectrums, and whether they are pro or con on explosive issues such as abortion. I must stress that no one is rejected as a reviewer because of personal views. The information is used to match reviewer and book and for no other purpose.

There is, however, one area in which I exercise total control that might well be properly labeled the height of authoritarianism. The cover letter that goes out to potential reviewers tells them point blank that they may not use phrases in a review designed to encourage subscribers to reject the book because of potential controversy. The reviewer's job is to adequately describe the content of the book in such detail as necessary for a reader of the review to be able to make a decision as to whether the book will fit into the collection that reader is building.

Personally, I don't much like it that there are librarians who will buy no book containing a homosexual character, thus depriving about 10 percent of their patrons of the right to find themselves in any book in the library. I don't much like it that some librarians have a long list of such banned topics, including such diverse subjects as suicide and witchcraft, but it is not my role to hide from these people the content of books, thus trying to "sneak" a book into their collection. Moreover, I don't much like it that not all library review media refrain from "warning off" potential buyers.

The system of matching reviewers with the right book generally works well with nonfiction titles; trouble arises when it comes to fiction. Many books are reviewed from galleys and contain no information about the book beyond its bibliographic data and suggested age group. Before pursuing this topic, this is a good time to point out that I do not ever read a book before publishing the review, unless I am its reviewer. Some publishers do send two copies of books, and I set aside the second copy of some titles to read at my leisure. However, if I were to read the book before I published the review, it would prejudice my editing of the review. I know that to be true, and any editor who claims otherwise is a fool or a liar.

The review belongs to the reviewer, not the editor. That is a second article of faith in publishing *Voice of Youth Advocates*.

Back to fiction. There is often no way to know that a book such as Bette Greene's *The Drowning of Stephan Jones* is going to be a searing indictment of fundamentalism's bigotry against those its followers perceive as violating God's will, in this case, homosexuals. This book is a perfect example of an editor's dilemma: the book can offend those who will object to the portrait of the evangelicals; it can also offend those who find homosexuality an abomination. *Weetzie Bat* arrives without any alert that it is breaking new ground in literary style for young adult literature. Thus it becomes the luck of the draw when a controversial title ends up in the hands of the reviewer most likely to appreciate its content. But then, that's what makes reviewing a horse race. It isn't for the faint of heart, either as reviewer or editor.

As an editor, I recognize when the reviewer is trying to warn off purchase of the book when a phrase such as "the extensive use of profanity will cause trouble in many communities." But when I see a phrase such as "the author depicts irresponsible sexual behavior between the two main characters," I have no way of knowing whether this means sexual intercourse without adequate safeguards against pregnancy and the transmission of AIDS and other sexually transmitted diseases or that the young people *had* sex, which is in and of itself irresponsible?

When I know the reviewer personally from encounters at ALA or other conferences, I generally know the answer. When the reviewer has been reviewing for a lengthy period and has a track record, I know the answer. With new reviewers, I am at a loss to determine what the phrase means and must query the reviewer before letting the phrase appear in print.

Whence the Books Come

No article on reviewing can be complete without a discussion of the publishing industry, upon which all else depends. An uninterrupted flow of review books depends on some individual within each publishing house whose job it is to see that the review copies reach the right person at the correct address. Unfortunately for a review editor, these people most closely resemble the marbles in a Chinese Checkers game: they hop all over the place.

The person responsible for sending review books usually works out of the publicity department. This is separate and apart from the library promotion department housing the person who works with schools and libraries. Juvenile publishers (from which stem the supply of young adult titles) generally bring their library promotion people to major conferences. Rarely is the publicist part of the group attending the American Library Association and other national conferences.

I have a theory about this that may, or may not, be accurate. I suspect the publicist responsible for young adult books is working as a minnow in a large department primarily concerned with getting adult authors on the *Today* show and other high-profile television programs. They are also busy planning a cross-country tour in which the adult author will make endless appearances on talk radio shows and local television programs. Publicity for young adult books (or children's books for that matter) is not among the first one thousand priorities in such departments.

However rotten that situation may be, it pales in comparison with the problem of trying to unlock adult books from adult publicists for review in a piddling magazine designed to reach professionals working with adolescents. Here again we need to understand that just because people work in publishing they are not very different from the general public. Many, if not most, people working in adult publishing simply do not understand that teenagers ought to be reading adult books by age fifteen or sixteen and that good readers are "into" adult literature.

Whenever possible, when requesting an adult title for review, my letter is sprinkled with the names of juvenile/young adult people within the publishing house who can verify my credentials. It is a sad commentary on the adult publishing world that it contains people who actually do not understand that Stephen King is even more popular with adolescents than with adults. But, as my favorite Kurt Vonnegut, Jr. character, Billy Pilgrim, would say, "So it goes."

These annoyances with the publishing world are nothing compared with how I feel about the current rash of supposedly nonfiction titles pouring into the office with the power of Niagara Falls. Good nonfiction requires passion! It is the most significant factor missing in the long series of what I consider expensive books that are little more than illustrated encyclopedia articles.

Librarians buy the books because they meet school assignment needs and that leads me to want to join the group bashing public education. (I don't, and never will, but it sure is a temptation!) *VOYA* reviews a cross-section of the books, most of them favorably, and I bite my lip and print those reviews. But I'd be lying if I said any of this made me feel good about the state of publishing or librarianship.

Since there is no way any periodical can review all of the nonfiction assembly-line books being produced, the situation leads me to practice what they may be called "selection by quota" or "affirmative action," depending on one's viewpoint. When a dozen or more books arrive, decisions have to be made, so the editor finds herself saying, "We'll do this Hispanic biography, this African-American, this Native American," etc. There is no way of knowing that the books selected for review are as well written as those donated to the school next door, and I worry about that, but space limitations impose decisions that must be lived with.

We need nonfiction with both passion and compassion written by authors like Milton Meltzer and Jim Haskins and Russell Freedman because only by involving the reader in ethical decisions does the reader have a chance of grasping that the past may tell us something important we need to know about how we live the present. Such books cannot be written by authors given specifications by editors to produce ninety-six pages of text to complement illustrations. Producing such books requires a lot more work by editors than they appear willing to give these days.

I am fully aware that this situation is not the fault of the editors working to produce books. The structure of publishing today has changed from the days when giants like Elizabeth Riley of Crowell gave us books to stretch the mind rather than meet the financial bottom line. The current gurus of big business seem not to have noticed that good books can sell every bit as well as mediocre books. What they notice is that it seems to cost a little more to publish a good book, and they figure the cost isn't worth it. No wonder the United States has a literacy problem.

Although I have very firm opinions about nonfiction, I plead guilty to mixed emotions about fiction for young adults. On the one hand, I don't ever want us to go back to the days of my youth when everything was squeaky clean and those of us who lived lives of quiet desperation never found any of our problems in books, yet I also wonder whether there can't be some balance in young adult fiction. Nobody needs to be hammered over the head all the time with the horrors of modern teen life: drugs, sex, incest, abuse, etc.

On the other hand, *VOYA's* attempt to be fair to the numerous Christian publishers usually results in reviews that at best can be termed "lukewarm." These books are squeaky clean; they also tend to be boring and preachy. The book editors in these publishing houses seem not to understand that putting readers to sleep isn't exactly the best way to convince the young that leading a religion-based life is worth considering.

In Conclusion

Being a review editor is really no different than any other job in society that requires judgment, intellectual curiosity, discretion, and a sense of humor. It isn't a glamorous position, but it beats digging ditches, and if it is done well, it can actually make a contribution to the intellectual wellbeing of the nation. It provides the opportunity to see a larger picture than is offered the individual author or book editor. That the picture is not all joyous or all disastrous would seem to indicate that librarianship and publishing are not in total disarray. Things could be worse; they could also be better. On balance, we're all doing just fine, thank you.

16

What We Know About Nonfiction and Young Adult Readers and What We Need to Do About It

Richard F. Abrahamson and Betty Carter

Some of the most satisfying stories in literature concern characters who triumph over adversity: the good-hearted Cinderella wins the prince from her selfish stepsisters; the ugly duckling turns into a glorious creature far more beautiful than his less glamorous tormentors; and Puss 'N Boots, a simple cat, outwits a selfish lord to bring honor and riches to his master. In each case, the main character works hard, endures ridicule, and succeeds alone without the outward trappings of wealth, beauty, or advantage.

These folktale plots apply to nonfiction for children and young adults in the 1990s. Today an elegant swan, a genre named nonfiction, now stands out among that once exclusive flock of stories, poems, and plays. For years fiction, poetry, and drama have persisted as the dominant components of children's and young adult literature in course offerings, annual awards, textbook content, and research studies.[1] Fiction particularly sets the norm for the very definition of genre, for the term nonfiction defines by exclusion and "tacitly implies these books are lacking a vital element."[2] Gradually, though, story is losing its exclusionary hold on literature, and nonfiction is emerging as a powerful and important force in the publishing world. Like Cinderella attending the ball and hearing the guests wonder "Who is she?" or "Where did she come from?" nonfiction has been sitting on the literary sidelines for years just waiting for recognition.

While modern nonfiction—with its stunning visual formats, highly readable prose, and appealing subjects—is currently enjoying a rebirth of interest among publishers, librarians, and teachers who work with literature for children and young adults, it has existed for over a thousand years. Far removed from the exciting volumes of today, early books of this type were primarily teaching devices not notable for style, organization, or format. In the seventh century, the monk Aldhelm wrote the first text for school instruction, an informational book in the form of a dialogue between teacher and pupil. At the same time, the Venerable Bede provided children with a catalog of scientific facts from the natural world. Four hundred years later, Alexander Neckham wrote *De Utensilibus*, a book for youngsters that describes everyday household utensils, as well as the diverse skills necessary for various tasks such as cooking, weaving, farming, and navigation.[3] Although each of these early works includes unique information, all were written with the same purpose: to teach youngsters.

The introduction of printing and the consequent proliferation of available books did not interrupt this pattern. Even the first picture book—*Orbis Pictus*, written in 1657—is best described as a "combination picture book, Latin text and natural history," which intended to show children a "graphic view of every one of the things in Heaven and Earth."[4] This function also characterized volumes in the English-speaking world. William Caxton, who in the fifteenth century introduced movable type to England, included a few works for children in his publications, believing that youngsters should read only books that would improve their minds, their manners, and their morals.

Not until the eighteenth century did children's literature begin the slow transformation from a cultural artifact, whose principal intent was instruction, to a popular product, which also attempted to entertain. Two nonfiction volumes anticipate this movement toward pleasure reading: Isaac Watts's *The Knowledge of the Heavens and the Earth Made Easy or the First Principles of Geography and Astronomy Explained* (1726), and Thomas Boreman's *A Description of a Great Variety of Animals, and Vegetables . . . especially for the Entertainment of Youth* (1736).[5] Although amusement may not have been the primary goal of these narratives, Watts's phrase *"made easy"* and Boreman's *"especially for the entertainment of youth"* indicate that the authors were sensitive to the recreational potential of literature.

John Newbery expanded upon that meager foundation and established it solidly in the publishing world with the 1744 printing of *A Little Pretty Pocket Book*, generally recognized as the first children's book written primarily for youngsters' enjoyment. In 1759 and 1761 he again stressed the importance of entertainment, this time through two nonfiction works, *A Pretty Book of Pictures for Little Masters and Misses; or, Tommy Trip's History of Birds and Beasts; with a familiar Description of each in Verse and Prose*, and *The Newtonian System of Phi-*

losophy, adapted to the Capacities of Young Gentlemen and Ladies, and familiarized and made entertaining by Objects with which they are intimately acquainted.[6]

Newbery, however important historically, remained a lone figure in children's literature in the eighteenth century. The influence of women known as "The Little Female Academy" dominated all other publishing by emphasizing moral instruction and strict realism in works for children. Over a fifty-year period they not only wrote didactic precepts couched within unimaginative stories, but also successfully directed publishers to print only moral treatises for children.

Adopting both the popular and the preachy, Americans eagerly seized upon these publishing trends from England. Isaiah Thomas emulated John Newbery's success by printing his books in the colonies, and American authors collectively known as "The Vale of Tears" wrote original works for children imitating "The Little Female Academy" in both tone and style.

By the end of the eighteenth century books to amuse children and those to teach them had both become established, although the latter enjoyed a firmer foundation than the former. Nonfiction works from within both camps differed only in methods of presentation. No matter what the focus, content consisted of descriptions of everyday items, instruction in manners, or information on the natural world.

During the nineteenth century, American authors for children began to influence nonfiction as we know it today. Thomas Wentworth Higginson, George Makepeace Towle, and Charles Carleton Coffin wrote histories, each focusing on a distinctive age to be experienced through both biography and event rather than on a series of facts to be learned. These authors brought fresh content and style to nonfiction books and thus encouraged others to take their infant field and nurture it by experimenting with format, presentation, and subject matter.[7]

By the early twentieth century, both technological advances in printing and philosophical changes in education had set the stage for the rise of the modern information book. For the first time, pictures could be reduced or enlarged without loss of quality, colors could be more faithfully reproduced, and illustrations could be located at any place in the text rather than having to be grouped for insertion. Such advances allowed authors to depart from their primary dependence on prose for content and signaled the birth of a natural partnership between text and illustrations.[8]

At the same time, Lucy Sprague Mitchell published her *Here and Now Story Book*, a popular work advocating "that children's earliest literature be about the real world—the 'magic' of plumbing and electric lights—rather than fairy tales of kings and princesses in the faraway and long ago."[9] Unlike similar statements from "The Little Female Academy" and "The Vale of Tears" two hundred years previously, Mitchell's viewpoints were allowed to coexist with those of authors who wrote fanciful works for children. What Lucy Sprague Mitchell did was both recognize and popularize the notion that youngsters find wonder in discovery.

Mitchell's advocacy for introducing science and technology to young people was accompanied by the appearance of several fine authors, such as Herbert Zim, who wrote science books exclusively for children and that newly recognized group of readers now known as young adults. Raymond Ditmars, Roy Chapman Andrews, Franklyn Branley, Carroll Lane Fenton, and William Scheele, adult authors and prominent authorities in their respective scientific fields, eagerly entered children's book publishing. These scholars lent a respectability to juvenile informational works as they introduced young people to fresh discoveries and new, exciting fields of study.

Unfortunately, this trend for information books to present facts and concepts which not only teach, but also entertain and delight, ends at the midpoint of the twentieth century. At that time, nonfiction publishing became the plain stepchild of juvenile literature with the proliferation of the informational series book, a product that marked nonfiction publications for the next twenty years.

In 1953 Jean Lindquist, then editor of *The Horn Book*, reviewed forty-nine books from five popular nonfiction series: *The American Heritage Series, Landmark Books, Real Books, Signature Books, and Winston Adventure Books.* Although predisposed to like the series books, Lindquist admitted, "I confess that I felt more in sympathy with them before I began to read the first book than after I had finished the forty-ninth!"[10] She concluded that although many fine authors, such as James Daugherty, Katherine Shippen, William Steele, and MacKinlay Kantor, were writing for series, none of these publications represented their finest work, and, "although there are some good books in all this mass-produced material, many more are pretty dull reading."[11]

Such utilitarian dispensation of facts continued in a flood of informational books which poured forth in the 1960s and 1970s. The publication of these works was encouraged by the availability of federal monies to libraries, the decline of textbooks in school curricula, and the proliferation of knowledge.[12]

Some authors took the practical advice of Illa Podendorf, first given in 1974, which, in effect, instructed them to examine the subjects of nonfiction and write books only in fields where information was lacking.[13] Gradually, this steady growth toward merely binding collections of facts with an eye on publishers' backlists was tempered by authors like Kathryn Lasky, who were "searching for the story among the truths, the facts, the lies, and the realities,"[14] or Robert Hofsinde, who wanted "to leave something of [his life's work] with the young people of America,"[15] or Milton Meltzer, who writes "to find some pattern or meaning in the struggle to realize his own humanity,"[16] or Laurence Pringle, who wishes to "acknowledge that the world is a complex place but that the complexity can be explored and understood."[17]

Authors like Hofsinde, Lasky, Meltzer, and Pringle reveal the same purposes in writing as did the scientists Scheele, Branley, and Ditmars in the early part of this century. These intentions are reflected in their works and represent an important shift in the writing of nonfiction. The didactic books published before the eighteenth century used facts as a weapon to instill moral beliefs in children. The utilitarian books of the 1960s used facts as morsels of information for children to accept and digest. And the personal books of the 1980s and '90s use facts as information to be shared with children trying to make sense of their world. All three styles appear in modern works for children and young adults, but it is the last that has been rewarded by increased attention from adult critics and young readers.

Format as well as focus characterizes the changes in the last two decades. James Cross Giblin, both an author and publisher of nonfiction books, describes four major alterations in informational books during this time. First of all, new titles often focus on one segment or aspect of a subject, a device intended to lead youngsters to generalizations about the whole. Second, text is more concise and tightly written, and fictionalization is allowed to bring facts into focus. Third, authors and publishers consider illustrations from the onset of book development, trying to fuse illustration and text into a unified whole. And last, visual appeal is considered. Type size is often larger than the utilitarian nine point, trim size is more generous than the minimal margins common just fifteen years ago, and page formatting, which places illustrations and text together, is an integral part of design.[18]

Reading Interest Studies

Yet, no matter how personable or how dressed up nonfiction became, it would have remained a literary wallflower unless children and young adults asked it to dance by paying attention to it. In great numbers they have. The majority of reading interest studies that include data about nonfiction preferences have been conducted in school settings. Although methodologies may differ, the conclusions remain identical: Children and young adults from preschool classes to senior high campuses read nonfiction.

In 1984, Glenda Childress, an elementary school librarian, analyzed the reading selections of her kindergarten and first-grade students over a period of eighteen weeks. Of the 1,184 books circulated during that time, 40 percent were cataloged as nonfiction, strongly suggesting that even the youngest children are drawn to informational works.[19] Slightly older children also read nonfiction. Ten years prior to the Childress study, Judith Blair reported that approximately one-fifth of the reading material chosen by the second-, third-, and fourth-grade students she studied consisted of nonfiction.[20]

Daniel Fader discovered the importance of nonfiction in the reading lives of teens more than twenty-five years ago when he conducted the research that led to his popular *Hooked on Books*. Fader's program, instituted in the Maxey Boy's Training School, involved surrounding these adolescents with paperback books and letting them choose their reading material. Fader writes: "Who among us would have bet on Wilford Funk and Norman Lewis' *30 Days to a More Powerful Vocabulary* or Ruth Gleeson and James Colvin's *Words Most Often Misspelled and Mispronounced* as best sellers in *any* school? Why should Adrian Paradis' *From High School to a Job* get almost as much action as certain lesser war, spy and detective novels?"[21]

Five years later, George Norvell used data collected from his massive nation-wide study and concluded that a strong interest in nonfiction emerges at about the fourth grade and that interest grows during adolescence.[22] More recently, Guy Ellis projected that at least 50 percent of the total reading among high school students was nonfiction.[23] Clearly, children and young adults are reading nonfiction. But what nonfiction are they reading?

That is precisely the question the two of us asked in 1985. We wondered whether nonfiction reading selections were idiosyncratic; whether common subjects and particular books appealed to a number of readers; or whether commonalities in format, structure, and methods of presentation could be found among books read by children. We first of all decided on a method for exploring these issues and chose to examine circulation records from three diverse junior high school libraries.[24] We investigated junior high readers because findings from this age group can be extrapolated to upper elementary-age children as well as to young adults in their first years of senior high school.

In order to determine what nonfiction books these teenagers were reading, we monitored the library circulation records of three junior high schools in Houston, Texas, for twenty-six weeks, from September 1985 until the spring break of 1986. Approximately 3,000 students and 50,000 circulations were involved in the study. Although 200 titles emerged as popular across all three campuses, these individual works are of less importance than are the common features we identified from the body of frequently circulated books. Because specific titles go out of print or are replaced by newer works, teachers and librarians armed with only a list of popular books can at best offer limited reading guidance. However, a knowledge of those features of favored nonfiction selections equips professionals with important information for evaluating existing publications, as well as for recommending new titles. Four such common characteristics stood out among the popular reading choices of these junior high students.

First, the majority of these books were not circulated for school assignments; clearly they were read for pleasure. Many adults erroneously suspect that junior and senior high students read increasing numbers of nonfiction books because they have more research requirements than do their elementary counterparts. Although the emphasis on research may exist, it does not translate into popular nonfiction circulations. For example, the most widely circulated book across all three campuses—hands down, fiction and nonfiction—was *The Guinness Book of World Records*. It was not accepted for book reports, it was not mentioned in classes, excerpts were not printed in the literature texts, and it was not read aloud by teachers. *The Guinness Book* had no formal ties to instruction, yet it remained the number one book circulated by the 3,000 youngsters in the study.

In addition to circulating *The Guinness Book*, these junior high students checked out great numbers of drawing books. Not only did these works not complement the school curriculum, they represented the antithesis of it. In all three schools the art curricula stressed free expression, color, abstract design, and collage. But these drawing books are copy books, and precisely the kinds of structured drawing negated by the curriculum.

The most popular of these copy books circulated came from a series by Lee J. Ames entitled the *Draw 50* series. These books, which have such diverse titles as *Draw 50 Dinosaurs, Draw 50 Dogs, Draw 50 Cats,* and *Draw 50 Famous Faces,* are all designed around the same format: Ames combines basic geometric shapes (circles, lines, rectangles) to create a specific illustration. Teenagers are shown how to start with a particular figure, add a few lines, draw an arc, shade certain sections, complete a circle, and conclude the exercise by producing a picture of Morris the Cat, Tyrannosaurus Rex, or the Taj Mahal. Ames was the most popular author in the entire study, and in may cases his works circulated more frequently than did novels by such perennial favorites as Judy Blume, S. E. Hinton, Richard Peck, and M. E. Kerr.

Lee J. Ames did not stand alone. Other authors of drawing books ranking at the top of the list were Paul Frame (*Drawing Cats and Kittens* and *Drawing Sharks, Whales, Dolphins, and Seals*), Don Bolognese (*Drawing Horses & Foals* and *Drawing Spaceships*), Jim Arnosky (*Drawing from Nature*), and Sam Savitt (*Drawing Horses with Sam Savitt*).

Other popular books, those that dealt with movie monsters, caring for pets, motorcycle racing, and scary or unusual stories, also had little relationship to what went on in the classrooms. Even those books that to outsiders appeared to complement courses of study in fact did not. Widely circulated volumes about World War II, for example, found no curricular home in these three junior high schools, where American history classes end with the Civil War. Such books were not read for course requirements or school reports.

Many of the frequently circulated volumes show remarkable structural similarity. Almost all of the books on pets cover a history of the animal, tips for choosing a pet, varieties of breeds, and first aid information. Many of the sports books, another popular area of interest, also follow a pattern. They provide a history of the sport; how to play the game; safety tips; necessary equipment; and organizations, interest groups, and clubs concerned with that sport.

Some readers find security in these patterns. During the junior high years many younger teens read series books like *Alfred Hitchcock and the Three Investigators, Sweet Dreams,* and *The Babysitters' Club*. Such readers find comfort in the predictability of these series, in knowing that the three investigators will never be placed in life-threatening situations; that a shy sixteen-year-old girl will win the heartthrob of her dreams; and that, as a group, the entrepreneurial babysitters will neatly solve problems for both their small charges and their increasing circle of friends. On the other hand, nonfiction readers find their patterns not in story but in the familiar structure of similar informational books.

Further, these young adults are reassured through their subject knowledge. With story, fiction readers understand and predict the basic plot structures the moment they pick up the next volume in a formal series. These readers read in order to confirm their preset expectations. Nonfiction readers enjoy another kind of knowledge—not about how story works but about how facts work. They may find gratification in discovering, in book after book, that Kareem Abdul Jabar still holds the record for the most field goals scored in a single basketball game, that Triceratops used its three horns to battle enemies, and that Howard Carter said "I see wonderful things" when he discovered Tutankhamen's tomb in 1921. Whether they choose fiction or nonfiction, unsophisticated readers seek to confirm what they already know.

The third feature about these frequently circulated books concerns subject, for circulations clustered among common areas of interest. The most popular books among these students were those that dealt with drawing and the decorative arts—drawing, comics, and handicraft books. Second in popularity were books on sports and movies. Engineering topics came in third, wild animals (sharks, snakes, dinosaurs) were fourth, and pets fifth. Yet subject similarities were more subtle than one might expect.

Two important points emerged. First, this subject interest crosses standard Dewey decimal divisions. For example, the three most frequently circulated drawing books were Don Bolognese's *Drawing Horses & Foals*; Lee J. Ames's *Draw 50 Dogs*; and Ames's *Draw 50 Airplanes, Aircraft and Spacecraft*. Horses, dogs, and airplanes all appeared independently as popular topics in other divisions of the study.

The general subject of airplanes follows a similar pattern. Airplane books accounted for a large segment of the engineering book circulations, but other books about airplanes, like *American Fighters of World War II* and *Air War Over Hitler's Germany*, came from history sections, while books such as *Airplanes and Helicopters of the U.S. Navy* were found on the shelves among books dealing with transportation. Still another popular title, Harvey Weiss's *Model Airplanes and How to Build Them*, was located with the handicraft, or how-to books. Frequently circulated fictional books, like Harry Mazer's *The Last Mission*, also concern airplanes.

An interest in a particular subject can thus manifest itself in different ways. Young adults may express curiosity about a single topic, but when recommending books to meet that interest teachers and librarians cannot assume book format. An inquisitiveness about airplanes, for example, does not predicate a preference for a fiction book, a history book, a drawing book, an engineering book, or a book on transportation.

On the other hand, an interest in format may well be just as nonspecific. Not all the drawing books received an equal number of circulations. Students certainly favored this type of book, but they also showed a definite preference for particular topics addressed. The secret of popularity lies neither in format nor in topic, but in the combination of subjects—like drawing and horses, drawing and dogs, and drawing and aircraft.

Equally important is the observation that not all books concerning a certain subject—like snakes, basketball, or movies—received the same number of circulations. Many books about favored topics failed to circulate at all. Just because young adults are interested in football does not mean that they will read indiscriminately in that subject.

The fourth feature we discovered from our examination of the popular non-fiction circulations is that many of these volumes demand some sort of active involvement on the part of the reader. Such books show their young audience how to draw, how to build model rockets, how to sing, how to tell a joke, and how to make presents. The involvement and character identification some adolescents have with fiction may well be substituted in the case of other teenagers by this active participation in nonfiction.

Young adults, though, will find themselves in many different books, even those that do not actively solicit participation. Few teenagers read books like *The Guinness Book of World Records* just to find out information or to gather facts to carry away from the book. When they read that Nolan Ryan threw a pitch that measured 100.9 miles per hour, they do not merely record that fact on a mental record sheet. They wonder, What would it be like to throw such a pitch? Would it dislocate a shoulder, harm their arm muscles, or completely bewilder the batter? Such identification comes from the reader, not the book.

A Balanced Reading Diet

Readers set their own purposes for reading, so they need to choose their own selections. What teachers and librarians must do, then, is provide a well-stocked pool, including both fiction and nonfiction, from which readers can select the books that appeal to them. As Daniel Fader reminds us, "Teachers, librarians and administrators who have participated in programs like *English in Every Classroom* have good reason to know that, given half a chance, the adolescent is more than likely to chose a balanced reading diet."[25]

For many readers, the most appealing bite of that diet is nonfiction. The most widely read single title in Fader's study was *Black Like Me*. Its popularity is testament to the reading motivation power of nonfiction when youngsters are free to pick what they want to read. Twenty-five years after Fader, teachers of adolescents are coming back to the importance of self-selected student reading using books written for young adults in reading/writing workshops. As professionals, we cannot claim to focus on what teenagers enjoy reading and, at the same time, offer students only a collection of fiction titles in these workshop classrooms. Nonfiction must be part of a quality reading/writing workshop in secondary schools.[26]

What we know is that young adults in the middle schools and high schools of America make nonfiction books a substantial part of their self-selected reading. What teachers and librarians do with that knowledge is the important next step. Educators must first of all recognize and reward the nonfiction reading that teens do just as they praise their reading of fiction. We do not think that happens at the present time.

Consider a recent ethnographic study conducted by Kylene Beers that examined aliterate junior high school readers. The United States has a growing population of students who can read but simply choose not to. Beers spent months in the classroom observing and talking to such youngsters. What she found was that even these uncommitted and unmotivated readers did read something: nonfiction. Whether it was the true stories in *Sassy Magazine* or the intramural handbook for soccer, these students read something. But, said one aliterate reader, "I don't think the teacher would call what I'm doing reading." Unfortunately what they have learned is that in the classroom fiction is reading; nonfiction is not. There is real power in this study. It tells us that nonfiction may indeed be the vehicle that moves the aliterate youngster into lifetime reading, but it also cautions that teachers must show students this reading is valued.[27]

There are many reasons why educators do not value the nonfiction reading their students do as much as they value the fiction reading. Perhaps teachers and librarians unconsciously perpetuate a bias toward fiction because nonfiction was not stressed in their own courses of study. Closely related is the observation that these educators are uncomfortable with nonfiction. They know how to probe fiction readers, how to ask questions that deal with characterization, mood, theme, and point of view. But what do they ask about nonfiction beyond, "What is the book about?" In *Nonfiction for Young Adults: From Delight to Wisdom*, we offer a set of ten questions that we think are worth asking about nonfiction books. Here are several that work well.

1. *What kind of teacher do you think the author would make?* This question gets at the issue of clarity in a nonfiction book. How does the author get you to understand what she is writing about? Is it a lecture? Conversation? Sermon? Does she have a sense of humor?

2. *Which photos or illustrations do you wish you had taken or drawn yourself?* Here we attempt to place the student reader in the position of artist/ photographer and think about the circumstances under which the illustrations were executed: How did David Macaulay get that perspective from the top of the pyramid? Was it dangerous to get those pictures of the men and women fighting in the Persian Gulf? What about the photos of molten lava from the volcano eruption? Or the pictures of the fire in Yellowstone?

3. *Compare this nonfiction book with another written on the same topic. How do they differ? How are they alike? Which one do you like better (or believe more)? Why?* This series of questions allows readers to look for conflicting information or points of view, to examine different sources, and to compare the veracity of each work.

4. *If you had a chance to interview the author of this book, what would you ask her?* This question allows the reader to go beyond the book to ask about more detailed information on the subject; to clarify things that are still vague; and to formulate questions that get at the issue of, "Here is what I now know, but here is what I need to know next."

Questions such as these are a jumping-off point for working with nonfiction in the classroom.[28]

Perhaps the most neglected classroom use of nonfiction is in the middle school and high school read-aloud programs. Teachers read aloud fiction.[29] In so doing, they further confirm the message that only when we read fiction are we really reading. Two questions need to be dealt with here. First, do adolescents enjoy hearing nonfiction read aloud? Second, what nonfiction books make good read-alouds?

In a 1990 study, Sue Griffiths, a ninth-grade reading teacher, read aloud to her class for ten to fifteen minutes per day. Over the course of one semester she read ten nonfiction books to her remedial readers and asked them to fill out a response questionnaire on each book. The students responded favorably to nonfiction titles as diverse as *Whales* by Eve Bunting, Edelman's *Dear America*, and the beautiful photo essay *Spaceshots*. These ninth graders wanted photos in the books to be in color. They wanted books that "set off your emotions" like *Dear America*. They also appreciated the knowledge gained from a book like *Whales*. One student wrote, "I was amazed to learn how gentle this giant is. How killer whales are not living up to their names was interesting."

Students also were aware of contrasting the fiction writing an author does with her nonfiction writing. This class had read an Eve Bunting novel earlier in the year. After hearing her *Whales* read aloud, one student said, "I think my feelings about Eve Bunting have changed. See, I thought Eve was just writing to make money, but she cares about young minds." Griffiths concludes, "Perhaps of most significance to this project is the information that surfaced regarding why students liked the books. In the responses, students mentioned time and again that the books were 'real,' 'true,' or 'actual.' As one student aptly stated, 'I like the fact it wasn't fiction.' "[30]

What nonfiction books make good read-alouds? "Nonfiction selections initially chosen for reading aloud should come from those works that incorporate some of the comfortable elements of fiction, such as plot development, characterization, and setting. Story narrative tells many tales—from ghostly legends to unusual adventures to biography—all popular among secondary students."[31] Alvin Schwartz's *Scary Stories to Tell in the Dark*, *More Scary Stories to Tell in the Dark*, and *Scary Stories 3: More Tales to Chill Your Bones* are always popular. True adventures such as Steve Callahan's *Adrift: Seventy-six Days Lost at Sea* provide the true-life counterpart to fictional survival stories such as Gary Paulsen's *Hatchet*. Then there are books that elicit the laughter and tears of life, from Fulghum's essays in his new collection *Uh-Oh: Some Observations from Both Sides of the Refrigerator Door* to Richard Lederer's books about puns and mangling the English language such as *Anguished English* to Milton Meltzer's powerful *Rescue: The Story of How Gentiles Saved Jews in the Holocaust*. By reading these and other nonfiction selections aloud in secondary classrooms teachers show, by example, that reading nonfiction is just as important and pleasurable as reading fiction.

Like much of literature, fine nonfiction recommendations will come to students from teachers and librarians. In our 1985 study we realized that young adults checked out—and checked out repeatedly—fine books like Archie Carr's *The Reptiles*, Alvin Schwartz's *Unriddling*, and Patricia Lauber's *Journey to the Planets*. But, along with these offerings, they also circulated many pedestrian volumes. Teenagers need guidance in locating nonfiction as surely as they do when looking for the latest novel. Adults do not leave them alone to discover fine fiction authors like Alden Carter, Robin McKinley, Nancy Bond, M. E. Kerr, Bruce Brooks, or Chris Crutcher. And we cannot leave them alone to unerringly discover the best of the nonfiction writers either. Books by Peter Parnell, Milton Meltzer, Melvin Zerman, Seymour Simon, James Cross Giblin, Franklyn Branley, or Brent Ashabranner will not automatically jump off the shelves into the hands of unsuspecting teen readers. But where do teachers and librarians find out about these books?

One source that offers some new nonfiction titles (along with popular fiction titles) every year is the Young Adults' Choices List published each fall in the *Journal of Reading*. The books on this list are selected by thousands of teen readers across the country. In 1990, nonfiction books selected by adolescents included Robert D. Ballard's *Exploring the Titanic*, Marilyn Greene and Gary Provost's *Finder: The True Story of a Private Investigator*, Milton Meltzer's *Rescue: The Story of How Gentiles Saved Jews in the Holocaust*, and Barbara Rogasky's *Smoke and Ashes: The Story of the Holocaust*.[32]

Other annual lists that include suggestions of fine nonfiction are the "Best Books for Young Adults" and "Quick Picks." Both come from the American Library Association. The former brochure annotates outstanding publications chosen by young adult librarians, while the latter represents a recommended reading list for reluctant teen readers.[33] In addition, the fine subject bibliographies printed in *Booklist* offer a wide variety of thematic recommendations.[34]

What we know about teenagers and nonfiction we've known for years: they read it, they find pleasure in it, and for many it is the literature that puts them on the path to lifetime reading. We now know more about what kinds of nonfiction adolescents read, and we know that more well-researched, well-written, beautifully illustrated volumes are available for teenagers than ever before. What we need to do is act on this information. As teachers and librarians, let's get comfortable with nonfiction and become more familiar with it. The young adult readers we serve already are.

Notes

1. Betty Carter, "A Content Analysis of the Most Frequently Circulated Information Books in Three Junior High Libraries" (Ph.D. diss., University of Houston, 1987).
2. John Warren Stewig, *Children and Literature* (Chicago: Rand McNally, 1980), 480.
3. Evelyn L. Wenzel, "Historical Backgrounds," in *Beyond Fact*, ed. Jo Carr (Chicago: American Library Association, 1982), 16.
4. Cornilia Meigs, Elizabeth Nesbitt, Anne Thaxter Eaton, and Ruth Hill Viguers, *A Critical History of Children's Literature*, rev ed. (New York: Macmillan, 1969), 101.
5. Wenzel, "Historical Backgrounds," p. 17.
6. Ibid.
7. Meigs, et al., *Critical History*, p. 245.

8. Meigs, et al., *Critical History*, p. 370, and Wenzel, "Historical Backgrounds," p. 22.
9. Wenzel, "Historical Backgrounds," p. 22.
10. Jean D. Lindquist, "Series," *The Horn Book* 29, 2 (1953): 137.
11. Ibid., p. 138.
12. Jim Haskins, "Non-Fiction Books and the Junior and Senior High Schooler: Changes in Supply to Meet Changes in Demand," *Arizona English Journal* 18 (1976): 78–82; and Alleen Pace Nilsen and Kenneth L. Donelson, *Literature for Today's Young Adults* (Glenview, Ill.: Scott Foresman, 1985).
13. Illa Podendorf, "Characteristics of Good Science Materials for Young Readers," in *Jump Over the Moon: Selected Professional Readings*, ed. Pamela Petrick Barron and Jennifer Q. Burley (New York: Holt, Rinehart and Winston, 1984), 214–219.
14. Kathryn Lasky, "Reflections on Nonfiction," *The Horn Book* 61,5 (1985): 530.
15. Robert Hofsinde, "Brother of the Indian," *The Horn Book* 35,1 (1960): 21.
16. Milton Meltzer "Beyond the Span of a Single Life," in *Celebrating Children's Books,* ed. Betsy Hearne and Marilyn Kaye (New York: Lothrop, Lee and Shepard, 1982), 104.
17. Laurence Pringle, "Science Done Here," in *Celebrating Children's Books*, ed. Hearne and Kaye (New York: Lothrop, Lee and Shepard, 1982), p. 110.
18. James Cross Giblin, "The Rise and Fall and Rise of Juvenile Nonfiction, 1961–1988," *School Library Journal* 35;3 (1988): 27–31.
19. T. Glenda Childress, "Gender Gap in the Library: Different Choices for Girls and Boys," *Top of the News* 42;1 (1984): 69–73.
20. Judith R. Blair, "The Status of Non-fiction in the Reading Interests of Second, Third and Fourth Graders" (M. Ed. thesis; Rutgers University, 1974, ED 095481).
21. Daniel Fader and Elton B. McNeil, *Hooked on Books: Program and Proof* (New York: Berkley, 1968), 67–68.
22. George Norvell, *The Reading Interests of Young People* (Lansing: Michigan State University Press, 1973).
23. W. Geiger Ellis, "To Tell the Truth or at Least a Little Nonfiction," *ALAN Review* 15,2 (1987): 39–40.
24. For a discussion of using circulation records to measure reading interests see Alan C. Purves and Richard Beach, *Literature and the Reader: Research in Response to Literature, Reading Interests and the Teaching of Literature* (Urbana, Ill.: National Council of Teachers of English, 1972).
25. Fader and McNeil, *Hooked on Books*, pp. 67–68.
26. Richard F. Abrahamson and Betty Carter, "Nonfiction: The Missing Piece in the Middle," *English Journal* 80,1 (1991): 52–58.
27. G. Kylene Beers, "Choosing Not to Read: An Ethnographic Study of Seventh-Grade Aliterate Students" (Ph.D. diss., University of Houston, 1990).
28. Betty Carter and Richard F. Abrahamson, *Nonfiction for Young Adults: From Delight to Wisdom* (Phoenix: Oryx Press, 1990), 186–187.
29. Betty Carter, and Richard F. Abrahamson, "Nonfiction in the Read-Aloud Program," *Journal of Reading* 34,8 (1991): 638–642.
30. Sue Griffiths, "Nonfiction: A 'Real'ly Appealing Read-Aloud," *Reading Education in Texas* 7 (1991): in press.
31. Carter and Abrahamson, "Nonfiction in the Read-Aloud Program," p. 639.
32. "Young Adult Choices List," *Journal of Reading* 34,3 (1990): 203–209.
33. Both brochures can be ordered from the American Library Association through the Graphics Department. Call the toll-free number (800-545-2433) and press 8 for the Graphic Extension.
34. Annually, the August edition of *Booklist* prints a retrospective list of these bibliographies.

Books Mentioned

Air War Against Hitler's Germany. New York: American Heritage Publishing Company, 1964.
Ames, Lee J. *Draw 50 Airplanes, Aircraft and Spacecraft*. Garden City, N.Y.: Doubleday, 1977.
____. *Draw 50 Cats*. Garden City, N.Y.: Doubleday, 1986.
____. *Draw 50 Dinosaurs & Other Prehistoric Animals*. Garden City, N.Y.: Doubleday, 1977.
____. *Draw 50 Dogs*. Garden City, N.Y.: Doubleday, 1981.
____. *Draw 50 Famous Faces*. Garden City, N.Y.: Doubleday, 1978.
Anderton, David A. *American Fighters of World War II*. New York: Crescent Books, 1982.
Arnosky, Jim. *Drawing from Nature*. New York: Lothrop, Lee and Shepard, 1982.
Ballard, Robert D. *Exploring the Titanic*. New York: Scholastic, 1988.
Bolognese, Don. *Drawing Dinosaurs and Other Prehistoric Animals*. New York: Franklin Watts, 1982.
____. *Drawing Horses & Foals*. New York: Franklin Watts, 1977.
____. *Drawing Spaceships and Other Spacecraft*. New York: Franklin Watts, 1982.
Bunting, Eve. *The Sea World Book of Whales*. San Diego: Harcourt Brace Jovanovich, 1989.
Callahan, Steven. *Adrift: Seventy-six Days Lost at Sea*. Boston: Houghton Mifflin, 1986.
Carr, Archie. *The Reptiles: Young Readers' Edition*. New York: Time-Life, 1967.
Delear, Frank J. *Airplanes and Helicopters of the U.S. Navy*. New York: Dodd Mead and Company, 1982.
Edelman, Bernard, Ed. *Dear America: Letters Home from Vietnam*. New York: Norton, 1985.

Ferris, T. *Spaceshots: The Beauty of Nature Beyond Earth*. New York: Pantheon, 1987.

Frame, Paul. *Drawing Cats and Kittens*. New York: Franklin Watts, 1979.

____. *Drawing Sharks, Whales, Dolphins, and Seals*. New York: Franklin Watts, 1983.

Fulghum, Robert. *Uh-Oh: Some Observations from Both Sides of the Refrigerator Door*. New York: Villard Books, 1991.

Greene, Marilyn and Gary Provost. *Finder: The True Story of a Private Investigator*. New York: Crown, 1988.

The Guinness Book of World Records. New York: Sterling Publishing, 1984.

Lauber, Patricia. *Journey to the Planets*. New York: Crown, 1982.

Lederer, Richard. *Anguished English: An Anthology of Accidental Assaults Upon Our Language*. New York: Bantam, 1989.

Mazer, Harry. *The Last Mission*. New York: Delacorte, 1979.

Meltzer, Milton. *Rescue: The Story of How Gentiles Saved Jews in the Holocaust*. New York: Harper & Row, 1988.

Paulsen, Gary. *Hatchet*. New York: Bradbury, 1987.

Rogasky, Barbara. *Smoke and Ashes: The Story of the Holocaust*. New York: Holiday, 1988.

Savitt, Sam. *Draw Horses With Sam Savitt*. New York: Viking, 1981.

Schwartz, Alvin. *Scary Stories to Tell in the Dark*. New York: J. B. Lippincott, 1981.

____. *Unriddling*. New York: J. B. Lippincott, 1983.

____. *More Scary Stories to Tell in the Dark*. New York: J. B. Lippincott, 1984.

____. *Scary Stories 3: More Tales to Chill Your Bones*. New York: Harper Collins, 1991.

Weiss, Harvey. *Model Airplanes and How To Build Them*. New York: Thomas Y. Crowell, 1975.

17

Eight Things I've Learned About Kids and Poetry

Paul B. Janeczko

I didn't start out to be a poetry anthologist. I started out as a kid in New Jersey who had two major goals in life: (1) survive one more year of delivering newspapers without being attacked by thugs from the public high school and Ike, the one-eyed, crazed cur that lurked in the forsythia bushes at the top of the hill; and (2) become more than a weak-hitting, third-string catcher on our sorry Little League team. I failed at both.

Had I announced at the dinner table, "Mom, Dad, I've decided to be an anthologist," my parents—especially my mother—would have been thrilled. In truth, they would have been thrilled that I'd decided to be *anything* other than the top-40 disk jockey, Edsel salesman, or bullpen catcher I constantly talked about becoming in junior high. But at that point in my life, poetry meant no more to me than gerunds, 1066, or the Belgian Congo.

I wasn't even much of a recreational reader. Beyond an occasional Hardy Boys book that my mother made me read, my reading was limited largely to baseball magazines, the daily sports page, and the backs of baseball cards old and new. I was captivated by those color pictures of men wearing five o'clock shadows and baggy pants, seduced by the sweet music of nicknames. Ah, the nicknames. I recall Whale, Runt, Blimp, and Porky. Boots, Bloop, Hoot, and Scooter. And Suitcase Bob, Jungle Jim, and Sudden Sam.

Maybe that's when the anthologist's bug bit me. While other kids were content to amass stacks of cards by playground gambling and trading, I actually collected, read, and organized my cards. On those evenings when I was supposed to be reading my geography, I dragged out my Keds box of baseball cards, rubber-banded according to teams, and rearranged them. I made a team of players born in New Jersey. I had my Alphabet Team on which each position was fielded by a player whose last name started with a different letter of the alphabet. I even had a team of Polish players.

Years later I found myself teaching high school, and reading poetry instead of the backs of baseball cards. Somehow, I had become a poetry junkie. I admit it. I read poetry the way people watch soap operas, work on cars, or follow the Red Sox: irrationally, compulsively, endlessly. Although I loved poetry, I doubted that my students would love it if they read only the poetry in the nine-pound anthology that served as their text. So, I took my first step as a poetry anthologist when I mimeographed poems and used them in my classes.

That was twenty-three years ago. Most of that time has been spent teaching high school English and gathering poems. Since I left the classroom two years ago, I've worked as a writer/consultant/visiting poet, working with teachers and young writers in grades 4 through 12, and with teachers and librarians in inservice workshops. The time I've spent with elementary and middle school students and teachers has shown me the flipside of my years in the high school classroom. It has allowed me to see what happens to children before they arrive at the door of the high school English class. And it has allowed me the chance to consider and consider again what I've learned about kids and poetry.

1. *Young readers will respond to good, carefully chosen poetry the same way they will respond to good, carefully chosen fiction.*

They will devour it. They will talk about it. It will get into their hearts and into their heads.

Things have changed since I was in grammar school and read poems from the Official Approved List of Subjects Poets Can Write Poems About. Among the subjects on the list were:

Tragic Ends
Pure-But-Usually-Brokenhearted-Love
Courage
Family (with a large dose of poems about pets that met Tragic Ends)
Patriotism

Poems were supposed to edify, enlighten, or illuminate. And a *really* good poem did all three. The problem was that I never seemed to "get" the poems, much as I rarely "got" the math problems. Poetry only puzzled, intimidated, and infuriated me.

Now when I visit schools and read my poems—from *Brickyard Summer* or a work in progress—or poems from one of my anthologies, many of the students are captivated by what the poet has been able to do with words. The poet has gotten them to think, to laugh, to wonder. I'm reminded of Stanley Kunitz, who said that if we listen hard enough to poets, "who knows—we too may break into dance, perhaps for grief, perhaps for joy."[1] The kids will ask questions about the poems and the poets. Occasionally, they'll even ask me to read another poem. One class of fourth graders even recited one of my poems as I read it.

2. *Young readers will tell us what they like and dislike about poetry . . . if we ask them.*

The young people I've spoken with tell me they enjoy short, humorous poetry. And younger children are particularly fond of rhyme. Hence the popularity of Jack Prelutsky and Shel Silverstein. Kids also like to read poems about things they can understand in a language that they can understand. What kids dislike about poetry should come as no surprise because, I suspect, they are the same things we disliked about poetry when we were in school: learning about the lives of the poets and studying the mechanics of poetry in order to become a World Class Poetry Scanner. The kids were most vocal about their displeasure with having to look for the Right Answer after reading poems their teacher selected for them.

3. *Choosers of poems—teachers, librarians, parents—must become readers of poetry.*

James Dickey spoke for me—and others, I'm sure—when he said, "What you have to realize . . . is that poetry is just naturally the greatest goddamn thing that ever was in the whole universe. If you love it, there's no substitute for it."[2] This is not to say that we must like and/or understand every poem we read. That's unrealistic. Just as it is unrealistic for us to expect that young readers will like or understand every poem we present in a book or a class. Young readers need to begin developing their own critical sense, not simply liking every poem the teacher (or anthologist) selects because it was presented by an adult, an "expert."

Becoming a reader of poetry is simple: read poetry. The more poems we read, the more we will have a sense of what has been written and what is presently being written. Let me offer a list of poets whose work I find interesting and provocative.

Gwendolyn Brooks, *Blacks*. David Co.
Jo Carson, *Stories I Ain't Told Nobody Yet*. Watts/Orchard.
Robert Currie, *Yarrow*. Oberon Books.
Robert Francis, *Collected Poems 1936–1976*. University of Massachussets Press.
Gary Gildner, *Blue Like the Heavens: New and Selected Poems*. University of Pittsburgh Press.
Dana Gioia, *Daily Horoscope*. Graywolf.
Langston Hughes, *Selected Poems*. Random House.
David Huddle, *Paper Boy*. University of Pittsburgh Press.
June Jordan, *Naming Our Destiny: New and Selected Poems*. Thunder Mouth.
X. J. Kennedy, *Cross Ties: Selected Poems*. University of Georgia Press.
Ted Kooser, *Sure Signs: New and Selected Poems*. University of Pittsburgh Press.
Maxine Kumin, *Our Ground Time Here Will Be Brief*. Penguin.
Stanley Kunitz, *The Poems of Stanley Kunitz, 1928–1978*. Atlantic.
W. S. Merwin, *Selected Poems*. Atheneum.

Robert Morgan, *At the Edge of the Orchard Country*. Wesleyan University
   Press.
Naomi Shihab Nye, *Hugging the Jukebox*. Breitenbush.
Linda Pastan, *PM/AM: New and Selected Poems*. Norton.
Marge Piercy, *Circles on the Water: Selected Poems*. Knopf.
Richard Snyder, *Practicing our Sighs: The Collected Poems*. Ashland Poetry
   Press.
Gary Soto, *Black Hair*. University of Pittsburgh Press.
William Stafford, *Stories that Could Be True: New and Selected Poems*.
   Harper.
John Updike, *The Carpentered Hen and Other Tame Creatures*. Knopf.
Paul Zimmer, *Family Reunion: Selected and New Poems*. University of Pitts-
   burgh Press.

4. *Good poetry explodes with possibilities, and we must share those possibilities with
young people.*

   Young adults need to recognize that poetry has functions other than to puzzle,
intimidate, and infuriate. Poetry can mesmerize, mock, and mimic. It can cel-
ebrate. Kids need to see that poetry can describe, confess, and lament. It can
provoke, praise, and remember. I want kids to know that some poems narrate,
console, and even commemorate. Above all, however, adolescents need to
know that poetry sings of human experiences, every so often, their own experiences.

   Young readers need to see that poetry is accessible, that it captures experiences, that it captures the meanings in life, and that it communicates through
intense, inventive language. I want young adults to feel that all poems have a
purpose, described well by Jonathan Holden: "to give shape, in a concise and
memorable way, to what our lives feel like, . . . Poems help us to notice the
world more and better, and they enable us to share with others."[3] And today,
with the planet minutes or a misunderstanding away from being destroyed,
we all need to share. That's what poets do. That's what I try to do with my
books. I want young readers to feel that each of my collections and every
poem in them is a sharing.

5. *Creating a good anthology is tougher than I thought it would be.*

   When I read poems for a collection that will be marketed for the YA reader, I
look for poems that strike me. Sounds simple, but those are the poems I've
saved, copying and filing in subject/topic folders where they wait to be redis-
covered like so many promising rookies. After the poems sit in folders for a
time, I read through them again, perhaps a folder at a time. This reading
refreshes my memory about the poems I saved. It also helps me make connections, to see similarities and differences in the poems that may help me place
them with other poems. But it does more than that. Some of these poems stick
in my mind where they rest for weeks, even months, until reading other poems may recall them.

It is during this gradual rereading process that the concept for a new anthology begins to take shape in my mind. I begin to see ideas and images that belong together. When I feel comfortable with a notion for a new collection, I pitch it to my editor. Sometime he immediately agrees that the idea would make a good book. Other times, he counters with a suggestion of his own. For example, after being moved by many poems about old age, I suggested that subject to my editor. He declined, saying that he didn't think young people were interested in reading an entire book of poems about old people. He suggested I work on a collection of family poems. After considering his idea, I decided I'd try it. The result was *Strings: A Gathering of Family Poems*.

About five years ago, my editor suggested I do a book of contemporary narrative poems. At the time, I wasn't interested, but as I worked on other collections, I discovered more and more story poems that I liked. I was ready to try the narrative book. I had tapped a vein of poets whose work was new to me, whose work was primarily narrative. The result was *The Music of What Happens*.

But files of poems do not an anthology make. Poems must connect with other poems. Some associations are obvious, but I look for the connections that aren't apparent at first reading. I want my readers to think about why poems are where they are. I want to bring order to the gathering of poems, an order that will bring out the order in the individual poems and that will give the timid, inexperienced reader of poetry a gentle nudge in a helpful direction. I discovered while working on *Dont Forget to Fly* that groups of two to six poems work better for me than larger groups. Small groupings, however, make the anthology more difficult to organize because I must not only connect the poems in each section but also connect the sections. All of my anthologies have an overall thread that holds each book together, which means that I arrange the sections almost as if they were chapters in a novel.

I go through a process of discovery when I read poems, when I look for order in disorder. I discover the possibilities of poetry, and I want to share those possibilities with my readers; possibilities in form, language, images, structure, rhythm, voice, sound, feeling. I want my readers to see that poems are expressions of human experience, that poems are as different as people. Further, I want them to understand that the feelings young readers have are shared by many people. At the same time, I'm looking for poems that will allow readers to expand their range of feelings.

6. *A good anthology should break ground.*

I certainly didn't realize when I was putting together *The Crystal Image* (Dell, 1977), my first anthology, that it would be followed by a long line of hardcover collections. I had no way of knowing that my anthologies would satisfy a need for good accessible poetry for the young reader.

Over the years, my anthologies have gotten better because of what I have learned about poets, poetry, and publishers. With *The Crystal Image* I relied, for the most part, on what was already on the library shelves. The collection did

include many good poems, poems not included in most classroom anthologies, but it was a safe book. When I sent a copy to Stephen Dunning—editor of
Reflections on a Gift of Watermelon Pickle, a modern classic poetry anthology—it
was months before he responded to my book. I was disappointed when Dunning did not dish out the praise I had anticipated. Instead, however, he gave
me some advice that has since served me much better: a good anthology
should "break ground."

Breaking ground meant that I needed to dig for the good stuff that is often
hidden in out-of-the-way places. I've looked for new voices that deserve a
wider audience, often young voices that will ring true for young readers. I've
searched for overlooked poems by frequently anthologized poets. And I've
looked for poets who can, at least on occasion, look at life with a sense of
humor.

The first place I still look for poems is in the books that I buy or borrow from
friends and libraries. When it comes to libraries and bookstores, I've become a
world-class browser, rivaling some of the tourists who cruise up and down the
Maine coast in the summer, hunting for bargain antiques. I head straight for
the poetry collection, often taking books of poems without any knowledge of
the poets whose work I am taking.

The problem with looking for books of poetry by younger, less well-known
poets is that most of them are self-published or published by small presses,
making them unlikely to appear on bookstore shelves. Major publishers keep
the tried and true names on their lists, rarely venturing to include the work of
a less-known poet. Because fiction outsells poetry, publishers are more apt to
take a chance on a new voice in fiction, paying, on occasion, obscenely large
advances.

And now come the disturbing results of a report prepared by the National
Writers Union. According to the NWU, three major national book chains—B.
Dalton/Barnes & Noble, Waldenbooks, and Crown Books—exercise a dispro-
portionate influence on what books are available to American readers. The Big
Three account for more than 40 percent of all retail bookstore sales. "In deter-
mining which books to support," the report said, "publishers must focus on
the kinds of books thousands of mall stores are likely to carry."[4]

Although you are not apt to find these books in a mall bookstore, let me
suggest some anthologies that I consider to be a sound foundation for a YA
poetry collection.

> *The American Poetry Anthology*, ed. Daniel Halpern, Avon.
> *American Sports Poems*, ed. R. R. Knudson and May Swenson, Watts/
>   Orchard.
> *Carrying the Darkness: The Poetry of the Vietnam War*, ed. W. D. Ehrhart,
>   Texas Tech University Press.
> *Geography of Poets*, ed. Edward Field, Bantam.
> *Harper's Anthology of Twentieth Century Native American Poetry*, ed. Duane
>   Niatum, Harper.

Love Is Like the Lion's Tooth, ed. Frances McCullough, Harper.
The Music of What Happens: Poems That Tell Stories, ed. Paul B. Janeczko, Watts/Orchard.
The New American Poetry, ed. Donald M. Allen, Grove.
Piping Down the Valleys Wild, ed. Nancy Larrick, Delacorte.
The Place My Words Are Looking For: What Poets Say About and Through Their Work, ed. Paul B. Janeczko, Bradbury.
The Poetry of Black America, ed. Arnold Adoff, Harper.
Poetspeak: In Their Work, About Their Work, ed. Paul B. Janeczko, Bradbury.
The Rattle Bag, ed. Seamus Heaney and Ted Hughes, Faber & Faber.
Under All Silences: Shades of Love, ed. Ruth Gordon, Harper.
The Voice That Is Great Within Us, ed. Hayden Carruth, Bantam.

7. *Many of the most exciting poetry books will not be reviewed or advertised in mainstream periodicals.*

I get leads on new books that I want to investigate by reading journals and book reviews. Some people spend their time reading the sports page, the stock reports, or obituaries. With notebook in hand, I read book reviews and book ads, looking for a book that I need to read. Sometimes it's a new title by an old friend. Sometimes a book (finally!) by a poet I've known only through poems in journals. Although I do read the *New York Times Book Review* and the *Washington Post's Book World*, and they review three or four poetry books each month, those are usually books written by Big Name Poets and published by the Major Publishers and, consequently, generally not books by women poets, poets of color, or poets whose work is published by a small press. I turn, instead, to journals that are more sensitive to the work published by small presses. *American Book Review, Voice Literary Supplement, American Poetry Review, Bloomsbury Review, Contact II, Poets and Writers Magazine,* and *Poetry* are a few of the periodicals that I rely on for information and poems not generally found in the mainsteam periodicals.

Another source of poetry books is catalogues of small or alternative presses that publish poetry. I'm on the mailing list for Broken Moon Press, Coffee House Press, Arte Publico Press, Graywolf Press, Milkweed Editions, Sheep Meadow Press, Copper Canyon Press, and Clark City Press, to name a few. Even the attractive catalogues of these small presses make for interesting reading. Ed Ochester's Spring Church Book Company puts out an excellent quarterly list of the latest small (and large) press poetry books.

Perhaps my best sources for fresh poems and new voices are the poets themselves. It started when I was working for *Poetspeak: In Their Work, About Their Work.* I wrote to the poets asking them each to send eight to ten poems they thought would be successful with YA readers as well as a comment on one of the poems or on writing poetry in general. The response was overwhelming. The poets were very generous with their time and effort. Many of them thanked me for reading their work and considering it for one of my books.

Since that time, I have continued to write to poets—a computer-generated postcard explaining my latest project does the trick—when I begin work on a new anthology. And, I always ask whether they can suggest poets whose work they feel deserves a wider audience. Any poets I learn about in that fashion receive an invitation to be part of my new book.

8. *Poetry is not read as much as it should be read.*

Why not? In researching their book, *What Do Our 17-Year-Olds Know?* Diane Ravitch and Chester E. Finn, Jr., discovered that poetry is "not in high favor" with 17-year-olds. Sixty-five percent of the girls read poetry on their own, while only 45 percent of the boys did. Ravitch and Finn seemed startled by their findings, but I would be willing to bet that these figures are higher than they would be if we put the same questions to insurance agents, bus drivers, accountants, or school principals. I suspect that somewhere along about eighth or ninth grade, kids, especially boys, end their love affair with poetry.

After visiting elementary and middle school classes for two years, I'd like to suggest The Law of Poetry and Kids: The younger a kid, the more he or she enjoys reading and writing poetry. A corollary to this law is: Teachers who teach younger kids (elementary age) enjoy reading and writing poetry more than teachers who teach older kids (high school age). I share Anatole Broyard's fear that we don't read enough poetry. "Where will our flair come from," he wrote in the *New York Times Book Review*, "our hyperbole, our mots justes? Unless we read poetry, we'll never have our hearts broken by language, which is an indispensable preliminary to a civilized life."[5]

Poetry—reading and writing—in the elementary classroom is fun. Kids read Karla Kuskin, Jack Prelutsky, Shel Silverstein, Myra Cohn Livingston, X. J. Kennedy, J. Patrick Lewis, Eve Merriam. A good elementary school teacher will let students discover the wild wonders of their language. Young author conferences are much more common in elementary and middle schools than they are in high schools, where, all too often, the teachers and students must follow a straitjacket regimen.

The whole-language philosophy is much more a way of life in elementary schools than in high schools, where teachers rely, for the most part, on a hardcover anthology and its teacher's guide. Some literature textbooks have improved since the day I first stood behind the desk of my own English classroom. More and more teachers' guides encourage teachers to go beyond the textbook. Still, the anthology, with its pattern of selections and questions, makes it easy for the teacher to ignore outside material. Many schools require American literature in the eleventh grade, British literature in the twelfth grade, and so on, further reducing outside reading possibilities.

Once kids reach junior high school, school becomes Serious. Kids begin planning for Their Future (i.e., taking the College Boards). Much of the material they read in language arts or English class is to prepare them for college. Poetry—language and subject matter—becomes further removed from their own experiences. The poetry many high school students are required to read is selected and presented in a way that is intended to prepare young readers for a standardized test (or a TV game show) or to demonstrate to some adults what kids their age do or don't know, rather than in a way that would allow young people to experience the fire and ice of words.

Philip Booth said that a good poem "makes the world more habitable . . . it stretches not toward mere pleasure, but toward joy." A poem "can be full of joy—no, that isn't true—a poem can *reach toward* joy and sometimes touch joy and touch in others, the reader, the joy of being so true to human experience that, however it may seem, it is finally sustaining. [Any good poem] changes the world. It changes the world slightly in favor of being alive and being human."[6] I can't think of a better reason why poetry should be a vital part of our lives and the lives of young people.

Notes

1. In Georgia Heard, *For the Good of Earth and Sun* (Portsmouth, NH: Heinemann, 1989), 8.
2. In *The Craft of Poetry*, ed. William Packard (New York: Doubleday, 1974), 151.
3. In *Poetspeak: In Their Work, About Their Work*, ed. Paul B. Janeczko (New York: Bradbury Press, 1983), 44.
4. Stan Luxenberg, *Books in Chains: Chain Bookstores and Marketplace Censorship*, National Writers Union, April 1991, p. 5.
5. Anatole Broyard, "A Narrow Escape from Poetry," *New York Times Book Review*, August 14, 1988, p. 14.
6. Stephen Dunn, "An Interview with Philip Booth," *New England Review/Bread Loaf Quarterly* 9,2 (Winter 1986): 134.

18

Reader Response Theory and the Problem of Meaning

Robert E. Probst

Reconceiving Literary Experience

We've known how to teach literature for ten or twenty years now. We should have known for fifty: the guiding principles have been available for that long. Since Louise Rosenblatt's *Literature As Exploration* was published back in 1938, we've had reasonable and comprehensible principles for guiding our teaching.[1] She articulated them well in that book, she and others have elaborated on them in the following years, and teachers at all grade levels have experimented with them in their own classrooms. Those principles have begun now to inform and guide ongoing literature projects and institutes such as Sheridan Blau's at the University of California at Santa Barbara and Rebecca Sipe's in Anchorage; and publishers of major textbook series are beginning to try to take them into account as they design their programs. Their influence is felt more and more widely.

Rosenblatt's principles tell us to focus on the meeting of student and text, on the transaction between the reader and the book. It is there, she argues, that the literature lives, not on the page, not in ink and paper, nor even in the mind of the author (except insofar as he is another reader), but in the mind of the reader during and after the act of reading. The poem is the product of a meeting, an exchange, a transaction between a reader and a text, a transaction to which each contributes.

The literary experience, then, is not dictated by the text, but is evoked by it. The words enter the reader's consciousness and awaken memories, associations, thoughts, questions, all of which become part of the reader's experience of the text. Meaning, in this conception of the literary experience, is not resident in the text. Rather, it lies in the mind of the reader, created and shaped as he works with the words on the page.

Relinquishing Old Goals and Living in Uncertainty

There are troubling aspects of this vision of literature and literary experience. One is, of course, that it deprives us of certain instructional goals that many of us have come to rely upon for our sense of direction and for the craftsmanlike satisfaction that some styles of teaching afford. We must, for instance, put the acquisition of information about literature in perspective. It is easy to conceive of the literature program in terms of the data we might teach, but to do so is to ignore the central importance of the encounter with texts.

More painful still, perhaps, we must forgo uniformity of interpretation as a pedagogic goal. If we accept the notion that meaning is not contained within the ink on paper but is shaped through the complex act of reading, then we have to acknowledge that meaning is variable, that one text will yield different meanings for different readers. As more teachers and researchers have looked closely at readers reading, that variability has become both transparently obviously and obviously respectable.

Although the legitimacy of widely differing readings of one text is now hard to deny, it does leave us feeling, at times, that we are trying to build on shifting sands. It can be disconcerting to remind yourself, as you prepare to face thirty or forty students, that you don't know what the text means. You may know what it means to you—or at least what it meant to you after the fifth reading last night as you planned today's work—but you can only guess what it will mean to each of the readers who are about to confront it for the first time, in an environment drastically different from your living room or study, surrounded by other students, carrying psychic burdens hidden from you and perhaps from themselves, disturbed or calmed by events of which you may not even be aware.

The situation is somewhat akin to that of the poet in Denise Levertov's "The Secret"—

> Two girls discover
> the secret of life
> in a sudden line of
> poetry.
>
> I who don't know the
> secret wrote
> the line. They
> told me
>
> (through a third person)
> they had found it

but not what it was,
not even

what line it was. No doubt
by now, more than a week
later, they have forgotten
the secret,

the line, the name of
the poem. I love them for
finding what
I can't find,

and for loving me
for the line I wrote:
and for forgetting it
so that

a thousand times, till death
finds them, they may
discover it again, in other
lines.

in other
happenings. And for
wanting to know it,
for

assuming there is
such a secret, yes,
for that
most of all.[2]

The poet can accept the situation, even rejoice in it—she doesn't have to face thirty students tomorrow morning—but the teacher who doesn't know the secret, who can't find what the two girls could find, still has to run a discussion for fifty minutes.

Respecting the Unique Reader

Nonetheless, that secret, unknown to the teacher, hidden in the mind of the student, is the core of the literary experience, if we accept the vision of literature offered us by Rosenblatt and others. That secret, that unique reading, the product of the coming together of text and reader, represents the idiosyncratic and personal nature of literary experience. Levertov seems to respect that uniqueness and does not demand that they find *her* secret, that they agree with one another about what the secret is, or even that they remember tomorrow what the secret was yesterday. She seems content to allow the poem, the reading, to evolve and change and grow. She would have little sympathy, I suspect, with a lesson or a test that required thirty young readers to ignore their own secrets, to disregard their own responses so that they might arrive at some artificial consensus about "the meaning" contained by the text.

Though contemporary theory urges us to stand with Levertov and give up uniformity of interpretation as a goal of literary instruction, not all of us let go easily. It is tempting to allow a bit of open response, personal storytelling, a few more-or-less relevant anecdotes, and then set them aside and ask the students to get down to the hard work of figuring out what the author really meant, what the text really says. To do so seems rigorous and intellectually demanding, but it is, in a sense, the easy way out of the dilemma. Rather than accept the notion that meanings will differ and figure out how to live with the uncomfortable multiplicity of readings implied, the teacher who slips quietly past the diverse responses of students, acknowledging but dismissing them, is still privileging one reading over others, still clinging to the notion that there is a *right* reading, a best interpretation.

That privileged reading is probably the teacher's own, unless in modesty or insecurity she defers to a critical authority; and though her reading is likely to benefit from broader literary experience, from knowledge of history, genre, biography, from the additional years she has lived, and from the energy she has devoted to preparing for the class, it nonetheless still betrays the inevitable limitations of her perspective: she cannot fully know the minds of each student, their history of literary experiences, their immediate circumstances, all of which will shape their understanding of the text. That is to say, experienced and well-trained as she may be, the teacher is in no position to do the students' reading for them. Rather, she must find ways of encouraging students to do their own reading, to make their own meaning, to assimilate the literary text into the ongoing stream of their own intellectual and emotional lives.

Pursuing Our Own Secrets—Ways of Talking

We are beginning to figure out ways of doing this with individual texts. Some obviously lend themselves well to the sort of discussion and writing implied in this conception of literary experience. We might, for instance, talk about Levertov's poem for a while, encouraging students to articulate their understanding of her vision of literary experience and inviting them to discuss its validity and their own reading history. Is Levertov suggesting that poems have no meaning? that they can mean anything? that the reader must create the meaning himself? that meanings differ from reader to reader? that meaning for one reader may evolve from day to day? In their own experience with literary texts, have students ever found that they discovered a unique secret, that they saw something, thought something, learned something, that the author could not have foreseen? Were those divergent readings accepted by other students? by the teacher?

The purpose of such discussion, of course, is to encourage students to reflect upon their own literary experiences, and we might hope that some students will remember that, indeed, there *have* been times when some valuable thought—their own, not the author's—took shape as they read.

And then, after some talk about the possibility that in reading poems we might find secrets that are not there, that we might open a small window into our own consciousness, we might read another poem, perhaps Stephen Dunn's "The Sacred":

> After the teacher asked if anyone had
>   a sacred place
> and the students fidgeted and shrank
>
> in their chairs, the most serious of them all
>   said it was his car,
> being in it alone, his tape deck playing
>
> things he'd chosen, and others knew the truth
>   had been spoken
> and began speaking about their rooms,
>
> their hiding places, but the car kept coming up,
>   the car in motion,
> music filling it, and sometimes one other person
>
> who understood the bright altar of the dashboard
>   and how far away
> a car could take him from the need
>
> to speak, or to answer, the key
>   in having a key
> and putting it in, and going.[3]

The discussion of Levertov's poem should have freed us to look for our own secrets in this new text, to reflect now upon our own places, our own readings of this poem. Our understanding of it, after all, is likely to be powerfully affected by our memory of our own sacred places, whether cars or rooms or mountains or back yards. Perhaps, for some of us, the absence of such a place in our lives may be the shaping factor. The point of such discussion, perhaps, is that *my* sacred place is more important, in my reading of this text, than is Dunn's. At least, it is more important for me. And by implication, your places and your students' are more important, as well. We make sense of this poem— we make meaning—by evoking related experience and reflecting on the connections. If we have no such related experience, if we can conjure no images of privacy, no memories of or desire for a solitude that gives access to elusive meditations and respite from the demands of others, then the poem may not work well for us. Furthermore, if we are restricted to what is there, in the text, to what Dunn says, to his experiences, reported or imagined, we may be deprived of the material we need to respond fully to the text. Readers must not be confined to extracting from texts: rather, they must be invited to create the texts, to bring them to bear upon their own history and forge something new from the encounter.

Various readers of Dunn's poem have, for example, read the text in differing ways. For many high school students, of course, the car *is* the sacred place. Why it is so, however, differs from student to student. For some it represents adventure, independence, excitement. They see it as an opportunity to be themselves, playing their own music, going where they want to go with friends they have chosen. For others the sacred place has a slightly different quality. It still represents freedom, but it is less the freedom of adventure and excitement than it is the freedom of escape and respite. There is a sadder note in their voices, and they speak not so much of what the car will take them to, but of what it will take them from. They speak less of the opportunity to be by themselves and to see more clearly for the moment who and what they are, than of the chance to be away from others.

The difference is important, and the chance to reflect on it, to talk or write about it, may be a chance to come to a clearer understanding of some small aspect of one's own life as well as the text. To dismiss those subtle differences as irrelevant or insignificant, or worse, to say to the student, It's all well and good that you feel that way about your car, but what does Dunn think? is to deny the student the opportunity to make significant meaning from the encounter with the text. On the other hand, inviting that free exploration of response may yield a sharpened understanding of oneself, of the text, and of the others with whom it is discussed. Literature is open, inviting us in to perform and to search rather than providing us with dogma. It offers us more questions than answers, prodding us to form tentative answers of our own, and to hold them tentatively, ready to rethink and revise when appropriate. The exploration of response does not disable student readers, encouraging them to intellectual laziness and emotional self-indulgence. Rather, it demands that they take into account the complex interactions of the words on the page, the history they carry with them, and the responses of other readers. The meaning they make through such explorations of texts and readings is potentially of greater significance to them.

Other readers have had strikingly different readings of the text. One, a teacher who had recently lost her son in an automobile accident, was barely able to read it at all. She left the group, returned thirty minutes later, and was at that point anxious to talk about her thoughts. Clearly, her reading departed from the text—there was nothing in "The Sacred" of accidents and dying—but it would have been inexcusable and insulting to tell her that her experience was irrelevant, that mentioning the death of her son betrayed a failure to concentrate on the task at hand, that her response was unfocused, undisciplined, and off the point. The memory of her son *was*, certainly, a central part of her reading of the text and to deny it would be to prevent her from coming to grips with her own experience, both her experience with the text, and her experience with loss.

I read the poem yet another way—neither better nor worse, but simply different—finding in it a condemnation of much of my teaching. Those last lines,

> . . . how far away
> a car could take him from the need
>
> to speak, or to answer, the key
>   in having a key
> and putting it in, and going.

reminded me of how often I'd imposed that need to speak upon my students, demanding that they answer my questions when they may well have had more important issues of their own to address. They suggest that I do not hold the key, that our students may have to provide their own key, their own questions, if they are to create their own meaning. The poem is for me a metaphoric comment on teaching—that is its meaning, for me. But my role as teacher in the classroom should not empower me to force that meaning on the other readers. Meaning must be forged by the individual out of an individual encounter with the text and other readers.

Where Are We Now?

And so where does this leave us at the moment? Our theories of literature are changing to respect individual, unique readings, and our principles of instruction are gradually coming along as we figure out ways of welcoming responses and investigating them productively. There are implications, though, that we have not yet fully respected or accepted. One of these is, obviously, that the curriculum itself needs to be reconceived. First of all, our ways of selecting works for the curriculum need to be rethought. The established canon, those works that have been in the textbooks for years, might be questioned and perhaps revised in the light of what we are coming to believe about the nature of literary experience.

Ever since the mid-1890s, when the National Conference on Uniform Entrance Requirements published its list of required texts for students who wished to enter college, there have been complaints about the rigidity of the curriculum. That some of the texts on that first list ("The Rime of the Ancient Mariner," for example) are still in the program today attests either to their eternal and universal appeal or to the inertia of the curriculum—probably the latter. The problem with many of those texts, however, is not that they are bad or outdated—"The Rime of the Ancient Mariner" is a magnificent poem; rather, it is that they have been chosen for the wrong reasons. We have looked for good literature, but the criteria by which we have judged whether a text is good tend to focus on features of texts and ignore the nature of the transaction an adolescent reader might have with the text. There is little question that Milton's *Paradise Lost*, to choose an extreme example, is an impressive literary work. But we may wonder whether there are many sixteen-year-old readers who are mature enough to have a satisfactory literary experience with it. If we considered, not the historical significance of a work, not its stature in the literary hierarchy, but rather its potential for awakening response and inviting students into dialogue about issues of importance to them, *Paradise Lost* might be postponed to some later date.

Competing for its place would be a great many texts perhaps less complex, less artistically sophisticated, less rich in many ways, but more likely to awaken interest and invite good, thoughtful reading. Among those books would be the best works of literature written primarily for young adults. Admittedly less likely than Milton's works to endure throughout the next century—though some undoubtedly will—they may nonetheless have the power now, with young readers, to sustain a productive literary experience, encouraging the students to reflect upon their own lives, to consider the differing readings of their classmates and teacher, to draw inferences and pass judgments on the skill, attitudes, and beliefs of the writer. Just as a beginning musician will have a more satisfying musical experience singing a simple folk song than struggling through the complexities of a Mozart aria, so too will the younger reader have a more productive literary experience with a text chosen for its suitability to his age and maturity and interest than with texts perhaps greater but less accessible.

Redefining the criteria by which we select texts would broaden the range, but it would not lead to a rejection of all of the works traditionally in the curriculum. Some of the standard items are perfectly appropriate for adolescents. What work could possibly be more suitable to adolescent readers, most of whose time is given to wondering about or pursuing the opposite sex, than *Romeo and Juliet*? But such works would be chosen not because the curriculum needs to have Elizabethan drama represented, but because the work invites students into talk and writing about love, conflict, family expectations, or other issues significant in their lives.

As we need to reconsider the content of the literature curriculum, so, too, do we need to rethink its organization. Again, as with selection of works, the guiding principles for their arrangement have arisen not from a close look at the transactions between reader and text, but from other sources. Most literature textbooks and curricula have found their organizing principles in the body of information we have about literature, the facts, the terms, the observable content, the testable data—knowledge, as compilers of dictionaries of cultural literacy conceive of it. The programs consequently do not sustain the sort of teaching that we would like to see, and, in fact, lure teachers away from it.

The typical twelfth-grade program, for instance, is British literature, and so works are chosen to represent the centuries and arranged quite logically beginning with Beowulf and marching forward to Virginia Woolf, or as far as the nine months of school allow. Similarly, in the eleventh grade we begin with sinners dangling over fiery pits and charge as far into the twentieth century as we can get by June. The earlier grades are likely to be arranged around genre. Curricula organized this way, by historical periods or genre, implicitly if not subtly encourage the teacher to emphasize history or genre to the neglect of the reader's transactions with texts. Even when the textbook series or the curriculum is arranged around themes, the themes chosen seem to have arisen primarily from a consideration of the texts, rather than of possible encounters with the texts. They seem to reflect more time in the library than with adolescent readers.

Still, we ought to be able to combine what we know about adolescent development, about the recurring issues and themes of our literature, about reading interests, about literary theory, and about learning to write, and find somewhere in all of it a structure that is not just logical, but also psychologically valid. The primary goal in such a curriculum would be to consistently encourage students to take responsibility for making meaning of texts and to assist them in learning how that might be done. That is to say, it would focus on the great issues of the culture, invite them into the dialogue, urge them to bring all of their experience to bear upon the literature and to allow the literature to inform them about their experience. The focus would always be on what the students might do with the literature. Works would be selected for their power to awaken memories, to raise questions about values and beliefs, to reflect the choices and dilemmas the readers themselves are likely to be facing, and those works would be arranged, insofar as possible, to coordinate with the patterns of adolescence.

Several examples illustrate the possibilities for such correlation between the concerns of adolescents and the issues of the great literature. One of the great themes of western literature, for instance, is romance and love; one of the great concerns of adolescence is chasing girls (or boys, depending on which you happen to be). Another of the major literary themes is the coming-of-age; one of the tasks of adolescent development is getting out from under the parental thumb, acquiring some autonomy. Such correspondences suggest that the literature curriculum could respect both the concerns of the kids and the literary heritage, allowing us to appeal to students' natural interests and at the same time present them with works that represent the best of our literature.

It should be possible for us to do that. We should be able to find some correlation between what children go through as they grow up and what writers have written about, and that connection should allow us to choose texts wisely. If, as Rosenblatt has said, "Of all the arts, literature is most immediately implicated with life itself,"[4] then we should be able to seize upon those implications in the classroom and design, ultimately, a literature curriculum that is itself deeply implicated with the lives of our students.

Notes

1. Louise M. Rosenblatt, *Literature as Exploration*, 4th ed. (New York: Modern Language Association, 1984).
2. Denise Levertov, "The Secret," from *O Taste and See*. Copyright © 1966 by Denise Levertov Goodman. Reprinted by permission of New Directions.
3. Stephen Dunn, "The Sacred," excerpted from *Between Angels* by Stephen Dunn. Copyright © 1989. Reprinted with permission of the publisher, W. W. Norton & Company, Inc.
4. Louise M. Rosenblatt, "Language, Literature, and Values,"in *Language, Schooling, and Society*, ed. Stephen N. Tchudi, 64–80 (Upper Montclair, N.J.: Boynton/Cook, 1985), 65.

Contributors

Richard F. Abrahamson is professor of literature for children and young adults at the University of Houston. He has been president of the National Council of Teachers of English Assembly on Adolescent Literature. He and Betty Carter edited the 1988 edition of *Books for You: A Senior High Booklist* for NCTE, and the two also published *Nonfiction for Young Adults: From Delight to Wisdom* form Oryx Press.

Dorothy M. Broderick is the editor of *Voice of Youth Advocates*.

Betty Carter, a former junior high reading teacher and school librarian, is now an assistant professor at Texas Woman's University in the School of Library and Information Studies, where she teaches classes in young adult and children's literature. She has chaired the American Library Association's Best Books for Young Adult Committee and is president-elect of NCTE's Assembly on Adolescent Literature.

Bernice E. Cullinan, professor of early childhood and elementary education at New York University, is a specialist in children's literature, language arts, and reading. She has been president of the International Reading Association, is a member of the Reading Hall of Fame, and received the Arbuthnot Award for Outstanding Teacher of Children's Literature. Her major publications include *Literature and the Child, Children's Literature in the Classroom: Weaving Charlotte's Web*, and *Children's Literature in the Reading Program*.

Judy Delton is the author of more than one hundred books for children and adults, among them the *Pee Wee Scout* series, *The Condo Kids*, and *Angel*. She has four children who are also writers and artists

Ken Donelson is professor of English at Arizona State University. He and Alleen Pace Nilsen are the authors of *Literature for Today's Young Adults*.

John Donovan is president of the Children's Book Council, Inc., a nonprofit association of children's book publishers. He has written several books for young readers.

Carol A. Doll is an assistant professor on the faculty of the Graduate School of Library and Information Science at the University of Washington. She has been active in library education since 1980 and specializes in training children's and young adult librarians, which includes teaching courses in children's literature. She is a member of the 1992 Caldecott Committee.

James Cross Giblin is the author of eleven nonfiction books for young readers, many of which have won awards and honors. His two most recent titles are *The Truth About Unicorns* and *The Riddle of the Rosetta Stone: Key to Ancient Egypt*. Mr. Giblin is also contributing editor at Clarion Book, and he lectures frequently at conferences of librarians, teachers and writers.

Violet J. Harris is assistant professor in the Department of Curriculum and Instruction at the University of Illinois at Urbana-Champaign. She teaches undergraduate and graduate courses in children's literature. Her current research interests are in the literacy materials created for African-American children prior to 1950 and literature reflective of the various ethnic communities in the United States.

Ted Hipple, a founder and past president of ALAN (the Assembly on Literature for Adolescents of the National Council of Teachers of English), currently serves that organization as its executive secretary. A professor of education at the University of Tennessee, Hipple has written widely about young adult literature.

Kathleen Howe completed her doctorate at the University of Minnesota. Her dissertation dealt with the use of children's literature trade books in the elementary social studies curriculum.

Paul B. Janeczko has edited a number of award-winning poetry anthologies for young adults. *Brickyard Summer* was his first book of poetry for young readers. He lives in Maine, where he works as a writer, consultant, and visiting poet.

Barbara Kiefer is an associate professor at Teachers College, Columbia University, where she teaches courses in children's literature, and reading. Originally trained in art education, she taught grades two, four, and five before completing her doctoral studies in language, literature, and reading. She was elected to the 1988 Caldecott Award Committee and has served on the executive committee of The National Council of Teachers of English.

Susan Lehr is an associate professor in the Department of Education, Skidmore College, Saratoga Springs, NY.

Maia Pank Mertz is professor of English education in the Department of Educational Studies at Ohio State University. Her areas of specialization include the teaching of young adult literature, literature study, and the impact of media on adolescents.

Dianne Monson is a professor in the Department of Curriculum and Instruction at the University of Minnesota. She is a past president of the U.S. Board on Books for Young People and has written and lectured on children's literature throughout the curriculum.

Robert Probst is a professor of English education at Georgia State University. A former English teacher, he is the author of *Response and Analysis: Teaching Literature in Junior and Senior High School* and part of the teach that prepared Ginn's *New Voices* series.

Sam Leaton Sebesta has taught reading and children's literature courses at the University of Washington since 1963, after completing his doctorate at Stanford. For several years he supervised the Children's Choices project sponsored by The Children's Book Council and International Reading Association, a field-based study of children's interests and tastes in reading. He wrote the book review column for *The Reading Teacher* for six years (1983–89), a text on children's literature (*Literature for Thursday's Child*, SRA, 1975), and received the Arbuthnot Award for leadership in children's literature in 1986. He conducts workshops and demonstrations on response techniques using children's literature.

Diane P. Tuccillo has been the head of the Young Adult Services Department at the Mesa (Arizona) Public Library since 1980. She has had articles published in a variety of professional journals including *Emergency Librarian, Voice of Youth Advocates (VOYA)* and *The ALAN Review*, and is regular book reviewer for *VOYA, Kliatt Young Adult Paperback Book Guide*, and *School Library Journal*.

DATE DUE